James Dobson's War On America

James Dobson's War On America

Gil Alexander-Moegerle

 Prometheus Books

59 John Glenn Drive
Amherst, NewYork 14228-2197

Published 1997 by Prometheus Books

01 00 99 98 97   5 4 3 2 1

Library of Congress Cataloging-in-Publication Data

Alexander-Moegerle, Gil.
    James Dobson's war on America / Gil Alexander-Moegerle.
        p.   cm.
    Includes index.
    ISBN 1–57392–122–X (cloth : alk. paper)
    1. Dobson, James C., 1936–   . 2. Christian biography—United States.
3. Focus on the Family (Organization)—Biography. 4. Conservativism—Religious aspects—Christianity—Controversial literature. 5. Christianity and politics—United States—Controversial literature. I. Title.
BR1725.D62A54   1997
269'.2'092—dc21
[B]   96–50183
                                                                              CIP

Printed in the United States of America on acid-free paper

✌ Contents

🌿 Dedication

In 1987 I became happily hyphenated.

    I had met and fallen in love with a marvelous woman named Carolyn. During our electrifying courtship, our last names became one of our favorite topics of conversation—the meaning and the power of the words by which people designate their identities. I learned that hers, Alexander, encompassed the rich heritage and epic adventures of a family of two doctors and five children whose nomadic journeys ranged from a drama-filled ER in a southern California hospital to boarding schools and earthen missionary clinics in Burundi, Africa. Alexander means a people of devout faith with amazing individual talents, including writers, teachers, surgeons, and gunsmiths.

    I associated equal riches with my name, Moegerle, the meaning of which included a western Pennsylvania family of faith made up of a hard working door-to-door bakery and dairy salesman and a multitalented homemaker as well as four children who grew up to be a small business owner, a teacher, a funeral home executive, and a marketer. Carolyn discovered that the meaning of "Moegerle" also included the treasure of three wonderful children of my own by a previous marriage.

    So on that emotional Easter eve in 1987, when I dropped to one knee and asked this special woman to marry me, I proposed that, instead of either of us parting with such riches, Carolyn attach my name to hers as I attached hers to mine. I am happy to report that she said yes. Later that spring, as we stood in a lovely southern California backyard surrounded by dear friends, we became officially hyphenated and infinitely wealthier. I therefore dedicate this, my first book, to the woman who gave me a great name and much more, the very sight of whom fires the soul of this white boy from Pennsylvania. To Carolyn.

Los Angeles, California
1997

🌿 Preface and Acknowledgments

There is a pivotal scene in the 1996 motion picture *Courage under Fire,* starring Denzel Washington, that reminded me of the experience we Americans are having with right-wing religious extremists like the man who is the subject of this book, James Dobson. The character played by Washington is in charge of a group of American tanks inside Iraq during the Gulf War. As the tanks advance through the Persian night, they suddenly find themselves under attack. The fire is close in. Washington quickly realizes that there are Iraqi tanks inside his own lines. His position has been infiltrated by the enemy.

In order to remedy the situation, he shouts to his weapons officer to find a target so that he can fire back. In the darkness and confusion the young boy accidentally locks his sight on an American tank. Washington gives the order to fire, only to discover moments later that he has just killed several of his own men. In a frantic effort to resolve the crisis now compounded by friendly-fire casualties, Washington radios his tank crews to turn on their headlights and watches through his night vision goggles as the American tanks, one by one, comply. And then he sees what he's looking for. Two tanks do not turn on their lights. In that instant, he orders his weapons officer to lock on those two dark hulks and blows away the enemy guns that had infiltrated his ranks.

The relevance of that story to this book on the secretive political activist James Dobson is that more and more members of our society feel as if they, too, are under personal attack, and the fire appears to be close in, adding a sense of betrayal to the confusion. In general, we fear that one particular religious sect within our ranks, ultraconservative Christians, led by fiery zealots claiming to speak for God, are trying to seize political power and force us all to be exactly like them. A friend of mine recently characterized her feelings about the religious right's political campaign as one of "terror." A local businessman spoke of his concern this way, "I was raised with a strong belief in the separation of church and state and, as a result, I'm very upset about the possibility of the religious right gaining significant control over Washington." But our fears are not only general, they can be highly specific.

For physicians who perform the legal medical procedure of abortion, and for their staffs, the analogy of a firefight in which people are dying is all too real. They have watched as activists mass in front of their offices and have feared for their lives. They have seen co-workers struck down by gunfire. They have been stalked in the privacy of their neighborhoods and have answered children's bedtime questions that are the same as those asked by children of war: "What's going to happen, Daddy?" "Will they hurt us?"

American women feel as if the private medical judgment they exercise with their doctor's advice is under vicious attack by fellow citizens. They hear voices within society's lines whispering that new laws are needed to control the pregnancy choices they and their trustworthy physicians make, even when their very health or even their life is at stake. Their enemy proclaims, "We will tolerate no exceptions to our new anti-abortion laws because you and your doctor cannot be trusted. We know you abuse 'health of the mother' exceptions." Why, these women wonder, would a complete stranger exhibit such disdain for their character and that of their physician? Why would these people try to remove from a woman the option to preserve her very life in a moment of medical crisis?

Homosexuals speak of the same close-in attacks; they sense that neighbors and countrymen despise them and are working to remove them from full membership in our society, all because of what gays and lesbians feel is an essential part of their identity. According to them, it's a little like being hated because you have blue eyes. They tell stories of friends who have been harassed, beaten, and even killed as a result of rhetoric that inaccurately depicts their lifestyle and grossly distorts their character. They talk of instances where they have been deprived of fundamental civil rights such as the right to work because of their private, personal orientation. Why, they ask in bewilderment and anger, do these attackers combine the words "homosexual" and "promiscuous" as if they were synonymous? Why do they claim falsely that homosexuals are wholly irresponsible and claim that they feel nothing of the commitment and responsibility toward their relationships that are felt by heterosexuals?

Similarly, many parents within our national community fear that their children will soon be forced by this same enemy to participate in sectarian public classroom prayers and indoctrination that makes them feel extremely uncomfortable; they feel as if the specific beliefs of the religious right are about to be imposed on their children. These parents hear the field generals of this adversary calling out, "Give us one generation of children and we'll reshape the entire society," and they know that it is their own sons and daughters who are being targeted for this conservative Christian revolution. They wonder why this foe is not satisfied that religion is so freely nurtured in three of the most powerful settings in children's lives—their home, their family's place of worship, and in broadcast radio and television. Why would fellow citizens open fire on America's public education system, using the war cry that diversity belongs outside the classroom and religion inside?

LOCATING THE ENEMY

In many other ways and places throughout the current American experience with the religious right, people are having the same experience the Denzel Washington character had that night in the desert firestorm. We sense something moving toward us in the dark. We feel a kind of tyranny slowly encroaching on our personal freedoms and the type of life we want for our individual families. Our assumption has been that America stands as a bastion of the individual freedom to make religious and other moral choices according to our own values, to design a life that meets our own needs and pleases us within very broad social constraints. And yet there is a group among us that seems, at times, to oppose our basic right to life, liberty, and the pursuit of happiness; that seems to relish social clashes, power politics, and forcing its own morality onto others. And our problem is that we're having difficulty locating the enemy tanks and determining how exactly to defend ourselves against them.

And so we scan across the society with our night-vision goggles, trying to identify who is shooting at us; trying to understand why these militant religious crusaders appear on news broadcasts, their faces sometimes etched in anger, using language that includes a specific declaration of hostility toward their fellow citizens. What does it mean that some within our society have declared war? We have proclaimed no aggression against them. They are welcome to their moral choices and their way of living life just as we thought we were welcome to ours. We were told that America is by definition a place of pluralism, of diverse views, of mutual respect, of governance based on the development of majority consensus, and of basic individual freedoms. We were told that our government was neutral and uninvolved in issues of religion. And yet this militant group is in our face almost daily, declaring that war is socially preferable to dialogue, and that raw political power is superior to mutuality and inclusion. Why have they chosen such a hostile, un-American, nonspiritual approach to our rich diversity? We ask. And we worry.

Allow me to extend the analogy of the story line of the motion picture *Courage under Fire* one step further. Imagine the movie's script writer taking a slightly different approach to the key battle scene I described to you. Instead of Denzel Washington ordering the headlights of American tanks turned on, picture him sneaking out of his tank, crawling across the skirmish zone, and switching on the lights of the two enemy tanks. Then imagine Washington racing back to his command tank and radioing to his crews, "Do you see the tanks with their lights on? They are responsible for the rounds you're taking. That is the enemy!"

One of my purposes in writing this book is to do just that, to call attention to the enemy, in this case one of the most powerful yet clandestine figures waging religious war against our beliefs, and many of our historic political values. The activist about whom I write employs a deliberate strategy of racing around the battlefield with his lights off. He prides himself in waging a covert war. He jokes privately about his ability to hide from the mainstream press and the scrutiny of the general public. I refer to the foremost guerrilla warrior within the religious right, James Dobson.

More broadly (and to paraphrase a current TV sitcom), this is a book about Christians behaving badly in the political arena, about people of faith doing politics ignorantly and dangerously. Finally, in its last two chapters, it is a book about what tolerant people of moderate persuasions, that "vital center" of American politics as some call us, can do about extremists in our ranks.

JAMES WHO?

The public has never needed a staff member of Jerry Falwell, Pat Robertson, or Ralph Reed to "out" them in terms of their political activism, to their credit. Whatever your opinion of their politics, generally they have done their political activism in plain view of the citizenry whose personal lives their policies, if enacted, would alter dramatically. Not so with the subject of the book you are about to read, to his discredit. This volume is being published on the twentieth anniversary of the founding of James Dobson's giant political action organization known as Focus on the Family, and yet most people who pick it up will begin by responding, "James who?" That is because of two important factors.

James Dobson lobbies Washington more powerfully than any individual or organization within the religious right. As a quick reference point, in December of 1996 the second most influential leader of the religious right, Ralph Reed of the Christian Coalition, announced excitedly that 1996 donations to his coalition had reached a lofty 26 million dollars—a 38 percent increase over the previous year's contributions.[1] In contrast, Dobson's organization, Focus on the Family, plus his Washington lobbying arm, the Family Research Council, raised approximately $125 million during the same period. But Dobson does his lobbying without answering to the mainstream public for his positions. He consciously avoids contact with the national press and shuns the media talk show circuit. He deliberately eschews the public spotlight choosing instead to do his political scheming in private so as not to be questioned or challenged. When he is queried about the size and nature of his political agenda, he responds with calculated deception, indicating that any activism on his part or his organization's is so minor as to be of no real consequence.

It seems to me that secrecy in public policy formation violates a basic tenet of the great American experiment in democracy. If you would lead this society in a particular direction, you must agree to be accountable to our citizenry for your ideas. If you would accumulate political power, you must accept our system of checks and balances to such power lest you abuse it. If you refuse to be accountable for your plans to change our national community, if you reject the challenges and critiques of the national media, then you are thereby disqualified from such leadership; you yourself make it necessary for an exposé such as this one to illuminate your intentions.

People know little about this particular powerhouse within the religious right because no one inside his organization has ever spoken out in this way before. Remarkably, this is the first published critique of the behind-the-scenes James Dobson in his more than twenty years in public life. And it comes to you from a somewhat unlikely source, a former devoted fan.

AN ATTEMPT TO DO BETTER

My part in this story begins in the late 1960s in the unimpressive studios of a small UHF television station in Lexington, Kentucky, where, as a seminary student preparing for the Christian ministry, I landed my first job in broadcasting. It was love at first sight. I was instantly fascinated by the way in which images and sounds merge to create communications products that either stimulate or bore. My primary preoccupation in those days, given the fact that I was a ministerial student, was the concern that almost all religious broadcasts fell into the boring category. I found myself making the career decision in 1970 to try to improve the quality of religious broadcasting rather than become a member of the clergy.

Many years later, having worked my way up the media food chain from camera operator to audio engineer to film editor to writer to television newscaster to director to producer to media consultant, I found myself vice president of a highly regarded Chicago advertising agency that specialized in providing professional print and electronic media services to religious broadcasters of national and international stature. It was there that I met James Dobson for the first time in late 1976, and agreed to produce for him the very first "Focus on the Family" radio broadcast for airing in March of 1977 on a small network of stations our agency signed up for his fledgling nonprofit corporation by the same name.

I worked closely with Jim for the next decade, first in an agency-client relationship and then inside Focus on the Family as a voting member of the board of directors as well as the corporation's senior vice president for creative services. In that role my staff and I had responsibility for creating the core elements of the Focus on the Family communications enterprise—Dobson's internationally distributed radio, television, and print media products, the contents of which focused on either family life or politics. If you were a consumer of this psychologist's best-selling products, you might think of him as a religious version of Dr. Benjamin Spock or Dr. Joyce Brothers. If you were a consumer of Dobson's political fare, you might regard him as a religious version of Pat Buchanan.

The enormous scope of the communications empire we were able to build will explain why James Dobson has such influence; why, for example, Dobson was selected by the staff of *Time* magazine to be a semi-finalist for its June 1996 list of the twenty-five most influential people in America. The daily half-hour radio talk show our Chicago agency launched in 1977 is now carried by over 1,500 stations in North America and 3,400 stations worldwide, with an estimated audience of well over five million loyal listeners. Richard Turner of *Newsweek* magazine reported in the December 16, 1996, issue on what he called "The Inescapable Voices of America." He referred to "A handful of radio personalities who reach listeners coast to coast. . . ." "Radio's most successful talking heads," he called them. According to Turner, the five most listened-to radio personalities are Rush Limbaugh, Dr. Laura Schlesinger, Howard Stern, Don Imus, and Dr. James Dobson.[2]

Dobson stated on his broadcast in the fall of 1996 that each week various editions of "Focus on the Family" radio programming air more than 100,000 times around the world. For example, the flagship broadcast, Dobson's daily half-hour talk show, is so popular that it is aired as many as four times a day on the stations that carry it.

The mailing list of donors and political constituents we began assembling in the late seventies is now approximately three times that of the Christian Coalition and produces annual contributions five times that of the coalition to Dobson's Colorado Springs-based corporation.

When Dobson opposes or supports legislation and calls on his followers to join him in pressuring Washington, it is quite common for 500,000 to one million phone calls and letters to rain down on the capital within hours. All five candidates for the 1996 Republican presidential nomination traveled to Colorado to seek Dobson's endorsement, some as many as four times. *Time* magazine was right. This is an American king maker. And he warrants our close scrutiny for a number of disturbing reasons.

From our first meeting in 1976 until our professional relationship ended, I worked more closely with this man than did any member of our staff except perhaps for one longtime personal secretary. For that reason I am able to offer you much more than an outside reporter's analysis or an inside admirer's praise. I can provide you with a broad view of James Dobson, the man whose political agenda would radically transform our nation, community, schools, and families. In so doing, my intention is to recognize Dobson's impressive body of work on family life, where recognition is in order, and to question and challenge conduct that has gone unchallenged for far too long.

The source material underlying this book begins with personal recollections from ten years of direct executive suite conversations with Dobson; talks in his office, car, and home; and conversations in mahogany board rooms where I attended virtually every board of directors and executive staff meeting over the organization's first decade of operation. I will also draw from thousands of hours of conversation with Dobson in the Focus on the Family radio studio where I served as his on-air co-host and announcer as well as the program's producer. And hundreds of pages of memoranda from and to Dobson have also been reviewed during the course of writing this book. In addition, this volume grows out of the content of thousands of pages of print media and hours of video and film media that I produced with and for James Dobson as the founding editor of the *Focus on the Family* magazine and executive producer of Focus on the Family films.

To ensure that my memory served me well, I requested a number of interviews with people whose stories I include here or who shared some of my experiences with Dobson. In the process, I encountered one or two interesting information roadblocks. For example, toward the end of the book I tell the eventful story of two Focus on the Family employees who sued Dobson alleging bizarre illegal conduct within the executive offices of Focus on the Family. Dobson obtained a gag order from the Los Angeles Superior Court prohibiting me from revealing to you some of the details of that case. Dobson refused to grant me permission to quote from his books and his three most influential executives, Paul Nelson, Rolf Zettersten, and Peb Jackson, refused requests for interviews regarding the accounts you are about to read. But, as you will discover, much can still be told.

BEWARE THE MAN

More than anything else, this book is a warning about the excesses within a powerful modern political movement—the religious right, a surging force within our culture whose continuing ascendancy has been well documented in the national media. In an article in the October 7, 1996, edition of *Christianity Today,* John W. Kennedy reported, "A recent Pew study concluded that 'religion is a strong and growing force in the way Americans think about politics.' " In the same article William C. Martin, author of a study of the movement, said, "Some believe the religious right peaked in 1980, but in every election since then they have always had 3 or 4 percent more of the electorate. The religious right is the single most important faction in the Republican party, perhaps in American politics." According to a scientific survey of 1,024 voters conducted by Wirthlin Worldwide of McLean, Virginia, immediately following the 1996 presidential election, the largest single voting block at the polls were born-again, evangelical Christian churchgoers—29 percent, almost one-third of the electorate. Their numbers had risen from 18 percent in the 1988 election and 24 percent in 1992 and were the reason why, for the first time in sixty-eight years, a Republican Congress was reelected.

This is the power surge that is producing fear and even anger in many

Americans. Albert Pennybacker, president of an association of people of faith opposed to the religious right, was quoted in the same *Christianity Today* article cited above as saying, "It is frightening to see Pat Robertson, a fringe element in American politics, wield such power over one of our nation's parties. His agenda is one of intolerance, exclusivity, and division." And sociologist Tony Campolo, a member of yet another more moderate association of Christians, Call to Renewal, observed that the religious right is not satisfied with their dominance of one of the country's two major political parties. "Christian [politicians] who want to stay in the Democratic party are often run out of office [by the religious right] because they're Democrats," he observed.[3]

Beginning with "born again" Jimmy Carter's campaign for the presidency, a formerly silent part of the electorate has begun to join in the great American political dialogue. Their awakening is a good thing because a democracy thrives on information and involvement. However, a large segment within this new block of voters is dangerously aggressive, intolerant, and uncivil. I believe that their rising religious militancy has brought our democracy to a crossroads. This is a time in our political history for vigilance and passion from moderates, lest something we take for granted, the tranquility that allows our society to thrive, be engulfed in the firestorms of violent religious wars so common to other societies and against which we are not at all immune just because we are America. It is not unthinkable that religious street battles and sectarian bloodshed might come to our society as they have to others that harbor uncivil religious zealots and factions. To believe otherwise is to invite the worst.

Mostly, though, this is a warning about a man, a power lobbyist who richly deserves to be labeled a true danger and a threat, a political influence peddler on his ascendancy about whom Barry Lynn, the executive director of Americans United for the Separation of Church and State, said in an October 1996 conversation with me, "James Dobson and Focus on the Family represent the greatest threat to constitutional liberties in our time."

The most serious of all menaces to our freedom to pursue the life we desire comes from the extremes within our society. Fringe political activism is an equal opportunity employer—it favors neither the left nor the right. Its threat is found not in its ideology, conservative or liberal, but in the extremist's bigotry and approach, his tone and temper, his self-righteous anger and aggression, his rigidity and intolerance. Neither the left nor the right, but rather, extremism in either camp, is the enemy.

The point of the book you hold is this: Beware the man who speaks not about that which is best for our society but that which is right according to his personal moral code. Beware the man who angrily pounds his fist on the table of democracy instead of using it as a listening post and an anvil of compromise and consensus building. Beware the man who sees society as a set of impersonal issues over which he wants to fight lest his cause be lost rather than as a set of real people with genuine concerns and honest differences with whom he must live with mutual respect and in social tranquility. Beware the man who despises the middle ground, whose view of public policy formation is a campaign of all or nothing, who thinks it best to dominate the public debate or to undermine it. Or, as Mark Hatfield, himself a person of devout faith, said when he retired from the United States Senate in 1996, "Beware of those who want to assume the power and the levers of Caesar to usher in the Kingdom of God."[4]

In short, beware James Dobson, the new faceless power broker of America's religious right whose corporate and personal headlights I would now like to switch on.

I gratefully acknowledge all who contributed to this book: who took my calls, answered my questions, agreed to be interviewed, or in various other ways assisted me: Noel Becchetti; Sam Ericcson; Scott Fagerstrom; Steven Gill, Ph.D.; Barry Lynn; Jarrell McCracken; John Murphy; M. Scott Peck, M.D.; Larry Richards, Ph.D.; Tim Stafford; John Stewart; Gary Warner; David Warren; Mel White; and others who preferred anonymity.

I am indebted as well to staff members of the following offices: Americans United for the Separation of Church and State; The Christian Coalition; the cities of Colorado Springs, Colorado, and Pomona, California; The Colorado Springs *Gazette Telegraph*; the Honorable Barbara Boxer; and the Honorable Mark Hatfield.

Special thanks to Steven L. Mitchell, Editor-in-Chief; my editor, Eugene O'Connor; and the highly supportive staff of Prometheus Books. The word here is "courageous."

And a special acknowledgment to the hardest-working man in the field of interpersonal reconciliation and conflict management, William Fields, executive director of Peacemakers, Wheaton, Illinois. A friend indeed.

NOTES

1. Christian Coalition Press Releases displayed on the coalition's home page, www.cc.org, December, 1996.

2. Richard Turner, "The Inescapable Voice of America," *Newsweek*, December 16, 1996, p. 25.

3. John W. Kennedy, *Christianity Today* 40, no. 2 (October 7, 1996): 76.

4. "With God on Our Side," Episode 6, November 1996 (New York: Lumiere Productions).

1   Moral Combat

The first time some of us heard that the religious right, or those cultural conservatives who have a religious component to their political activism, had actually declared "war" on the rest of us was probably during Pat Buchanan's infamous speech at the 1992 Republican National Convention. He spoke combatively, in terms that chilled many listeners, of a religious war in America, something few thought possible. His eerie words brought home to millions of us that repulsive feeling associated with holier-than-thou moralists who presume to have a corner on right and wrong and who seem to be itching to fight about it:

> My friends, this election is about much more than who gets what. It is about who we are. It is about what we believe. It is about what we stand for as Americans. There is a religious war going on in our country for the soul of America. It is a cultural war, as critical to the kind of nation we will one day be as was the Cold War itself.[1]

Two years earlier a secretive but increasingly powerful political organizer, psychologist, radio talk show host, millionaire businessman, and author by the name of James Dobson had spoken even more bluntly of hostilities within our society—not differences or debates, but war. Dobson wrote his particular declaration of war, his manifesto of contention, in a book titled *Children at Risk* that was published in 1990. In it he spoke of a "Second Great Civil War":

Nothing short of a great Civil War of Values rages today throughout North America. Two sides with vastly differing and incompatible worldviews are locked in a bitter conflict that permeates every level of society. Bloody battles are being fought on a thousand fronts. . . . Open any daily newspaper and you'll find accounts of the latest Gettysburg, Waterloo, Normandy, or Stalingrad . . . someday soon, I believe, a winner will emerge and the loser will fade from memory.[2]

On reflection one wonders what it is in a man that causes him to see in the faces of all around him only the enemy; what it is in his spirit that causes to be reflected back to his gaze only images of conflict, hostility, and war, struggles to the death where there must be a winner and a loser whose memory is obliterated from the earth. I believe James Dobson's declaration of war is a reflection of his own temperament and disposition. He is a man at war because *he* is a man of war. An outsider might speculate in reading Jim's assessment above that Dobson either sees a real threat or he's more than a little paranoid, prone to hyperbole, believes in conspiracy theories, and is given to doom-and-gloom prognostications. But I was an insider. No speculation needed here. The answer is the latter—it is not that he *sees* a problem, he *is* a problem.

If our children came home talking like Dobson we'd take them directly to a psychiatrist because these ruminations of death and bloody conflict are not the outlooks of the healthy, balanced psyche we wish for them, one that would enable them to be productive members of society. We would worry for their well-being. It is no less worrisome a worldview in the grown man and self-proclaimed moral leader whose declared intention it is to reshape America's public policy to his own ultraconservative religious liking.

In *Children at Risk,* Dobson goes on to explain that on one side of the enormous chasm dividing Americans are those people of traditional beliefs which he describes as rooted in the Bible, the Ten Commandments, the New Testament, and the gospel of Jesus Christ. Dobson believes that Christian, biblical understandings underlie almost every moral issue of the day. What we hear in this assessment is that traditionalists and conservatives, those who vote with Dobson, do so because they are oriented toward the New Testament and Christianity. What Jim means here is that if you are a conservative Jew or a traditionalist who is also an atheist, you have political beliefs that are Christian. You just don't realize it. In other words, political values like Jim's—lower taxes, smaller government, larger defense, the elimination of the Department of Education and the National Endowment for the Arts, the barring of women and homosexuals from military service—represent Christian politics, right politics.

Dobson claims that until thirty years ago the basic values and beliefs in the West, which Congress and the judicial system reflected, were biblically based concepts. If you're wondering about the time our "biblically based" Congress and judiciary determined in their "biblically based" wisdom that blacks were personal property and slavery was moral and it was irreligious for women to vote, I'm not sure what chapter and verse of the Bible Jim would point to for an explanation. But if you gave him sufficient time, I'm confident he could offer some reason for his sweeping generalization.

Dobson then describes the other side of the rift dividing society, those with whom he sees himself locked in a bitter, bloody moral struggle for the very soul of America. They are the secular humanists, people for whom "God isn't," and for whom right is determined by whatever seems right at the time. According to Jim all manner of evil, such as abortion, infanticide, and euthanasia, flows from these godless Americans. Because of them "everything emanating from the Creator was jettisoned, including reverence for Scripture or any of the transcendent, universal truths."[3]

Perhaps you are surprised to learn that "everything emanating from the Creator was jettisoned" from our society years ago and that the national community each one of us helps create each new day no longer contains any reference to transcendent, universal truths. Is that your experience with America? Let's see, we have more churches in our country and more religious involvement by our citizenry than any nation in the world. Our coinage still declares that we trust in God and we still refer to God every time we recite the pledge of allegiance. And as I write, there are more individuals holding seats in the Senate and the House who openly declare activist religious commitments than at any time in recent history. Nevertheless, to Dobson's eye, everything transcendent has been jettisoned.

Dobson goes on, in *Children at Risk*, to lament that his values are incessantly mocked by the media, children are corrupted by TV, obscenity abounds, and government is encroaching upon his constitutional freedoms. Humanistic values dominate in the power centers of society, in Jim's view. They have outstripped Judeo-Christian precepts in the news media, the entertainment industry, the judiciary, business, medicine, psychology, law, the arts, and the halls of Congress. To Jim's way of thinking, unlimited resources are available to the incredibly well-organized secular humanists among us for their expansive agenda and for their calculated attack on him and his values. Dobson believes that his opponents are highly motivated and armed to the teeth, but that many on his side are unaware that they are even under attack. He then goes on to tell us that warfare is dangerous, exhausting, and expensive, but that he cannot remain uninvolved.

As you hear these opinions and try to picture the mind and temperament behind them, allow me to apprise you of the following: When Jim
says that Judeo-Christian precepts have been outstripped by those of secular humanism you have, in my view, one of the central reasons why
James Dobson has declared war on virtually every sector of society. He
perceives that his belief system is losing ground and he's angry about
that. He's a poor loser. The idea of holding the minority opinion in America, the minority value system, minority power, or minority control of any
situation is anathema to James Dobson. Again from *Children at Risk*:
"The humanistic system of values has now become the predominant way
of thinking in most of the power centers of society. It has outstripped
Judeo-Christian precepts . . ."[4]

You are not reading the words of a man of peace, a reluctant warrior,
who is deeply saddened by the moral decline of his beloved nation. These
are the words of a man of competition who is deeply offended and
angered that his side is losing and who intends to take back lost ground
by sheer political force.

FALSE ALARM?

As Dobson's declaration of war and its imagery of bloody civil combat
has entered our social discourse during the past several years, it is important to try to distinguish between two possibilities: (1) Our culture may be
at war and Dobson may be serving as a wise observer. If so, it is generally assumed that war is dangerous and we should be discussing publicly
such things as how this conflict began, how we can end it and return to a
more peaceful and productive society, and, perhaps most important, how
we can defend that which deserves defending from the raining shells of a
civil war. Or (2) Dobson and religious zealots like him may be provoking
us toward civil unrest. Our problem may be a little boy crying, "Wolf!
Wolf!" or, more appropriately, a bully on the block trying to pick a fight
with us, attempting to disrupt our diverse and functioning neighborhood
because of his desire to create by force and intimidation a more homoge-
nous village.

As I have already suggested, from my perspective the war to which
Dobson refers is primarily a conflict that has its origins within himself, a
type of moral tension he personally experiences over individuals and
movements within our society that are different from him, not a legitimate
conflict that he reluctantly joins for the greater good of our country. I fear

this is a fight he is picking with us and I'm concerned about just how bloody it may get.

As we turn toward a new century, the truth behind Dobson's belligerent words and views is that, to some moralists like him, America has become an inexcusable, intolerable place to live. He takes it all very personally. His moral system is losing ground and he's mad. And he doesn't plan to tolerate it or you if he thinks you're the enemy. He refuses to put up with America as it has become. He has declared war to take us back to the past. This is his own fist fight with anyone different than himself, his beliefs, and his America. We have a word for this type of intolerance. We call it demagoguery.

I am reminded of a highly descriptive line from the film *The American President.* The Democratic president, played by Michael Douglas, and his love interest, played by Annette Bening, are taking time out of a busy election year schedule for an evening at Camp David. They're going through scrap books of the president's college days and watching TV. The president's Republican challenger appears on the screen ranting and raving about the moral deficiencies of the president and his girlfriend and everyone else except himself, or so it seems. Bening turns to Douglas and says, "For a man who says he loves America, he sure hates Americans."

The following is the story of a man who loves one idea of America and of Americans and hates all the rest. And it is my hope that by recounting my years at Focus on the Family and by explaining the previously undisclosed personal ways and means of this particular enemy of the social calm I will make a small contribution to our exciting yet vulnerable American experiment—a secular government run by and for a wonderfully diverse people, religiously and otherwise; one in which demagoguery has no place.

NOTES

1. Internet, Buchanan for President Campaign.
2. James Dobson, *Children at Risk* (Dallas, Tex.: Word, Inc., 1990), pp. 19, 20.
3. Ibid., p. 21.
4. Ibid., p. 22.

2 🌿 Who Is This Belligerent?

Describing for you exactly who James Dobson is and precisely what his goals and objectives are is surprisingly complex. But we can start with the fact that he's an extremely popular American religious broadcaster.

I worked for twenty years inside the cartel of conservative Christian radio and television ministers that blankets the American airwaves with their approach to religious truth, appeals for donations, and their passionate pronouncements about a wide array of political issues. Ten of those years I was James Dobson's right-hand man, during which he first entered the media and went on to become the most listened-to religious broadcaster in America.

Speaking of radio and television fund raising, I'm reminded of a friend who received a monthly "appeal letter" sent out by one of these listener-supported organizations in which the broadcaster pled, "If I don't receive an adequate response from this letter we may be forced to shut our ministry down. I am trusting God to speak to you about sending me some special message about the future of this ministry in your return envelope." My friend wrote back, "God's message is—shut it down." The broadcaster was not amused. These businesses die hard.

The exact religion to which I am referring is a colorful fundamentalist conservative wing of American Protestantism, whose broadcasters include such bright lights as Billy Graham and such low lights as Jim and Tammy Faye Bakker and Jimmy Swaggart. By and large the faithful in this wing of the Christian Church do not introduce themselves by a subgroup label that helps you pinpoint their perspective, say, Episcopalian or Methodist. These followers of Jesus Christ generally refer to themselves simply as "Christians," which can be good or bad depending on the exact person using the label. The desire of most conservative Protestants to identify themselves more with Christ than a denomination is probably noteworthy and commendable. But this label can also mask a fairly heavy dose of religious egotism on the part of many within the movement. Everyone else who follows Christ, including members of churches hundreds of years older than theirs, can find some other term for themselves such as "Roman Catholic" or "Greek Orthodox" or "Church of England." *They* are the true Christians, thank you very much.

This untidy bit of religious arrogance pops up daily on thousands of radio and television stations across the United States that this branch of the Christian faith owns and operates. I recently heard a conversation between a radio talk show host and a caller that illustrates this hubris. The caller began, "I have a problem with my husband. He refuses to go to church with me." The all-knowing radio host responded, "Tell me more." To which the caller stated, "Well, I'm a Christian but my husband isn't." "I'm sorry," said the loving host. The caller continued, "He's Catholic." At this point the host never interrupted because, in his view, nothing inaccurate had been said by the caller.

During the ten years I worked with Dobson, from 1977 to 1987, I was his daily radio announcer and co-host. In that capacity I opened and closed each program, including making appeals for financial support from our listening audience. In the body of the broadcast I posed the family life questions of the day for Jim to answer. And I provided the friendly banter that helped make our highly successful format of conversational talk radio an award-winning production. We became the number-one-rated program on most of the stations that carried us.

IDENTIFY YOURSELF

We had three primary objectives when we started "Focus on the Family." Actually, Dobson sometimes spoke of four and, on occasion, five. And the professional identity that Jim projected was a little changeable also. Now that I reflect on those years, we were none too clear about who we were. In the course of Dobson's career, he has presented himself primarily as a down-home family psychologist, a dispenser of commonsense advice on marriage and the family. But within that core image there seemed to be something of an identity crisis. He lurched, sometimes wildly, from one professional identity to another to suit his purpose at the moment. At times this pitching about seemed little more than the machinations we see too often in politicians—saying whatever the crowd they're addressing wants to hear. At other times, it seemed rooted in something less corrupt, as if he had never made peace with the adult he'd become. What were these various alter egos?

One day you would swear Dobson is a straightforward Christian minister. This impression comes quickly and easily to a radio listener because Jim is a fourth-generation religious professional with deep roots in a small, fundamentalist denomination, the Church of the Nazarene.[1] He comes by his steady stream of earnest God talk honestly. His southern father, grandfather, and great-grandfather were all Bible-belt preachers of the gospel. He has often said, when the identity on display for the day is his religious worker persona, that every single aspect of the work of his organization is designed to advance that gospel.

In a story you will hear in detail later, in 1991 Jim was taken to court by two employees who alleged significant misconduct within Focus on the Family. Dressed in his finest liturgical identity, and with God talk fairly deluging the courtroom, Jim successfully evaded judicial scrutiny. He did so by telling the court that his company was actually a "Church" and thus was protected from civil accountability by the First Amendment. In one court filing he wrote:

> In Evangelical Christian theology all believers constitute a Church—the universal Church. Indeed, any gathering of believers constitutes a "Church." Focus on the Family is part of the universal Church. It is a localized Church to the extent it has an identifiable audience. Hence, theologically speaking, it is a Church unto itself.[2]

During the summer of 1996, Dobson could be seen listing heavily toward this man-of-the-cloth image on a radio broadcast he titled "Focus on Jesus." During that particular half hour he explained to his listeners that the real purpose of Focus on the Family was to do just that, to focus on Jesus. Toward this end he announced that he intended to devote himself to a campaign for "spiritual righteousness in America." If you were to conclude that that sounds very much like someone who views himself as a minister, you'd get no argument from me.

Senior writer Tim Stafford, profiling Dobson in *Christianity Today,* perhaps the most respected magazine within conservative Protestantism, said of him: "Dobson has chosen channels of influence closer to a radio evangelist's than a psychologist's. Dobson's peers are preachers Charles Swindoll, Jerry Falwell and Robert Schuller."[3]

But I have mentioned that he has several identities. On a different day

Dobson might be seen lurching toward what appears to be a 100 percent nonreligious presentation of himself, anything but a Christian worker. I've seen him become angry on several occasions at those who referred to his ministerial persona when he wanted his image to be nonreligious. Follow him around the corridors of Congress, for example, in and out of the offices of senators and representatives, and count the number of references to *Dr.* James Dobson, *Ph.D., in child developmental psychology from USC, seventeen years on the attending staff of Children's Hospital in Los Angeles, etc.* The identity of choice for Dobson on such occasions is one tied firmly to his secular credentials. Absent is any reference to a religious broadcaster or a central corporate mission of "focusing on Jesus." On these occasions Focus on the Family is presented as a nonprofit educational institution and he is presented as a behavioral scientist, certainly not the head of a "church." When Jim's nonreligious self was on display I often saw him become incensed when reporters referred to him in their articles as a minister or evangelist, or addressed him, God forbid, as the Reverend James Dobson. He complained bitterly that these were deliberate attempts by the media to discredit him. I often thought that reaction contained in it two interesting revelations about the inner workings of Jim's mind, first, his tendency to irrationally demonize the press. After all, Jim's books and broadcasting are filled with religious language. What is there to criticize when a member of the press corps makes the assumption that someone who constantly talks like a minister might actually be a minister? And, second, it seemed at times as if Jim were subconsciously radiating a disrespect for the clergy. Dobson reacted violently to being called a minister as if experiencing a personal revulsion at being identified with the profession.

THE BUNDY INCIDENT

You would have encountered a heavy dose of Dobson's nonreligious persona had you been standing among the mob of national media representatives outside Florida State Penitentiary in February 1989, the evening serial killer Ted Bundy was executed. Dobson had been invited inside with his video cameras to tape a sensational execution-eve interview with Bundy, which Jim later used as a fund-raising incentive in his war against pornography. Had you asked one of Dobson's people for a write-up about him, here is exactly what you would have been handed. Please look carefully for the religious elements of this very detailed introduction to Jim and his business that Jim personally authored:

James Clayton Dobson, Ph.D., is a founder and the president of Focus on the Family. He was for fourteen years, an Associate Clinical Professor of Pediatrics at the University of Southern California School of Medicine, and served for seventeen years on the attending staff of the Children's Hospital of Los Angeles in the Division of Child Development and Medical Genetics. He has an earned master's degree in the field of education and a Ph.D. from the University of Southern California in the field of child development. In addition he was awarded an honorary Doctorate of Laws from Pepperdine University, an Honorary Doctorate of Humanities from Franciscan University of Steubenville and an Honorary Doctorate of Humane Letters from Seattle Pacific University.

He is a licensed Psychologist and Marriage Family and Child Counselor.

Recently, Dr. Dobson has been heavily involved in governmental activities related to the family. He served on the task force that summarized the White House Conferences on the Family and received a special commendation from President Jimmy Carter. He was appointed by President Ronald Reagan to the National Advisory Commission for Juvenile Justice and Delinquency Prevention. From 1984 forward he has regularly been invited to the White House to consult with Presidents and their staffs on family matters. He served as the co-chairman of the Citizens Advisory Panel for Tax Reform, in consultation to President Reagan and served as the chairman of the United States Army Task Force Staff. He was appointed to the Attorney General's Commission on Pornography and to the Attorney General's Advisory Board on Missing and Exploited Children and to Secretary Otis Bowen's Panel on Teen Pregnancy Prevention within the Department of Health and Human Services. He received the Marion Pfister Anschutz Award in recognition for his contribution to the American family.

When handing out this résumé to members of the media at the Bundy execution, Dobson attempted to get them to sign a statement pledging that they would refer to him in these secular terms. Many, however, observing the heavy religious content of Jim's materials and approach—for example, Bundy and Dobson took holy communion together—referred to him quite naturally as a minister and evangelist, which infuriated him. He referred to such caricatures as deliberate attempts to demean him.

When Dobson did the final production work on the Bundy video footage, the opening interview stood out as a classic example of James don't-you-dare-call-me-a-religious-worker Dobson. Remember, Jim scripted and then approved his announcer's segments:

Announcer: It has been fascinating to read the aftermath in the press of this event that happened at the Florida State Prison. The circus that occurred outside, the interview inside and then what happened afterward. And it was curious to me that more criticism was leveled at you than was leveled at Bundy. That's why I would like to establish first of all who you are and what your credentials are in the professional community. Can you do that for me?

Dobson: It is interesting that I come off bad in comparison with a man who killed twenty-eight women and children. I mean, I need a new press agent, I suppose, under those circumstances. I think what that reflects is an effort to discredit the messenger. What we had to say, what Bundy had to say, and some of my own conclusions about it are unacceptable to the media. And so there has been this effort to confuse who I am. I have been called a tele-evangelist to identify me with some of the embarrassing things that happened in Christianity a few years ago. I have been called a minister, and so on. It is true that I have a radio program on 1,300 [the 1989 total] Christian radio stations. But to say that that makes me a minister, is like saying if you live in Orange County you are a citrus grower.

Announcer: You were called a religious broadcaster, in fact, in most of the articles that I saw. I wouldn't characterize you as a religious broadcaster. How do you characterize yourself?

Dobson: I have a Ph.D. in child development from the University of Southern California, I served on the faculty of the medical school at the University of Southern California for fourteen years. I served at the same time for seventeen years on the attending staff at Children's Hospital of Los Angeles. So my background is in the area of research and child development. I am not a minister. I have never been in the seminary. I have absolutely no credentials there.[4]

This is one of the more fascinating secular self-descriptions by Jim on record, a man who later swore to a court that he heads a church, stating that the "sole purpose" of his professional work was to promulgate "the gospel of Jesus Christ." Here Jim gives us one of the clearest snapshots of a man deeply at odds with himself in terms of his professional identity as he publicly attempts to deny even being a religious broadcaster.

POLITICAL ACTIVIST

And so we have James Dobson, minister, and James Dobson, psychologist. Yet another of Jim's multiple identities and a further example of his strange lurching from one to another can be observed when one examines James Dobson, political activist. Remember the words Jim wrote about himself in the Bundy press packet? "Recently, Dr. Dobson has been heavily involved in governmental activities related to the family. . . ." From my perspective, that was factual. Jim became deeply involved in politics in 1979 and has never looked back. Jim's 1990 war book, *Children at Risk,* was co-written with former domestic policy advisor to President Reagan and undersecretary of education, Gary Bauer, who is now a Dobson associate and one of the most influential conservative lobbyists in Washington.

One of the six distinct daily radio broadcasts Dobson produces is called "Family News in Focus," which addresses only political issues. He also publishes a magazine, *Citizen,* which is devoted exclusively to politics. Early in Dobson's political activism he began organizing grassroots chapters of like-minded religious conservatives to work at the local, state, and federal level. Some would argue that there is no more important feature of James Dobson's rise to the most powerful role on the religious right than this one; he has been working for fifteen years to set up coalitions of local political action groups in every state. One way he forges that link is by offering such groups publicity and copy space in special state-by-state press runs of his *Citizen* magazine.

And Jim devotes a large part of his personal schedule to building his Washington power network of congressional contacts. Tim Stafford said in his profile: "He has spent a substantial portion of the last year in Washington, much of his involvement revolving around governmental panels."

Notwithstanding such intense commitments to political action, Dobson sometimes pitches irrationally in the opposite direction relative to this aspect of his identity. For example, when talking to reporters such as the *Washington Post*'s Marc Fisher. Fisher wrote in a 1996 profile: "Dobson's insistence that public policy is a tiny, almost insignificant part of his work has led his critics to accuse him of running a stealth campaign to impose a Christian agenda on the nation."[5]

WEALTHY SHOW HORSE OWNER

Yet another feature of the fluctuating Dobson identity is the fact that he has made a great deal of money within the conservative Protestant religious marketplace and is one of the most successful businessmen in that market. Nevertheless, he constantly attempts to present himself as essentially uninterested in money making. He's become very wealthy by writing more than a dozen national best-sellers and producing related highly

successful audio and film products, and also by keeping most of the proceeds as personal income rather than deeding such products to his nonprofit corporation.

I recall once in the early eighties walking to a computer printer in
Jim's office to retrieve a document, only to discover, sitting on the printer,
a financial statement. In the second it takes the eye to flash from the top
of a piece of paper to the bottom, I suddenly realized that I was looking
at a printout of Jim's personal worth and the bottom line was in excess of
a million dollars. And that was fifteen years ago, before many of his most
lucrative business ventures.

With wealth comes the role of investment manager and for Jim that
has included, at times, owning a small bevy of Arabian show horses with
all the associated anxieties that go with that investment. Dobson doesn't
approach the financial aspect of his life in a casual, carefree manner, no
matter how much he talks about material possessions being of little
importance. I recall, for example, a time when he began to suspect his
publishing friend Jarrell McCracken, who owned the Arabian horse farm
where Jim's horses were kept, of misleading him about the well-being of
his herd. Dobson told those of us close to him of dispatching a trusted
aide to travel to the farm unannounced and perform a surprise audit of his
possessions to "get to the bottom of it." It turned out to be nothing more
than an unfounded suspicion, something Jim frequently displayed as you
will learn in the pages ahead.

An accurate portrayal of the many identities that make up this man
should place near the top of the list the passion and drive for success you
will find wrapped up in the description "James Dobson, wealthy businessman."

GOALS AND OBJECTIVES

Along with these multiple personae, I mentioned that Jim seemed to have
fluctuating objectives for Focus on the Family. Allow me to explain.

We started Focus on the Family in 1977 with two very simple goals:
(1) to strengthen the marital skills of our constituents and (2) to add to
their parenting skills. We did this by producing educational materials for
our customers: radio and television programming, audio and video cassettes, magazines, and books and pamphlets. Actually, we didn't call our
customers "customers," even though we produced products for them and
they bought them in incredible quantities from us. Dobson often referred

to the company we created as a "marketing machine," so successful was it from a business standpoint, but Dobson the minister didn't think it wise to speak in such business terms to his faithful donors. But a marketing machine it was and is.

Reporter Fisher observed this bustling product creation and sales engine when he toured Focus in 1996. He wrote:

> Here, hundreds of operators, most of them women, wear phone headsets and sit poised over computer monitors, processing 10,000 letters a day whose orders for Focus products will be filled within three days, 3,500 phone calls that will be answered within 30 seconds. There are 6,000 items in the Focus warehouse—books with titles such as "Someone I Love Is Gay" and "The Cheapskate Monthly Money Makeovers," how-to guides such as "Internet for Christians," and brochures on how to fight against sex ed courses in public schools.[6]

A 1995 ABC television news profile of Dobson reported the organization processes over 300,000 letters and orders from customers every month. The report stated: "In sixty countries Dobson's advice is heard over the radio by tens of millions of people [in] Russian and Spanish, French and Korean and Portuguese."[7]

More than 100 million dollars of this type of commerce goes through Focus on the Family bank accounts each year. But we called it by religious terms. In that culture "business" was called "ministry," our customers were "friends" or "donors" or "listeners" or "partners," and the bottom line was said to be of no concern even though it was a prime concern.

In terms of corporate objectives, what started as an enterprise to provide educational materials about marriage and parenting to these customers expanded to include a third specific objective about two years into Focus's history: political organizing, lobbying, and activism. Here, in addition to Jim's personal work in Washington as a lobbyist for issues he considered family-oriented, our staff recruited, financed, and orchestrated the work of many lesser-known activists, from grassroots chapters of community activists to owning and operating the powerful Washington lobby, the Family Research Council, headed by Gary Bauer.

And, as mentioned, along with these goals of producing educational products and conducting political activities, a fourth religious objective was touted, at times, as our sole objective—to spread the gospel of Jesus Christ. If you're having difficulty keeping all this straight, perhaps this comparison will help. The goal of the Billy Graham organization is to spread the gospel. That's exactly what Graham does in every radio and television broadcast and piece of literature he publishes: he speaks of

Christ's life and death and how one becomes "a Christian." But it is clearly not the sole objective of Focus on the Family.

This aspect of Jim's fluctuating professional goal and identity became bizarre at times; as if this son of generations of evangelists could not quite make peace with the fact that he had broken a powerful religious lineage; as if he feared that one or more of those preacher forefathers might be looking down and scowling at him. If you caught him in this slightly defensive, unsure-of-himself, I-am-too-faithful-to-my-heritage mood, you might hear from his lips the most amazing contortions of logic regarding how a psychologist, a multimillionaire businessman, and a CEO of an educational products and political action organization is doing just what his daddy did, spreading the gospel. Note this observation from the Stafford profile:

> James Dobson, who may well be the most famous and influential psychologist in the world, was born in 1936 in Shrevesport, Louisiana, by Cesarean section. The doctor told his mother she might not live through another birth. Thus, the man who counsels millions about family life was raised an only child.
>
> A great-grandfather and a grandfather on his mother's side had been charter members of the Church of the Nazarene, a holiness denomination headquartered in the Midwest. A prophecy had come to the great-grandfather [In Jim's religion, a "prophecy" is a mental impression that a person concludes may be a message from God giving them a special revelation of future events] that all his family for four generations would belong to the Lord. That prophecy has held true and with interest.[8]

In terms of how funny Jim can be when he's trying to equate his work to that of his forefathers, I offer you this hypothetical interview based on my decade of close work with and intimate knowledge of the man. There is no humor intended in the words chosen, just in the contorted logic.

Question: So, everything you do promotes the gospel of Jesus Christ?

Answer: Yes.

Question: Everything. That seems a little broad. By the way, what is the gospel of Jesus Christ?

Answer: Well, that's the brief set of beliefs at the heart of Christian doctrine. It goes like this—Christ was God's Son, he died for our sins; if we believe in him he forgives us and gives us an eternal home in heaven. Those beliefs represent "the gospel." That's it.

Question: Okay. Please explain how a program you aired within the past year on understanding early childhood memories from a psychological perspective represents broadcasting the gospel of Christ.

Answer: Well that's easy. The better we understand ourselves, including whether we're dealing with real or imagined memories of our childhood, the more integrated a person we become, and the more integrated we are the easier it is for us to understand the gospel message and to become born again.

Question: But isn't that torturing language like a prostitute saying she's in the business of "love"? Take your daily "Family News in Focus" radio series. Your literature describes it as "a close-up look at news headlines that impact the listener's home, a daily information and analysis radio feature that keeps you up to date on important family issues and then challenges you to take action on pro-family matters." I'm searching in those words for anything about Christ being the Son of God or how I reach heaven.

Answer: Well, if we all work together to create a more family-friendly America by being active politically, then families will have more time to concentrate on the important things, and one of those is parents spending time with their children explaining spiritual truths like the gospel. Get the connection?

Question: Not really.

Keep in mind that on any given day one or more of these objectives may mysteriously vanish depending on which identity Dobson is emphasizing, who he is talking to, and what influence he is attempting to exert over them. In retrospect, this facet of James Dobson has all the appearances of a control issue. Jim decides, hour by hour, what Focus on the Family is and who he is, depending on who he's talking to. He is a Ph.D. from USC when power brokering in Washington about legislation. He is the leader of a "church" when called into court. He is a businessman and Focus is an educational and communications empire at other times. And he is sometimes on a "Campaign for Righteousness" when talking to his conservative Christian donors.

One of the New Testament writers spoke of Christians needing to be "all things to all men," but I doubt that sending mixed messages and spinning manipulative images was what he had in mind.

NOTES

1. See chapter 9 for a description of the Nazarenes.
2. Declaration of Dr. James Dobson, executed August 3, 1989, in Sydney, Australia, and part of the public record of Los Angeles Superior Court Civil Case EAC 71129.

3. Tim Stafford, "His Father's Son," *Christianity Today,* March, 1988.

4. Ted Bundy Interview, video, Focus on the Family, Colorado Springs, Colo.

5. Marc Fisher, "The GOP, Facing a Dobson's Choice," *Washington Post,* July 2, 1996.

6. Ibid.

7. "Day One," ABC Television News, October 18, 1995.

8. Stafford, "His Father's Son."

3 🌿 Into the Fray

The James Dobson I knew well is nothing if not a lover of power. Whatever influence he has amassed as the chief managing partner of the religious right political movement has come to him quite on purpose.

Jim's temperament is, worst case, that of the stereotypical only child who grew up having a little too much of his own way around the house, never sharing with siblings because there were none, and enjoying too much attention from doting parents.

Stafford writes:

> Dobson was known for his searing memos even in his medical school days. He told me that he wrote memos to his parents as a child, protesting when he considered their treatment unfair. The best guess is that he got such traits from being raised an adored only child. One close friend says, "I really love the guy, he's been terrific to me. He's loyal, and a tremendously faithful friend. But there is one area in his life that he cannot be aware of: it's being an only child. You don't have to share. You don't have hand-me-downs. You get your own way."[1]

I refer you to the now infamous "tolerance" debate during the pre-'96 convention meeting of the Republican Platform Committee. You heard that the religious right refused to allow language into the platform that acknowledged that many members of the party held views other than pro-life. I wonder if there is a hint of the origins of that extraordinary level of intolerance within the following observation by Jim's wife, Shirley Dobson, about how Dobson was raised. She told Stafford during an interview for his profile:

No matter what Jim said to [his mother], even if she didn't agree with it, she would never put it down. She would always let him say whatever he wanted to say, and then she would ask questions. She would never give an opinion.

Many would say that the outcome of that approach to child raising has been a control-hungry, nonsharing, demanding and pushy adult. Stir in an overdeveloped ego and you have a man who disdains the weaker, servant role in human relationships, and strives instead for the stronger, controlling role, either grabbing it or leaving town in search of new arenas to dominate.

Stafford continues:

James Dobson once wrote that, had he been asked to write a theme on himself during adolescence, he would have begun, "I am the number-one tennis player in the high school."

There's a puzzling difference between the normally gracious and self-effacing James Dobson, and the accusing, domineering character who can surface. . . . Many of Dobson's friends, though they genuinely love him, seem intimidated by him. "It's very difficult to confront him," one told me.

Dobson leaves a trail of bruises. He does not leave a trail of bodies [Stafford, an outsider, just didn't know where to dig]. His friends tend to be old friends and his closest employees extremely loyal. Many, though, would echo his old friend and USC medical school colleague Mike Williamson: "I realized that the only way we would work together was if I let him be the pilot of the ship."[2]

Dobson has his brighter sides, as we all do. But anyone who knows Jim well and will speak of him candidly will tell you that two of his least endearing qualities are arrogance and control and that he is often a royal pain to be around because issues must be resolved his way. This is especially true if you have an eye for doing business in the niche market he dominates—that of conservative American Protestant purchasers of self-help products—where he is something of a commercial godfather. The waves of business synergism that roll off any association with James Dobson are so great then you endure his idiosyncrasies for the sake of a buck.

An example of this synergism and its effect on how, as a result, people refrain from criticizing Dobson publicly can be found in my relationship with a friend I will call Ted. I value Ted's perspective on the Dobson religious subculture, so I called him and asked to interview him about some of the ways I would be describing Jim's world to you. His response was that he would not want his name to appear in a book critical of Dobson, because when he wrote his first book he needed a celebrity within this marketplace to endorse it. Jim did so. My friend was virtually unknown at the time. He told how Dobson had read his book, invited him to appear as a guest on the "Focus on the Family" radio program (I remembered the story, I was the radio co-host at the time and had suggested that we interview him), and gave Ted and his publisher a strong endorsement that went on the front cover. My friend indicated that his book had just passed the milestone of one million copies in print. "How," he asked, "could I say anything that might be construed as critical of the man who did that for me?" That is commercial synergism and its ability to produce interpersonal indebtedness. It is a powerful force, both for good and bad, within the religious marketplace. And Dobson is a master at trading on the currency of indebtedness.

Those who do speak openly about Dobson invariably refer to his lifelong addiction to power. My wife and I are friends with a retired couple who have known Jim even longer than I have. In their younger years they had occasion to work on several business and church-related projects with him. They tell stories of a young Ph.D. who was arrogant, pushy, demanding, and difficult to work with in every arena in which they met him. In short, they indicate that Dobson has never been what might be called a team player.

Now flash forward to a telecast featuring ABC television reporter John Hockenberry and Dobson at the beginning of the 1996 presidential primary season. Watch for clues as to whether today's sixty-year-old version of that young Ph.D. has mellowed and is less pushy.

> **Hockenberry to viewers:** Even though nearly every one of the Republican candidates have met with Dobson, none of the front runners or any one on their campaign staffs would agree to speak with us about it. But Dobson was happy to talk about one meeting he had.
>
> **Dobson to Hockenberry:** I had an encounter with Phil Gramm a number of months ago that did not go well. And it didn't because he said he would never talk about those issues, he would never talk about the moral issues. He said, I'm not a preacher and I can't discuss those things.
>
> **Reporter to candidate Gramm:** "You did say the other day, 'I ain't running for preacher, that's your job.' And you were talking to people like James Dobson of the Focus on the Family and the religious right. Can you really get away with that? Such an important [constituency within] the campaign?"
>
> **Gramm:** "I'm not going to go around reinventing myself like Bill Clinton does. Or like Bob Dole does."

Hockenberry to viewers: But after four more meetings with Dobson, it was a reinvented Phil Gramm who stood up this month at the Christian Coalition Convention and pledged his support for making abortion illegal.

Gramm addressing Christian Coalition convention: "I signed the pledge [to support a constitutional amendment outlawing abortion]"

Dobson to Hockenberry: Don't ignore the traditional conservative vote. You do so, as a Republican, at your own peril.[3]

I've mentioned that Dobson and his associates frequently try to throw reporters off the scent of his being the single most powerful figure within the religious right. Some of these efforts to distract the media are laughable. Take the following comment in Marc Fisher's *Washington Post* profile:

Gary Bauer says Dobson became involved in politics only "defensively, when he saw government destroying the family."[4]

Wrong. I was there the day Dobson decided to add political activism to his agenda, long before he met Bauer, and Jim's involvement in politics was an outgrowth of his combative temperament and his competitive desire to beat the opposition.

Two years after we started Focus on the Family, Jim got his first taste of the surreal sense of power and control Washington offers. The flavor was sweet to this only child and, ever since, Focus on the Family's component of political activism has been a central feature of the life and work of James Dobson, one that he personally relishes perhaps more than any other aspect of it.

In 1979 Dobson heard that President Jimmy Carter was organizing what became known as the White House Conferences on the Family. He gave several reasons for the decision he eventually reached to become involved in that conference and in politics in general.

Before I describe those reasons, there is a little known aspect to Jim's first involvement in Washington that shows him to be, from the outset, as facile a spin doctor in his political activism as the most seasoned political operative inside the beltway. There was a small problem with his decision to get involved in Carter's Conference on the Family: he hadn't been invited. Dobson was virtually unknown at the time. Jim set about devising a plan to make himself known and to finagle an invitation to the conference. He refers publicly to that invitation as coming from the president himself. It was a great honor, he says, to be invited to serve the country. But the truth is that he contrived his way into the convention hall. Dobson went on the air and told his listeners how despicable it was that such conventions were dominated by "Eastern establishment, liberal, secular humanists." In his finest conspiratorial and fear-evoking style, he warned that such liberals gave government officials only one perspective on the needs of the American family—the view from hell. Then he suggested to listeners that he would be willing to present the "right" perspective on the family if invited and indicated that they might want to write to James Guy Tucker, Jimmy Carter's conference director, and urge him to invite the good doctor. It is estimated that 80,000 Focus on the Family listeners did just that—a phenomenal bit of pressure on Tucker, who proceeded to extend an invitation to this unknown religious radio psychologist from Los Angeles.

The rest, as they say, is history. Jim was bitten and smitten with the infection called Potomac fever, the symptoms of which are a rash of wild feelings that there is power in Washington to solve the nation's moral problems. I think one reason Dobson was vulnerable to this very contagious illness was a measure of boredom I detected in him with what we were doing at Focus on the Family in 1979. Long before we incorporated in 1977 and began our radio, television, and print enterprise, Jim had been delivering speeches and writing books on the right way to raise children. My sense of him in 1979 was that he had grown weary of helping parents with their bed-wetting, sibling-whacking, slow-learning, discipline-needing children. He seemed somewhat like the mother of three preschoolers who wanted a break; not to abandon parenthood completely, mind you, just to add something to it that injected a new vitality into life—say, an affair with Fabio. And the feeling of power and control one gets pressing the flesh in the hallways of Congress and speaking to presidents in the Oval Office is revitalizing by any standard.

In addition, can there be any question that the one commodity, the one product and service, the one reality that is closer to the essence of Washington, D.C., than any other is raw, unadulterated power? And since gaining and using power are so central to the essential lifelong disposition of James Dobson, you can imagine the fundamental attraction of one for the other. It's my opinion that these were the central motivations for Jim's campaign to go to Carter's Conference on the Family and why that trip was not a onetime experience of political activism for him. It has represented a large part of the work of Focus on the Family ever since. Despite his vehement protest to the contrary, a significant portion of his time and energy, and that of his staff and budget, was thereafter devoted to changing the American way of life to one more compatible with Jim's "Christian" perspective.

I do not mean by this that there was no reasonable justification for Dobson to attend the White House Conference on the Family or to involve Focus on the Family in political activism. But this turn of events definitely represented an altering of the original purpose of the organization and one which has not gone without controversy and criticism in the years since. Unconfirmed reports surfaced after a spring 1996 closed-door meeting of the Focus on the Family board of directors that serious divisions persist to this day over Dobson's intense political agenda.

Immediately after the White House conference, Jim began speaking out on this new third objective of the organization. We began using phrases on the air and in fund-raising letters that it was now our goal to make America a more family-friendly society.

One of the first things we discovered was that this was a powerful organizational change in terms of fund raising. Focus on the Family is listener and donor supported, much like your local PBS television station. While some revenues are generated by the sale of products, the bulk of income comes from radio listeners writing out a donation check for fifteen or twenty dollars. We repeatedly acknowledged to each other during those early days of political activism that it was a remarkably effective fund raising technique to talk to our constituents about the great danger secular humanists in Washington represented to their families and to offer our services as a shield against that danger. We witnessed a much larger financial return on appeal letters requesting a ten-dollar donation to keep the nation's liberal monsters away from the donors' children than resulted from asking them to send a donation to help us print a new pamphlet on sibling rivalry. If I were asked to quantify the difference, I would estimate that a fund-raising letter based on the formula "Your family is under attack, give so we can help protect you" drew ten times the volume of donations as any other type of letter. Don't misunderstand; Jim was convinced that we were indeed under attack, so the point here is not that we were manipulating the donor. We may have been wrong in our assessment of society, but at least we were sincerely wrong.

We learned that it is very easy to frighten people in this society if you have the adroit verbal ability that Jim has, and if you yourself are genuinely frightened of the future, as Jim is. Listen to a sample of Dobson's fear language taken from his July 1996 fund-raising letter:

> It is a fact that nations, as well as individuals, suffer from bad choices made by leaders who place millions of people on the cusp of the slippery slope. That is what is occurring today in these United States. In my general letter last month, to which many of you responded, I tried to illustrate how radically we have departed from the values and beliefs of our founding fathers. Most of their public policy decisions were in harmony with the scriptures, which established our nation on the bedrock of eternal truth.

Unfortunately, those spiritual concepts on which the new nation was built are being superseded now by philosophies and judgments that are rooted in atheism. The God of the Bible has been removed from every vestige of public life, as though He were a cancerous growth that threatened the life of the organism. Our public policy decisions increasingly reflect the humanistic and pagan notions of the day. This transformation is occurring, not by the will of the people who remain overwhelmingly religious, but by our elected representatives and by liberal judges who seem determined to recast society in their own image.[5]

Jim got into politics out of a combination of genuine concern for his country mixed with less noble ingredients such as a life long need to control, a love of Washington power, boredom with answering the same old questions about how to raise kids, fear of the future, and the financial benefits of basing a publicly funded nonprofit corporation on political activism. How successful has he been? How much power has he amassed? The answer is breathtaking.

HOW POWERFUL HAS JIM BECOME?

Allow me to take you, rapid fire, through the observations of numerous professionals regarding the question of Jim's influence. For example, in the lengthy Stafford profile of Dobson, Tim Stafford observes:

[Dobson] is heard on more radio stations than anyone but Paul Harvey. But while Paul Harvey offers news and cracker-barrel philosophy, James Dobson asks his listeners to take action: to organize against pornography in their communities, to write to Washington. And they do. Few organizations anywhere can mobilize the supporters that Dobson can.

In early 1987, angered that government officials had silenced Joanne Gaspar [a member of Reagan's domestic policy staff] for her anti-abortion decisions, Dobson inspired 100,000 letters to the White House. Gaspar was restored to power. Largely because of such public clout, Dobson has developed considerable influence in Washington.[6]

In the fall of 1995 ABC television did a prime time profile of Jim that included this opening statement by "Day One" anchor Forrest Sawyer followed by the second observation by ABC reporter John Hockenberry:

He is one of the most powerful men in the country, and yet few people even know his name.

On Capitol Hill he's treated like some kind of powerful lobbyist. You've probably never heard of him but James Dobson is one of the most influential leaders of the religious right. Dobson's vision to transform America is known to every member of the House and Senate and he's been delivering his message to the White House in person for years.[7]

In advance of the August 1996 Republican Convention, Barry Lynn, executive director of Americans United for the Separation of Church and State, observed in an ABC television interview,

In many ways James Dobson is the ultimate stealth campaigner. He is a person who likes power, who likes to be a king maker. I think you could make a strong case that if you had a deadlocked Republican convention, if you were a candidate you'd be more interested in getting the support of James Dobson than the support of Jerry Falwell and Pat Robertson combined.[8]

In a July 2, 1996, profile of Dobson, *Washington Post* writer Marc Fisher reported that every major candidate for the Republican presidential nomination had gone to see Dobson during the primaries; Phil Gramm made the pilgrimage to the Holy See of the religious right no less than three different times. Marc wrote:

To each man who would be president, James C. Dobson, head of the powerful Focus on the Family organization, offered his genial smile, heartfelt prayers and a stern message. The wrath of America's army of evangelicals, he said, awaits any Republican who strays from the hardline anti-abortion fold and embraces the Big Tent philosophy of pluralism in the GOP.

"Dr. Dobson is one of the best-kept secrets in America," says Howard Phillips, the former Reaganaut who created the U.S. Taxpayers party, a stalking horse that's on the ballot in thirty states this fall. "He's extremely well known and respected everywhere except the secular world of Washington, New York and Hollywood. That makes him extremely influential."

The GOP knows the numbers: Dobson's Focus family is twice the size of the Christian Coalition. The audience for his daily radio show is right up there with those for Paul Harvey and Rush Limbaugh. His mailing list dwarfs anything Pat Robertson or Jerry Falwell can put together. He's got 3.5 million families on that list, and he didn't buy a single name from the telemarketing industry. They all came to him, for advice, for the love and biblical wisdom he dispenses on the radio.

All Dobson need do is mention disparagingly a piece of legislation and the Hill is bombarded. When Dobson asked listeners to protest a bill that he believed would restrict home schooling, the congressional switchboard was paralyzed by nearly 1 million calls.[9]

If, at this point in the book, you find yourself disbelieving the possibility that someone you've never heard of before could have gained this much influence over society and issues that affect you personally, your surprise is due not to the exaggeration by any of these reporters regarding the lofty heights to which Dobson has risen, but rather to the effectiveness of his systematic campaign to disguise his activism, to do politics as a "stealth campaigner." This mild-mannered southern family counselor regularly dashes into a phone booth and reappears in cape and tights to strike fear in the halls of Congress, only to reappear in street clothes with a boyish "Who, me?" look on his face. I will explain exactly how he achieves this sleight of hand, but first allow me to describe how he put together the power base that has made him one of the most feared men on the right.

NOTES

1. Tim Stafford, "His Father's Son," *Christianity Today,* March 1988.
2. Ibid.
3. "Day One," ABC Television News, October 18, 1995.
4. Marc Fisher, "The GOP, Facing a Dobson's Choice," *Washington Post,* July 2, 1996.
5. Focus on the Family, July 1996.
6. Stafford, "His Father's Son."
7. "Day One."
8. Ibid.
9. Fisher, "The GOP, Facing a Dobson's Choice."

4 ❧ Accumulation of Power

Barry Lynn, of Americans United for the Separation of Church and State, made an interesting observation in an interview with ABC News about the means Dobson employed to reach his desired ends of gaining political power:

> **Lynn to reporter:** A lot of the names in his database came, not because somebody said, We seek your advice about legislation. It's because they called in at a time of great personal trauma in their life and those names have now become a part of a gigantic mailing list of James Dobson.
>
> **Reporter:** So James Dobson has turned a family crisis hotline into a political army?
>
> **Lynn:** That's absolutely right.[1]

I had never considered that linkage between the way we built our constituent base and the power we gained politically while serving as senior vice president of Focus on the Family. But now that I've distanced myself from the organization, and can view it more objectively, I believe Lynn has made a provocative and accurate point. And to understand that point, allow me to explain how Focus on the Family makes its money.

Everything about the economics of Dobson's business is geared to obtaining a written and financial response from the organization's millions of radio listeners, as often as possible. As I indicated, Dobson broadcasting is not commercially sponsored, it is paid for by asking the listener to fund it with a tax deductible contribution. Every day, in every reasonable way conceivable, appeals are made to listeners and constituents to write and donate. And the cadre of aggressive young business people Jim has surrounded himself with know how to move products and generate revenue. This is one of the great American business success stories. Make no mistake about it, if you're looking for one particular skill or achievement by which to characterize this man, nothing he is or does surpasses his ability as a fund raiser and a marketer of product. He is variously praised as a great speaker, a gifted family advisor, a knowledgeable psychologist, a loving man of ministry, and a crafty political organizer and power broker. But none of these skills suppresses his incredible ability to analyze a market, determine its needs for new products and services, and then create that merchandise and derive enormous personal and corporate income in the process.

If you ever have occasion to see Dobson speak in public you may make the mistake of thinking that that's all he is doing—speaking. That is not the case. He has developed remarkable abilities to do market research as he speaks. By that I mean, if you had X-ray eyes and could study his mind while he's talking, you would see that, more than concentrating on his remarks, he is scanning the faces in his audience and asking himself, "Is she interested? Is he with me?" "I'll shorten this section next time because I'm losing them." "That worked better than I expected, I'll make a note to repeat it next time."

Dobson's first book, *Dare to Discipline,* was a runaway national bestseller. His first book! How did that happen? Because of his academic research? His originality? His writing skill? No, because of his marketing prowess. Stafford writes:

> Trying out topics [during his extensive public speaking work] he found a subject that made audiences buzz: discipline. Eventually he set out to write a book [on what his research had discovered the market wanted].
> *Dare to Discipline* was published in 1970 when Vietnam War protests reached their height. The book caught the wave of reaction to the excessive sixties, and made James Dobson suddenly well known.[2]

Then, when Dobson became the CEO of his own communications company, he transferred that skill at market analysis from his personal writing and speaking to his business. Again, Stafford observes accurately:

> Focus on the Family is the most powerful organization in the [American religious market] at moving books. They choose two main premiums (books offered for a certain donation) each month, and will generally buy about thirty thousand copies of each. Their promotion also stimulates sales in bookstores. Ron Land, Vice President of Sales and

Distribution for Word Books, estimates that a book Focus selects will double its retail sales.

Recently Focus has begun publishing books of its own. So far it [Focus's first self-published book] has sold over 200,000 copies. A book that Focus chooses to promote is a guaranteed success.[3]

THE PREMIUM STRATEGY

The way you wed this type of marketing savvy with a publicly funded broadcast that solicits donations is through the use of incentives, or "premiums" as they're called in the trade. And here is where Focus becomes a powerful direct marketing business, one of the very best in the nation. The incentive for your donation is an exciting new product, say a book or cassette. The Focus announcer, or sometimes Dobson himself, appeals to listeners to write and include a contribution and, in return, offers to send them a valuable product for their family. In this regard the marketing is as creative and powerful as you can imagine. Authors who have written simplistic but wonderful-sounding how-to books about stubborn family problems, say, "How to Get Your Teenagers to Stop Acting Like Teenagers," are invited onto the program to offer their ten-step solution for every parent's teenage dilemma. Listeners eat it up. During the interview Dobson drops in numerous well-placed endorsements about the book's effectiveness in solving this never-before solved family problem: "I know what you've written is going to be so helpful to our listeners. What a great set of ideas!" And then the co-host (once upon a time yours truly) takes the final three minutes of the broadcast for "the close," which sounds like this (I can still do this in my sleep):

> Well, I'm sure you agree, listening friend, that it has been extremely helpful to have Dr. Joe Author with us today talking about a problem that every single one of us faces—how to handle our teenagers. I certainly agree with our host, Dr. Dobson, that this is exactly what we parents need to understand how to successfully raise our adolescent youngsters.
>
> But the half hour has gone by so quickly I'm sure you're already feeling that it's going to be hard to remember all these helpful suggestions Dr. Joe gave us. And besides, we only covered part of the doctor's book due to time constraints. There's so much more helpful material in these pages.
>
> Why don't we send you this entire book, *Dr. Joe Author's Simple Plan for Eliminating Adolescence,* highly recommended by our own Dr.

James Dobson. We can do that in return for your contribution of eighteen dollars to Focus on the Family.

By the way, you can also request an audio cassette of our discussion today, including the observations you've heard Dr. Dobson make about this difficult problem faced by every family, advice which is not contained in Dr. Author's book. We'll include it for an extra contribution of just seven dollars. You can listen to it and then share it with other families wrestling with teenage problems.

And remember, when you send that donation you're not just ordering a book, you're making it possible for us to carry on all the projects underway here at Focus on the Family to ensure that America will be a more family-friendly place in the future for you and your children.

Here's that address. . . .

Did the image of a television infomercial just flash across your mind where an entire half hour, rather than just a sixty-second commercial, is designed to point out a need you have and then a product that will meet that need? That is the marketing formula here. Most Focus on the Family broadcasts give the appearance of a half-hour talk show but are actually thirty-minute infomercials for a Focus product. It's ingenious as well as perfectly legitimate.

Once listeners write, whether or not they contribute, their names are added to a mailing list: one of those infamous donor data bases from whose bowels flow endless direct mail pieces known disparagingly as "junk mail," although I would argue that our junk mail at Focus was the best junk in the marketplace. And placing a new name and address into the mailing list is the means by which the next level in the business relationship is reached. This type of business is conducted with a progression in mind: Get the listeners to provide their mailing address, get them to give their first contribution, get donors to give more regularly, get them to make a "pledge" that they will donate so much per month, get contributors to make a large one-time gift at the end of the year (December and January are the peak months for gifts to charities) in addition to their pledge, and then get them to include Focus on the Family as beneficiaries in their wills.

To help nudge this progression along, a complimentary magazine is mailed monthly to all households added to the list. The magazine, also called *Focus on the Family*, contains an exact replica of the marketing formula used on air. It has self-help how-to articles on nagging family problems that give the appearance of being solely an informational service to the reader, although they are not. In addition to providing information they are intended to draw the reader to the centerfold which reads like the finest mail order catalog Madison Avenue can design, pulling effectively on the purse strings of donors. That's where readers discover that the helpful article they read on page 1 by Dr. Joe was actually an excerpt from Dr. Joe's new book which can be ordered for a gift of eighteen dollars.

In addition to the magazine, Dobson writes a "personal letter" to his list six to ten times each year addressing some new concern about the survival of the family and asking for yet another donation to the cause. Often his letter reinforces the value of some product of the month, lending yet another marketing voice to this "buy now" atmosphere and this marketing juggernaut.

KEEPING ACCOUNTS

By the way, the accounting on products that go to customers is done as precisely as you would find at any commercial mail-order house. When donors contribute, the computer creates a positive balance on their account. When they request a product the computer debits the account. So if listeners hear about a book offered for a donation of eighteen dollars and a cassette for seven dollars and send a check for twenty dollars requesting both, there is a distinct possibility they will receive only the book and a note that the cassette could not be included because the donation ("purchase remittance") was insufficient. Dobson brags about the flip side of this policy, the company's occasional willingness to send products to those who state that they have no funds at the moment, but has never to my knowledge spoken publicly about this side of the policy. It's true that Focus even maintains a "Benevolent Fund" to send cash to listeners who state that they are destitute. But the fact remains that donation amounts are tracked against product value and constituents are sometimes refused products if their "donation" is not sufficient. It's called doing business.

But we're not done with our lesson in Focus on the Family economics. Sprinkled generously throughout Dobson's broadcasts and written communications is a generalized offer to listeners that sounds like this—If you have a family problem, a need regarding your children or your marriage, and you don't know where to turn, we're here for you. We will do everything in our power to help you. One report stated that Focus is receiving approximately 300,000 letters and phone calls *per month* as of this writing, most containing contribution/product purchase checks. This "river of Focus-sustaining mail," as Dobson calls it, breaks down as follows: 10 percent of those writing include in their letter some need or family life question with which they would like assistance. And 10 percent of those, or 1 percent of the overall mail, contains emergency, crisis requests for help from constituents.

In response, two different departments at Focus swing into action. The 10 percent of letters containing general questions is routed into a correspondence department, where computerized answers to the listener's questions are generated and mailed back. The department's data base has been programmed with hundreds of Dobson formulaic answers to family life questions which are merged with word processing text so that the outcome is a personalized, well-designed letter from Focus addressing your specific need. There is a problem here that many feel is serious: the answers cranked out by such a system tend to be simplistic. That's one of the issues which Stafford comments on:

> James Alsdurf, court psychologist for Hennepin County [Minneapolis], notes that, "you find that people want short-term answers. The problem is that that doesn't work in families. There are no short-cuts. I'm not saying Dobson says there are. But the way he packages his show [and materials and counseling letters], you come away with a sense that there are."[4]

The crisis portion of the river of mail, the 1 percent, is then routed to the counseling department, where phone calls are placed to listeners to offer a twenty-minute "stabilizing" counseling session and refer the listener to therapists across the country who have passed the Dobson litmus test of beliefs (i.e., "Do you, in your practice, condone abortion?").

This 1 percent group—those writing because they are experiencing severe personal circumstances; or who have just been diagnosed as terminally ill; or who are penniless, abandoned, or suicidal—is also added to the Focus on the Family mailing list. And this mailing list is exactly the same list used to mobilize Americans for political action.

RECRUITING THE TROOPS

So Rev. Lynn makes an intriguing point: Dobson has built a powerful grassroots political machine by appealing first to people's everyday parenting and marital needs (and is there a parent among us who doesn't need a little help?) and then by offering to assist with crisis needs and, finally, by having gained the constituents' trust and perhaps even a sense of indebtedness. Jim then asks if they will help him by writing to Congress in opposition to some bill that displeases him. Do they respond? Of course they do. And it is that powerful stimulus-response mechanism that drives Dobson's political machine. When he tells his constituent base that Washington needs to be pressured, they put on the requisite pressure as well as any political machine in America. Is this observation by Lynn the description of a crassly manipulative ploy, to pretend to care about people's personal needs in order to recruit them for political action? No. But it is an accurate description of one of the ways Jim rose to power.

One can find additional explanations for his rise to prominence as a leader of the religious right beyond the I-help-you-you-help-me element of Focus's relationship with its constituents. For example, a reporter named Scott Fagerstrom, formerly the religion editor of the southern California *Orange County Register* newspaper, observed during a recent telephone conversation:

> If you are not a conservative Protestant of the Dobson variety you probably don't understand the kind of power a religious leader like Dobson has over his followers. It's one thing when our boss tells us we have to do something or we'll get fired or when our parents say we must do a chore. But the kind of feeling that moves in the heart of the faithful when a religious leader says, "We must do this," is on a much higher plane.
>
> A man like Dobson rises in the minds of his followers to a level that people believe he speaks with the authority of God. He has gained the stature of a pope in the Middle Ages, the ability to direct the masses politically one way or the other in the name of the Almighty. And, unfortunately, the masses don't question him.

Scott is right. If you had been raised in my religious world, you would have grown up with an indoctrination more pervasive and more powerful than you could consciously assess of the concept that God places in certain people special gifts and callings for leadership and the rest of us must fall into step behind them. A favorite Bible phrase used by conservative ministers when they want to remind parishioners of their obligation to do so states: "Touch not mine anointed, saith the Lord" (Psalm 105:15). It means what it says—keep your hands off God's leaders. And we dutifully do so. We follow. We follow very well.

Closely akin to this aspect of Jim's influence is another source of power on which Jim trades—hero worship. This characteristic of Jim's particular religious sect leads to all manner of failings and dangers. He is one of the top two or three heroes of this particular group; similar in stature in their minds to, for example, Billy Graham. Because of this elevated stature, Dobson represents as a hero a validation in their minds of the truth of their position. He is right, which means they are right. His powerful support for certain views, perspectives they hold but may not be able to articulate, makes them feel better about holding those views. And he is their standard bearer when he goes to Washington, the one who speaks for them and holds the key to saving them, their family, and their nation.

This mindless hero worship is one of the reasons, in my view, for the strange phenomenon we observed of donors continuing to send contributions to Jim and Tammy Faye long after it was clear that the donations were being improperly managed. How could their supporters doubt their hero without doubting themselves? So they didn't. And very few people within Dobson's religious world question him either.

ARTIFICIAL INTIMACY

One final reason why Dobson commands so effective a political following, perhaps the most difficult area to describe, has to do with the offer he extends of an artificial replacement for the lack of community in the lives of so many; the absence of caring relationships and friendship experienced by many in our culture. James Dobson offers to be your "friend." And at a time when love is in generally short supply, people bite on that offer with ravenous hunger, with the result that a very strong but artificial bond develops between them and this leader.

On the air, Jim refers to his audience as his "listening friends." Every fund-raising letter he has ever written has begun, "Dear friend." His radio guests are introduced as "good friends of Focus on the Family," thus creating an air of warmth and intimacy extremely attractive to those wanting to be included as friends. Donors who, instead of making random gifts to Focus, make a written pledge of a regular monthly contribution are enrolled in a special category of relationship with the organization called "Friends of the Family" and receive special attention and benefits.

The on-air version of this friendship banter sounds like this:

> I was thinking, dear listener, as I was looking through some recent mail
> to our organization, of the special friendship that exists between you and
> us. I realize that we meet around these microphones each day rather than
> in person but, in all honesty, we feel a closeness to you that is no differ-
> ent than if we were right there sharing a cup of coffee and whatever you
> enjoy baking up in your kitchen. It's clear that we share common inter-
> est and concerns; that we laugh at the same things and cry over the same

problems in our country. Thank you for extending your friendship to those of us here at Focus on the Family and, rest assured, we love you, care about your family and pray daily that God's very best will be yours.

Warm words in a cold world. That is, until you open the dictionary, read the definition of friendship, and suddenly realize that what you experience listening to a broadcaster is, by definition, a quasi-relationship at best. Imagine if your favorite television news anchor concluded each broadcast with, "Thank you for watching tonight's edition of the news. I just want to remind you that we at the station feel such a bond of friendship with you. We thank you for being part of our family here and feel like a part of yours in return. We love you. Good night."

For Jim the accumulation of power has come through superb marketing; through the offering of friendship and caring; by touching highly sensitive nerves of family need; by building trust and indebtedness; and then by addressing this vast constituency, currently some five million people strong, just as an Old Testament prophet would, "Our nation is in danger of damnation. I cry against it. You cry against it with me." And they do just that.

NOTES

1. "Day One," ABC Television News, October 18, 1995.
2. Tim Stafford, "His Father's Son," *Christianity Today,* March 1988.
3. Ibid.
4. Ibid.

5 ❧ Guerrilla Warfare

How did James Dobson, perhaps a man you've never heard of, become so powerful without more people hearing about him? How did this son of a rural southern preacher rise to the status of one of the most influential political figures on the nation's right without becoming a household name in the process? In a word—by design.

Throughout the birth and the development of the public policy dimension of Focus on the Family, one of the most interesting and, frankly, disturbing aspects of what Jim has done, has been to establish a powerful political action enterprise while working hard to deny its size and purpose, to keep the American press at arm's length, and to sidestep the scrutiny of him and his political work that is a prerequisite for such leadership.

Members of the media have been systematically subjected to a two-part strategy by Jim ever since he became politically active: (1) Their requests for interviews are greeted with a sincere sounding "Regretfully, Dr. Dobson is too busy." And (2) if fortunate enough to get an interview, the media are informed that Dobson has very little involvement in politics. Neither of these is candid or responsible in my view.

This element of deceit and disrespect for public accountability to the press is one of the reasons why James Dobson has disqualified himself from public policy leadership. James Dobson deserves to be acknowledged as a legitimate contributor to family life in the same spirit as T. Barry Brazelton and other family life professionals are appreciated for similar contributions. His resourcefulness is immense and deservedly appreciated by the millions who have purchased Dobson's products and who feel they have gotten their money's worth. But it is an altogether different issue whether Jim should be revered, applauded, and listened to in the area of public policy formation and political activism.

I assert that, by definition, if you offer yourself for leadership in this area you must accept the consequence that what some call the fourth branch of government, the free press, will be allowed access to you and will be given an honest and forthright disclosure of your goals, opinions, and objectives; that you will accept their legitimate role to question you and will make yourself accountable within reason. It is nothing more than a fair and essential contract between a public policy leader and the people who are affected by his policies, that if the leader wants to be listened to and his ideas considered and eventually enacted, then the people who would be affected by his policies must have access to the information they want about that leader, not just the information the leader wants them to have. And that access is best gained through the work of members of the American press whom Dobson wrongly demonizes and bars from the door.

I refer to the press as the fourth branch of government in the most positive and constructive sense, while realizing that they are subject to excesses of power as are the executive, legislative, and judicial branches. The power to be grasped and exercised in this country by those in public leadership is incalculable. By definition, if we have the most powerful economy and the most influential political state in the world, then the pieces of that power that are sliced up and handed out to people in various leadership roles are greater than those conferred on humans in any other place or at any other time in history. And it is and always will be true that such power corrupts. The only cure we've ever developed for this weakness within the human temperament is what we call the "balance of powers" or the system of checks and balances whereby someone goes nose to nose with you as you possess and exercise your part of the power; challenges you; and gets the information that they're asking for to allow the public, from whom, in a democracy, all the power arises, to evaluate you and to take your power away if need be.

James Dobson fails that fundamental test of how power is and must be handled within our system. Jim, by nature, by temperament, and by upbringing, recoils against scrutiny and tough questions, and any suggestion that he must be accountable to others. As you read, you will find more striking evidence of that fact than you may imagine possible. But for now, the point I'm making is that when Jim developed the political arm of Focus on the Family, he made a conscious decision which represents, I believe, one of the greatest flaws in this man and his organization. And that decision was that he would try to work in public policy, but not be publicly accountable.

NOW YOU SEE ME, NOW YOU DON'T

This stonewalling of the media and the public it represents is spoken of blatantly by Dobson in private office conversations. One favorite metaphor Jim uses is that of guerrilla warfare.

It became excitingly evident early in our political activism that we had the power to create as much or more public response to Congress as any organization in the country when we asked listeners to contact their representatives on Capitol Hill. When we first tried our hand at letter writing campaigns we began to get reports from friends on the Hill and at the White House of quantities of mail, postcards, telegrams, and telephone calls hitting Washington that were historic in their numbers. Never before had so great a public response to legislature been received, we were told. And that provided a type of emotional rush for Jim and all of us that prompted the following line of reasoning.

Jim would say, a broad smile on his face bordering on a smirk, that he envisioned us waging guerrilla warfare. He would laugh as he spoke of our listeners' letters and calls striking Capitol Hill like mortar shells. He would say that he loved the thought of the political power brokers in Washington grabbing their binoculars and running onto the balcony of the Capitol trying to spot where the mortar shells were coming from. Jim enjoyed the idea that Washington could be taking a massive hit of public opinion for which he was responsible but that they couldn't locate him for any responsive or defensive action. Hit and run. Jim likes that approach to politics.

Dobson frequently told us that he refused to give the press access to him the way Jerry Falwell and Pat Robertson did, because he thought it was a serious mistake on their part to allow the ridiculing liberal media the opportunity to attack them. So the plan was to strike Washington but not give the media a target at which they could return fire. Jim avoids the media because he believes them to be unfair, inaccurate, and unreasonably critical of people in his position. So many conservatives confer credibility on that perspective that we should pause to examine it. I don't think an American leader has the right to say, "Because I perceive the media to be of a different general persuasion politically than I am, I therefore unilaterally make the decision not to make myself available to them. I want power and I want to change the society, but I refuse to be scrutinized by the press." The hysterical, conspiratorial perspective about the media that Jim nurses in his mind and fosters in so much of his literature is just that—irrational. He tends to play the whiny victim in this area, complaining constantly about the excessive power of the media, the liberalism of the press, the conspiratorial tendencies of the networks, and how his views never receive a fair representation because the media are biased against him and people like him.

Beyond this reason for stonewalling, I came to recognize an even deeper cause during my tenure with Dobson. A general lack of maturity in certain areas also drives this press-bashing aspect of Dobson and his organization. He is basically afraid of the media. The James Dobson into whose face I looked hour after hour across a radio studio table, whose comments and observations I heard when he was feeling confident and on days when he was not, that Jim Dobson harbored substantial insecurities and fears relative to any tough, intellectual challenge to his positions.

The James Dobson who prides himself on his intellect and on his silver tongue also has, in the unseen parts of his person, deep feelings of inadequacy. And he projects onto meetings with the media an overwrought hysteria that a more mature, seasoned person would recognize is unnecessary. By that I mean he perceives representatives of the media to be godlike in their power to influence the public and Mafia-like in their power to hurt him. Therefore, he experiences encounters with them to be the emotional equivalent to the early Christians willingly agreeing to go into the center of the Roman Coliseum for a struggle to the death.

A Consuming Antagonism

As I said earlier, any analysis of why Dobson functions as he does must keep in focus the issues of power and control. Since Jim is not in control when he's dealing with the media, he therefore thinks an appropriate response is avoidance. This may be fine for a writer of books on family life or a radio talk show host. But it is not, in my view, if he desires a significant role as a formulator of American public policy.

I viewed with humor the many occasions on which members of the religious media approached Jim for an interview. Jim's response would often be: "I will grant the interview but only on the condition that I get to see the article before it's printed and make changes." Now the remarkable thing is that even though members of the mainstream press would laugh in the face of someone making this demand, Dobson is so powerful and interviews with him so coveted inside his specialized marketplace, that reporters from the religious media agreed to this controlling condition. What resulted was a remarkable abridgment of the independence of the press where Jim would edit what he had said to the reporter interviewing him so that it turned out exactly as he wanted it to.

Such is the style and the manner, the desire for power and control, and some would say, the megalomania of James Dobson. And such was the guerrilla-like development of the political ways of this activist. To this day, it's very difficult for reporters to get interviews with him. I spoke recently with a member of the staff of Jim's hometown paper, the *Colorado Springs Gazette Telegraph,* who volunteered his shock at how little access even the local press has had to Jim since he arrived in town in 1991. The reporter said that he knew of no personal visits made to the paper by Jim and of only two or three opportunities for the paper to visit with Dobson at his massive new headquarters building. He spoke of being invited once to the Dobson home for an interview with Dobson's wife, Shirley. During the visit Jim refused to participate in the interview or even to be photographed with his wife.

Then, when members of the press do succeed in getting a few fleeting moments with Dobson to probe his political opinions, what they hear is that his political activism is a very minor, almost incidental part of his work. And yet something approaching the opposite is a more accurate portrayal of this master of clandestine politics.

6 ❦ Streetfighter

One of the most carefully papered-over aspects of the true James Dobson is the fact that he is by nature a fighter—a combative person whose temperament is to dispute rather than dialogue. The James Dobson I observed in private and worked with daily for a decade often displayed irrational animosity toward people of opposing viewpoints, demonizing them rather than acknowledging gracefully the obvious—people of good faith can interpret facts differently and can come to differing conclusions.

This fighter instinct causes him generally to proclaim his views to the marketplace in a monologue rather than looking for opportunities to engage in a positive exchange of views in the best tradition of public discourse and debate—cardinal rules of a democracy. You will never see James Dobson in a public debate with a philosophical or political opponent. You will never have the experience of seeing him participate, for example, in a give and take of social ideas with a Ted Kennedy or a Mario Cuomo on the left or even with a William F. Buckley, Jr., on the right.

When you view such a public debate you have the distinct impression that the participants understand the distinction between themselves and the ideas they're presenting. You detect a lightness in how they handle their own thinking, a personal security with which they present them to their listeners, as if they hold ideas at arm's length so as not to suggest that the idea is the person. They can offer their opinions with a sense of humor, evenness, and proportion even though they may be talking about the explosive issues of the day and facing someone passionately opposed to their thinking. These characteristics are not present in James Dobson or in his style of communication. His approach is domineering, controlling, and uncontested; it is a monologue.

IT'S PERSONAL

James Dobson takes it quite personally when someone disagrees with his views, often becoming insulted and angry, lashing back in an emotional rather than rational manner. In his view of people and relationships, someone who disagrees with him is criticizing him, trying to discredit his intelligence and ability to process philosophical and theological truth. He experiences such a personal affront when dealing with people who strongly disagree with his ideas that he simply does not place himself in a public setting where his ideas will be strongly contested.

My current work is in the field of marketing and customer service. We have a term in the customer service industry for the mistake Jim makes in responding to differing perspectives. We tell trainees, "Don't allow yourself to get hooked by angry customers." By that we mean it is almost unavoidable in human discourse to feel yourself beginning to take critical statements personally and to feel reactive emotions rising when hearing a customer criticize you and the company. The pathway through this type of encounter can be found first by acknowledging the reason for the customer's strong feelings, treating that reason with respect, and then addressing the root problem, not the emotion being displayed. Meanwhile, you guard against allowing yourself to feel that the customer actually means "you" when he says "you." Place Jim in close contact with an opponent with passion and he will invariably swallow the bait, the hook, and the line rather than simply address the root issue and leave his personhood out of the discussion.

I remember suggesting to Jim early in our work in the radio studio that we should host debates; that we should invite someone of the opposite viewpoint to join us from time to time for an honest dialogue on a subject. His response was that Phil Donahue could host the debates, he intended to use his program to promote his own personal perspective—period. The reference to Donahue said it all.

Shortly after "Focus on the Family" began, Jim had been invited to participate in a debate on Donahue's national television show, a plum of an opportunity for public exposure. Jim accepted. The topic of the day was spanking children and opposite Jim was a family life professional whose thesis on the subject he summed up with the phrase, "Children are people and people are not to be hit." Jim lost the debate on points. He was not able to prevail in the contest of ideas that took place in that Chicago TV studio that afternoon. And he never got over it. To this day he will bend your ear with excuses about the loss such as, "You can't believe how Phil stacked the audience against me and then worked them into a fever pitch against spanking before the taping began." Or, "If you added up the on-air minutes Donahue gave my opponent for his position and the time I was given to respond it was a joke. The whole thing was rigged." I was there that day. Actually, Jim just lost the debate. And, to my knowledge, he has never accepted another invitation where the ideas he espouses, views he now presses on members of Congress and presidents, are openly contested.

FIGHTING FAIR

This refusal to enter the arena and honestly debate his public policy ideas, considering respectfully the views of his opponents and weighing the relative merits of the two sides that exist to every public issue, discredits Jim's claim to public policy leadership from my perspective. Consider, for example, how ideas become laws in our society. We begin with widely diverse views on how to resolve a particular problem. Those perspectives are discussed in the public square by means of conversations, citizen to citizen, talk shows, newspaper editorials, and other forums. Then they make their way to our representatives in government who, through the committee process, subject various ideas for problem solving to rigorous debate. Then comes "the floor debate," where a legislative idea comes to the floor of the House of Representatives or the Senate and is once again subjected to a pounding from all sides. If a proposed solution passes both chambers, but in a slightly different form, it is refined still further by a "conference committee," where the pros and cons of differing perspectives are debated once again. Finally, this idea must pass the test of the executive branch. If constitutional objections to its application arise, the judicial may need to resolve the dispute. What is that process if not one long debate, in the best sense of what we learned in high school debate class, regarding how best to solve a problem? It is a contest of ideas, not in the gaming sense but in the competitive sense, to see which idea can stand the test of tough questioning. If people refuse to debate, if they opt out of the contest, they have, by definition, opted out of the American way. They stand outside the system, pitifully yelling at it, red faced, angry about its so-called wrongs. That's where you will find Dobson much of the time.

Not being a mental health professional by training, I must refrain venturing too far into the issue of why Dobson came to adulthood and now to his sixties so angry and intolerant of people with differing views. But, once again, the factor of his being an only child comes to mind. He often acts like somebody who did not grow up around people who challenged his ideas, who didn't acquire the requisite humility that we all gain during adolescence by standing fervently behind an idea only to have it decimated right before our eyes by an older sibling's wiser ideas. Obviously Dobson met people with different views as he grew to adulthood and obviously he handles many lesser contests of ideas well. But what I'm describing to you is a basic character flaw that I observed over the years that he has neither faced nor corrected. Jim's career is replete with intemperate flashes of anger and unattractive reactionary responses to what were simply encounters with people of differing views.

NOT IN MY PARKING LOT

The first time I witnessed this side of Jim's temperament took place during a visit to the southern California office Dobson occupied when I met him. It was a modest-sized suite on Duarte Road in Jim's home town of Arcadia, the community next door to Pasadena, the famed home of the Rose Parade and Rose Bowl. At that time his staff was composed of a secretary and a part-time bookkeeper. The suite consisted of a large inner office that Jim occupied, a combination lobby and secretarial area, and then a third room where a desk for the bookkeeper was located.

I was the vice president of the Domain Agency in Chicago and Jim was my client. We provided religious broadcasters with a wide array of professional services they needed to carry on their work. These included what we called "creative services," including skilled radio, TV, and print writers; producers; directors; engineers; editors; and artists to create the communications products they wanted to market. We also offered the support of media researchers and buyers who would determine which broadcast stations in which markets across the country should be pitched to carry the broadcaster's product, how much should be paid for the air time, and what level of donor response from that market was adequate to continue airing the program. And there were the tape duplication and mailing services by which a program reached the station broadcasting it and the satellite distribution systems that allowed live programming. And, finally, we provided those all-important fund-raising services designed to successfully appeal to listeners and viewers to write the broadcaster with a donation.

Each of these services is a skilled function. None is exercised in a casual or haphazard way by broadcasters who are successful. Each has a science behind it. You may view the financing of religion as the leaders of a particular faith offering little more than a prayer and a hope that sufficient revenue will be generated to meet obligations. That's not the way it works. There is as much business strategy and as many tactics behind the scenes at a religious organization as there is at a nonreligious one.

On one particular day early in my agent-client relationship with Dobson, I witnessed what for me was a very surprising exchange inside Jim's office suite. A man walked into the front lobby and asked to see my client. Jim dismissed himself from our conversation and walked out of his office leaving the door open. The man asked if Jim owned the large red Mercedes sedan parked directly behind this gentleman's car and blocking him in his parking slot. Dobson responded that he did, and asked the stranger in a curt tone if he had taken the time to notice that the office building had reserved parking slots and that he had parked in Dobson's personal slot. The man said no, he had not, that he had just been visiting the building and hadn't noticed any lettering or numbering on the slots. Dobson proceeded to inform the surprised visitor that he had deliberately blocked him in the parking space in order to teach him to be more careful the next time he came to the building. With that Dobson walked down to the parking lot, backed his Mercedes off the man's bumper, and allowed the shell-shocked visitor to escape.

That incident has repeated itself and grown in intensity with the passage of time as Dobson's power has increased—from consciously interfering with people's cars to consciously interfering with their lives and their civil rights.

Unfortunately, James Dobson is not a moral crusader about whom you would say his motives and the energy driving his crusade are pure. He is not a man on a mission that arises simply from a divine impulse and is driven forward with charity for all. His focus is not simply the benevolent reformation of a nation's morals for the common good of all. James Dobson is, in short, a man of mixed motives and mixed morals.

His is a drive to win. His is a passion to beat the opposition. His is a desire to prevail. He is angered at losing. Although Jim works hard to craft a public image characterized by high levels of intelligence and sophistication, of great Christian love for everyone, the truth is he is incensed at those whose beliefs are different from his own and who are projecting those views more effectively in the public square than he is. The emotion that I observed time and time again was simple anger. I looked into his eyes in thousands of private conversations, whether in our radio studio, his office, the Focus board room, the front seat of his car, or at executive staff retreats in beautiful Mammoth Lakes, California, where the men who ran his company would sit on the floor of his condominium and talk into the small hours of the morning. I looked into those eyes as he spoke about the leaders of the American women's movement, the American Civil Liberties Union, or Congress, the media, fellow psychologists and educators. I listened to him talk about individuals he had come face to face with in the marketplace of ideas. There was often little charity or understanding in those eyes or in the tone of that voice. His was frequently a response of anger and disbelief that people could accept opposing viewpoints.

IF YOU CAN'T BEAT 'EM, DENOUNCE THEM

One of Jim's worst traits is that of demonizing those who differ with him by exaggerating or omitting part of their reasoning in order to make their view seem preposterous. I remember, for example, when Jim was serving on the Attorney General's Commission on Pornography during the Reagan administration. Jim would come back from Washington with hair-raising stories of the idiocy and corruption of the positions on pornography being taken by one Barry Lynn, who was representing the ACLU at the hearings. If you study Jim's literature you'll see him use Lynn as a whipping boy even today, long after their encounter at the commission.

Jim repeatedly made the point, for example, that Lynn had taken the position that even child pornography should be protected by the First Amendment. Then Jim would lapse into one of his eloquent, golden-tongued soliloquies—phrase turning that comes so easily to his fertile mind—describing the most revolting examples of child pornography, explaining in graphic terms what it must feel like as a young girl to be abased and abused at the hands of greedy adults. And then came the powerful verbal punch line: This is the kind of thing, said Dobson, that Barry Lynn and the ACLU support. Jim included this morally shredding description of Lynn in his best-seller *Children at Risk,* "Mr. Lynn sat with a straight face and told us it was the ACLU's position that the sale and distribution of child pornography, once it is in existence, should not be prohibited by law."[1]

I had never met Mr. Lynn personally, but with Jim's help I came to view him as the very worst example of an American free speech advocate—ungodly, immoral, base, perhaps a consumer of child pornography himself, someone with no redeeming sense of societal values whatsoever. That is the powerful effect of Jim's demonizing language relative to his ideological foes.

Several years after I left Focus on the Family I had the opportunity to become acquainted with Barry and I discovered, not at all to my surprise since I had by then begun to awaken to Jim's distortion of opponents' views, that the facts about what happened at the Pornography Commission hearings were very different than Dobson's description.

First, I learned that Lynn is a clergyman with deeply held spiritual and moral values—they just happen to be somewhat different than Jim's, for which he has been condemned to hell by Dobson. He and his wife have been married for more than twenty-five years and have two children. Once in 1996, when we talked at length by phone, he was at home taking time away from work so that he could participate in an event at his son's school. Let's call that, for lack of a better phrase, focusing on one's family.

Two insights from that conversation with Mr. Lynn: First, the words that make up the quote in Jim's book are essentially accurate but deviously out of context and blatantly misleading. In other words, they are offered to Jim's customers in the finest demonizing tradition. Barry testified before the Attorney General's Commission on Pornography with only one objective, to urge the commission not to recommend government actions which infringe on the freedoms of adult citizens. Lynn appeared as an advocate for permitting *Playboy* to be freely available to adults. He did so in keeping with the fundamental perspective of the ACLU, that if a government is to err with regard to censorship, it should always err on the side of granting the governed too much rather than too little freedom, leaving to citizens the ultimate decision about what type of society they will create. Let adult citizens decide whether *Playboy* should be on a rack behind a counter at the local 7–11, Lynn would say, not the government. If the citizen doesn't purchase, the magazine will disappear. Meanwhile, individual liberties are unencumbered.

And here is where Dobson's streetfighter approach to social intercourse leaps into plain view. While testifying on behalf of this broad basic precept, that adults should choose for themselves, Lynn was asked by Dobson to articulate for the commission the ACLU's position on *child* pornography. It was Dobson, not Lynn, who introduced this subject. And the question was not how Lynn himself saw the issue but how the ACLU saw it. The distinction is important because it so happens that Barry differs with the ACLU's perspective here. So committed is the ACLU to fighting censorship, the organization extends its opposition to government controls even to materials containing child pornography. Lynn, however, believes such materials should be restricted and even attempted to change the ACLU's position without success. But Dobson solicited the organization's hard line position, knowing what Lynn would be forced to answer, and then turned that answer into a bludgeon against his ideological opponent for the next twelve years. That is the streetfighter style.

The Joys of Uncompromising Beliefs

Barry told me a second story about his work in the field of censorship that serves as yet another example of the contrast between the Dobson approach to public policy debate and that of productive participants in societal discourse. At issue was the question of whether children should have free access to Dial-a-Porn messages via the telephone. Ultraconservative activists of Dobson's stripe, including Don Wildmon, famed boycotter of virtually everyone and head of the American Family Association, mounted a campaign years ago to make Dial-a-Porn illegal. Lynn and the ACLU took their traditional position that American adults can decide that on their own; they don't need the government to make such decisions for them. However, Barry tells of his attempt to find some common ground on the issue that would satisfy at least some of the concerns of the conservatives in the spirit of that fine American public policy endeavor of compromise, building consensus, and striving toward a meeting in the middle. An idea was fashioned and proposed to the Dobson and the Wildmon forces. What if providers of telephone pornography were required to issue PIN numbers like banks provide adult customers? The telephone messages would still be available to adults, thus respecting the views of advocates of free speech, but children could not access them because you would have to be an adult to acquire a PIN number, thus respecting the views of conservatives.

I was fascinated to learn from Barry that Dobson and Wildmon rejected this compromise plan because, in their view, to accept it would have meant supporting the existence and sale of pornography. As a result of that rejection, our children can freely access telephone pornography today. In other words, conservatives like Dobson are responsible for American children being unprotected from Dial-a-Porn because their conservative approach to public policy issues is all or nothing, take it or leave it, rather than compromise and consensus.

The perspective I offer to you is this: I found James Dobson, family advisor, to be a source of encouraging homespun commonsense wisdom about marriage and raising children, but the James Dobson I helped become a powerhouse in the political arena is more than wrong: he is out of step with the American way and even, at times, dangerous to great principles of democracy such as diversity, tolerance, and compromise. Surely at work here is the proverbial "Peter Principle," the management theory that companies have a tendency to promote successful people until they reach a job at which they fail. A man who by all accounts was a capable member of the research staff at Children's Hospital of Los Angeles was promoted by society to a position of capable writer and speaker on family issues and then to capable national broadcaster and publisher of family life materials. Then we made the mistake of promoting him one more time, to national public policy leadership. There, sadly, he failed because, among other things, the requisite skills of crafting compromise and consensus had not been essential in his previous roles and successes, but they were crucial in this one.

Democratic government is the search for a middle ground between conflicting positions that can provide all parties with at least some of what they feel they need and with the satisfaction of knowing that their views are represented in society's resolution of its conflicts. And that's why we hear it said of the political process that those who are mentally agile at the business of compromise are our statesmen and women. These are the individuals who walk into the well of the Senate or House chamber and do aggressive battle with those of differing views and then have the remarkable ability, after the battle is resolved, to speak so graciously of the esteemed gentleman from Virginia or the distinguished gentlewoman from Pennsylvania. Those of us who have never worked in the political arena sometimes wonder what is going on. It's the process of debate, of give and take. It's the search for common and middle ground.

This, it seems to me, is critical to our success as a democracy. At the end of any given day it would be appropriate for congressmen and women to return home, nourishing the positive feeling within them that they have helped to craft some very strong compromises between conflicting viewpoints that have led the country forward. It is important that you understand of James Dobson that there is nothing about that type of process or about the word compromise that is positive for him. There are few conservative American Protestants who grow up believing that compromise is a good thing. We are taught to see the world as black and white, as good and bad, as right and wrong; to defend the right, to oppose the wrong. And so, unless we adopt a different paradigm as adults, we come to public policy issues not with the view that compromise is a good thing but with the view that we must prevail in our position. There are no right-wing religious types involved in public policy who go home at the end of the day and say to their spouses, "I had a wonderful day compromising." To say those words would be exactly the same for someone like James Dobson as saying, "Today I set aside part of that which is right and accepted some wrong into my position so that in the process my new position, partly right and partly wrong, could be agreed to by many people with whom I work." For a person like Dobson to pursue the work of compromise would mean saying at the end of the day, "During the course of my day I incorporated some sin into my position so that in the process I was able to achieve some unanimity with my fellows."

Compromise of a certain type is literally impossible for James Dobson. He is a combatant in part because of his religious ideology. He is an antagonist in relation to his foes. He is poorly equipped, dangerous, and not to be trusted as a leader in the public policy arena. His objective is not to meet those who disagree with him on some common ground; it is to overcome and dominate them.

NOTE

1. James Dobson, *Children at Risk* (Dallas, Tex.: Word Inc., 1990).

7 ❧ Fighting Words

It is not only those who stand outside Dobson's particular religious group who encounter and question his streetfighter tactics; a growing number of those within his own religious tradition are doing so as well. I want to tell you four revealing stories about Dobson's mini-wars with his own beloved "brethren."

In recent years the name Ralph Reed has become a household word. He is head of the Christian Coalition, the politically active group associated with televangelist and former presidential candidate Pat Robertson. From what you've heard here of Dobson, you might assume that Ralph and Jim are close friends; they probably talk together daily and golf on weekends. Right? Wrong. There is an interesting myth on both sides of the political fence that the other side is extraordinarily cohesive, unified, and well funded—virtually unstoppable. It's simply not true on the right any more than on the left. And Dobson's personality is one of the reasons. He does not build coalitions. He does not share power, even with brothers in the faith.

Regarding Reed, if you surveyed Dobson broadcasts over the past several years as well as his written materials, you would be surprised to discover that it is almost impossible to find any reference to Ralph or his politically active boss, Pat Robertson. Jim has a polished, ready-for-the-public answer for this, having to do with the fact that Ralph and Pat are both busy doing their thing and Jim is busy doing his and they simply don't have the time to get together, but they love each other dearly and wish they could see more of each other. The truth is that Pat and Jim are rivals more than allies. I can offer you four primary reasons for this estrangement.

First of all, Robertson and Dobson are very different men and have chosen differing strategies for their political activism. Robertson has clearly selected a very "up front" style, going so far as to run for president in 1988. Dobson, as I've explained, has chosen a behind-the-scenes stealth approach, being every bit as active as Robertson but disguising his political reformism in order to avoid the scrutiny of the press. Jim often ridicules the approach Falwell and Robertson have taken as that of a soldier in a fox hole close to the dividing line between the two warring armies who suddenly stands up and shouts to the enemy, "Here I am, shoot at me."

Second, they do their religion very differently. Robertson is a "charismatic," believing in such sensational religious experiences as a person being given the ability to speak another language, including the language spoken in heaven, as well as the ability to touch a person and heal them of disease. Dobson, on the other hand, cannot abide the charismatic wing of the faith, viewing "speaking in tongues" as potentially demonic and disease as inevitable and sometimes even helpful to our spiritual development.

Third, both men have enormous egos and getting them to work together would be like getting two highly strung entrepreneurs to abandon individual corporate dreams they're pursuing and merge forces. It might happen, but only as a marriage of extreme necessity.

Finally, they don't like each other very much. Ralph Reed's book *Active Faith* describes some of the suspicions between the two men and their respective staffs. More than anything, it reads as if he and Dobson and the two camps they represent are virtual strangers.

The root of Dobson's dislike for Robertson can be traced back to an incident in which I participated. During the early years of Focus, when Robertson's television program, "The 700 Club," was successful but we were not, we worked with the producers of Robertson's show to secure a guest appearance for Jim. It was arranged that Jim would fly to Virginia Beach on a particular date for a twenty-minute interview segment on a book he had just released. The first discomfort that Jim encountered was that Pat did not meet him at the airport. That mattered to Jim. And that affront, in Jim's thinking, was compounded by the fact that the staff member who did meet Jim clearly had no idea of his accomplishments. But it was to get worse. As that day's interview assignments were organized, the Dobson segment was not taken by Robertson but given to a subordinate. Jim did not merit the "A" team. And the final insult came when Pat did the live on-air introduction of the upcoming segment between the subordinate and their special guest, "psychologist and author Dr. James Dotson." Right, he mispronounced Jim's name.

Jim never forgot it. In the years of association I had with him thereafter, he never showed the slightest interest in working with Robertson. Nor did Pat court Jim's friendship or partnership. And I'm certain that Jim's streetfighter temperament played a part in this nonalliance. Take, for example, a story Reed tells in *Active Faith*: Ralph explains the strategy he developed during the fall of 1995 for dealing with the potential presidential candidacy of Colin Powell. Reed took a publicly cordial, noncritical approach to Powell on the hunch that he would not run and therefore there would be no need to publicly attack Powell's unacceptable positions, most especially his pro-choice stance. But Dobson read into Reed's public cordiality sinister motives. Reed tells of receiving what he called a "heated letter" from Dobson expressing outrage that in his cordial let's-wait-and-see approach in the pre-primary period, Reed had begun to "skirt the great moral issues of the day." Dobson chastised Ralph for conveying the impression in appearances on national talk shows that "politicians who promote abortion can still get our support, and that hypocrisy is a respectable avenue." Reed tells also of the intense wrath Dobson expressed toward William Bennett for his public support of Powell despite his pro-choice position.

Reed writes of needing to move quickly to deal with Dobson's explosion because, without ever bothering to speak with Reed personally or to work through his disagreement directly with Ralph, Jim's hot letter had already been "copied to numerous people and was in the process of being faxed all over Washington."[2]

I was taken by Reed's repeated references to Dobson's anger. At one point in the book Reed tells of attending a meeting between Dobson and presidential candidate Phil Gramm, where Gramm made his famous "I'm not running for preacher" statement in response to Dobson's call for Gramm to speak out on moral issues. Reed reports that as he and Jim filed out of Gramm's office, Dobson turned to him, cheeks flushed with anger and exclaimed, "I walked into that meeting fully expecting to support Phil Gramm for president. Now I don't think I would vote for him if he was the last man standing."[3]

FIGHTING WORDS

In 1995 a classic Dobson firestorm broke out on the pages of a highly respected magazine within Dobson's religious community, *Christianity Today*. A member of the academic community questioned the belligerent battle language used by some Christian political activists like Dobson in an article called "Culture War Casualties." Dobson was not the focus of the article; in fact, he was mentioned only once in its introduction. But he responded in true fighting form in what became a very telling portrait of his streetfighter disposition, setting off an extended three-article series.

John D. Woodbridge, Ph.D., author of the first article, is a professor of church history at Trinity Evangelical Divinity School in Deerfield, Illinois, and is a visiting professor of history at Northwestern University in Evanston, Illinois. His article offered five examples of why he had come to believe that warfare rhetoric in the political arena is hurting the work of the Christian church:

> First, culture-war rhetoric can be self-fulfilling prophecy, exacerbating the very conflicts it seeks merely to describe. Repeated recourse to the language of war makes it harder to love our enemies—and it is already hard to do so—because it inflames angry feelings. Second, culture-war rhetoric leads us to distort others' positions, to see enmity in place of mere disagreement. It leaves no room for nuanced positions, or for middle ground. Third, culture-war rhetoric distorts our own position too— making our message seem mainly to be angry criticism when it ought to be mainly the reconciling gospel of Jesus Christ. Fourth, culture-war rhetoric plays into the hands of extremists on the Left, who would like to convince Americans that "the religious right" seeks to impose a theocratic state on them. Fifth, culture-war rhetoric tends to create division among Christians, even evangelical Christians—for in war, there is no room for question or hesitation, and those who are slow to march in lockstep seem to be cowards or traitors.[4]

Woodbridge went on to suggest that not only is the war language used by militant activists counterproductive, but that it may also be an overstatement, a point I made in chapter 1:

> The vast majority of Americans are not hostile toward Christians and are not ready to shoot anybody. We would be more accurate to portray the bulk of the American public not as belonging to two giant phalanxes of the Right and Left engaged in mortal combat, but as religious centrists, remaining to varying degrees committed to Judeo-Christian values and to First Amendment guarantees regarding freedom of religion. There are theaters of cultural warfare, but millions of Americans are not self-consciously enlisted soldiers in them.[5]

Dr. Woodbridge has expressed, more eloquently than I could, one of the central theses of this book—James Dobson has not uncovered moral conflagrations within our society and resolved them; he has uncovered differences of opinion and enflamed them. James Dobson has not discovered a civil war of values; he has started one. If there is moral discord in the land, James Dobson is not part of the solution but part of the problem.

Several issues later, *Christianity Today* published Dobson's rebuttal. It carried the catchy title, "Why I Use Fighting Words." In it he never once acknowledged even the possibility that the struggle to address difficult social issues like abortion and to raise society's moral climate might be enhanced by avoiding frightening and oftentimes incendiary metaphors of war. Woodbridge was not part right and part wrong, his views had zero merit.

He began his defense with the argument that if war words were good enough for Christian song writers of a hundred years ago, they should be good enough for those of us wrestling with complex issues here in the late 1990s. He then quoted such lyrics as "Onward Christian Soldiers" and "The Battle Hymn of the Republic." He next cited the Salvation Army whose military-style uniforms, job titles, and brass bands supported his rhetoric. Next came a recitation of Bible verses intended to show that the writers of Scripture were certainly not shy about using such martial language.

CHEAP SHOTS

Peppered throughout Dobson's arguments were numerous cheap, childish shots at his opponent, many of which smacked of outright sarcasm. "How could the writer have overlooked dozens of biblical references?" And "Surely Dr. Woodbridge must not have pondered his thesis before deciding to write about it." And "[Some] fellow Christians invest their energies not in the struggle itself, but in criticizing those who are putting their lives on the line. . . ." And "Instead of decrying the evils around us, they [*Christianity Today*] conclude that the real problem is one of inappropriate language used by alarmed Christians." And ". . . there are those who wish we would ignore the social issues altogether and seem to resent our refusal to do so."[6]

At one point Jim wrote, "The author implied that those who use the analogy of war are pretty unpleasant people. After having mentioned my name, he went on to write generally about Christian activists who are unloving, vindictive and lacking in compassion." Jim was correct except for one small detail. In between Woodbridge's use of Jim's name and the unattractive characterizations Jim objected to were no fewer than thirty-one paragraphs of copy with no intervening references to Dobson. To suggest that Woodbridge meant to connect the two can only underscore Dobson's uncivil and nonintellectual approach to public debate.

Jim concluded with a melodramatic appeal to sentiment that would be laughable were it not so important an issue:

> Let me conclude with a request of those who choose not to help fight the civil war of values. May I ask you to extend a little charity and grace to those of us who feel called to this cause? We are ordinary people trying to deal with incredibly powerful and dangerous institutions. But while you're there on the sidelines, I ask that you not make our task any more difficult than it already is. The world of the Christian activist can be a very lonely place. War is always tough on those who are called to fight it.[7]

Several issues of *Christianity Today* went by and then came the Woodbridge response to Dobson. I'll quote only one revealing paragraph:

> In my article, I cited Dr. Dobson of Focus on the Family as an example of a Christian leader who has chosen to use warfare rhetoric to describe the "ongoing civil war of values." But neither Dr. Dobson nor Focus on the Family was the focus of the article. To my mind, he and his organization have served as a great force for good in helping many parents with their awesome, God-given responsibility of raising children in these troubled days. Focus on the Family's literature arrives in my own home and has been valuable to my wife and me. But like a man who sees his profile transformed beyond recognition in a distorting mirror, I did not recognize a number of Dr. Dobson's characterizations of my essay.[8]

Notice three points: (1) Woodbridge did not write his article with Dobson as the focus, but Jim took it that way; (2) Woodbridge felt his points were distorted by Dobson, as indeed they were; and (3) even so, Woodbridge spoke with civility and charity toward Jim while Jim spoke sarcastically and disrespectfully about him. Meet James Dobson, streetfighter.

FREEDOM OF THE PRESS, SORT OF

But Jim's name need not even show up in an article for him to decide it is direct and unacceptable criticism of him. Witness a 1988 street fight he picked with Gary Warner, past executive director of one of the four major professional religious press organizations in the country, the Evangelical Press Association (EPA), which claims 350 member publications with a combined readership of twenty million.

When Warner wrote an election year editorial in the association's house organ, *Liaison,* cautioning against conservative Christians always lining up behind certain political perspectives and practices that Dobson and others like him employ, Dobson mounted a remarkable assault on the EPA aimed at coercing its board of directors to end Warner's ability to editorialize in *Liaison.*

It was March of 1988. The country was in the throes of presidential primaries and Pat Robertson, the CEO of an EPA member organization, was running for president. As head of the association and a professional source of input and ideas for writers, editors and researchers of member publications, Warner concluded that he should direct an editorial at the issues on the political table. Whereas he would normally have devoted himself to topics related to raising the level of journalistic quality exercised by those who read him, this was the moment, he felt, for a general piece about the right way and the wrong way for a conservative Protestant religious publication to relate to the political issues of the day.

Warner told me that he had a specific concern about the Reagan years that were coming to an end. He thought they had been divisive, leading to a weakening of the middle class, an increased number of people in poverty, and the rise of a "ruling class" or a "wealthy class" in America. In case this book is your very first introduction to Robertson-type or Dobson-type Christians, allow me to point out that Warner's concern was atypical of the ultraconservative Protestant majority of the EPA. Most viewed Reagan's place in history as somewhere just under the Messiah.

Warner, by contrast, viewed the Reagan years as a disaster of greed and other un-Christian outgrowths of the great communicator's public policies, and was alarmed about what might happen if a person like Robertson, or, for that matter, someone from the extreme left, such as Jesse Jackson, got into power. And so he wrote his member editors and writers about his concerns, urging them primarily to think through the issues of the day rather than to parrot the conservative Christian party line of the moment. There are Christian people, Warner wrote, who have feelings that are not the same as those on what is called the religious right, Christians who are at different places up and down the political spectrum. So, he urged, let's give readers more to consider regarding the issues of 1988 than simply what the Falwells and the Robertsons of the day are saying.

Warner's concern expressed itself in a general call to members to avoid being single-issue people; to offer views about the entire spectrum of issues; to widen their horizons. In addition, he made such specific observations as: "Society would be far better served if students learned to pray in church and to read and write in school," and "Marching in front of convenience stores to have *Playboy* removed is, by and large, a waste of time."[9]

You can see the problem, can't you? Dobson was a great Reagan fan. Jim had spent virtually one entire year in Washington during that administration, serving on not one but six different administrative commissions, including the famed Attorney General's Commission on Pornography. And Jim believes in prayer in school and in banning *Playboy*.

I Know You're Talking about Me

Jim reacted hot-headedly to the editorial even though it never named him. He directed three members of his publications staff to inform the EPA board of directors at a May meeting of the association that either they terminate Warner's right to write editorials as the association's director, or Focus on the Family would leave the association and take with them as many other members as they could persuade to join them. Streetfighting at its best, don't you think?

The board did not buckle. A straw vote of the members on the issue, taken at the business session of the convention, overwhelmingly supported Warner's role as an editorialist. For a consensus builder that would have settled it. But not for Dobson. He wrote Warner after the convention that he was extremely disappointed by the EPA board's decision to support political editorials in official publications. Warner recently showed me that letter, and I was struck by its intolerance. "Given the liberal perspective from which you write," Jim stated, "we do not want to be identified in any way with your forthcoming editorial opinions."

Jim's seeming paranoia was also on display in the letter. He said, for example, "Without provocation, you attacked virtually everything we stand for. . . . It is difficult to understand why an executive director would seek to undermine confidence in several of its member organizations in this way, especially if he valued their continued participation. . . . We believe we will again be implicated or hurt by the publication of your political perspectives."

To fully understand Jim's skirmish with the EPA, it's important for you to know that from the beginning Dobson bypassed problem solving and consensus building directly with Gary and the association board as a means of addressing his concerns. Jim turned instead to the EPA membership by way of a letter in which he attempted to mount a mutiny as leverage to get his way with the board.

The EPA's board continued to stand with Warner. The association's ethics committee reviewed the matter and said, among other things,

"Does the article attack EPA members or their organizations? No." And "Is the text of the article unfair? No." And Dr. Mark Fackler of the committee wrote poignantly in the final review, "An editor's job and salary should not be used as a lever to tone down opinion or to adopt a more conservative or liberal agenda."

Dobson withdrew his organization from the EPA, and convinced only 3 percent of the membership to stomp out with him. Within months every organization that pulled out rethought their reaction to the editorial and returned—all except one, Focus on the Family. Along the way Dobson never met with or spoke with Warner in person. But he did write several times, including in his letters the syrupy language religious types often use to disguise their true feelings. He told Warner in another letter shown to me, "I want to emphasize that our reaction is not intended as an expression of anger or opposition to you personally." And in another letter he invited Gary to stop by some time and finished with, "May the Lord bless you and yours."

I think Warner summarized well the Dobson characteristics showcased by this incident. He said to me during a recent conversation, "I think the story speaks to Dobson's occasional paranoia, his resistance to even perceived direct criticism and his penchant for using whatever means are necessary to accomplish his ends, and, all the while, his tendency to gloss over his tactics with words of Christian love and strange invitations to stop by for coffee—as if no negative response to his power plays were expected." To which I would add: does it send a chill up your spine, as it does mine, to think of someone who tries to muzzle differing opinion having national political power?

HIS MOTHER'S BOY

One of the most perverse examples I witnessed of Jim's penchant to pick fights with those he opposes rather than to engage in civil discourse and mature resolution practices revolved around the sad final chapter of his mother's life.

If you're a consumer of Dobson's writings and other communications pieces, you are aware that he has devoted enormous quantities of tape and ink to the subject of his parents. You know that he had a very close relationship with his father, and that no one contributed more to his thinking about the family than did his dad. You have heard that it was out in the woods during the frosty mornings of childhood, there with his dad, a couple of shotguns and a favorite dog, that he learned how to be "a man." When his father died, Jim could be excused for becoming a bit overwhelmed with his telling and retelling of the death and its meaning to him. There was the plane flight to the bedside when he reviewed with his wife his childhood. And then there was the description of the man himself—large hands, soft spoken, a reader. You can even find the exact inscription on his dad's tombstone tucked within the complete works of James Dobson. What you hear about all this seems a little overstated, but it's certainly effective sentimental communication.

When Jim's mother died several years later, Dobson devoted four full half-hour national radio broadcasts to her memory—hours of programming on thousands of radio stations. On one program we listened to a scratchy old tape recording of Mrs. Dobson playing the piano and singing a hymn, complete with Jim's commentary that "it was her favorite." A friend of ours, after hearing the first two broadcasts of Jim's eulogy of his mother, made an offhand comment that he sounded to her like a guilty son trying to make it right with his mother. There is evidence that that's exactly what was happening, and therein lies an amazing story.

We sometimes describe a man's personality and even physical appearance as that of a "teddy bear." Usually what we mean by that is that he's gentle, loving, and harmless, perhaps even large and bear-like physically, often with a ready smile and a kind word for everyone. Dobson and I worked with a textbook teddy bear on the staff of Focus on the Family, a man I will call Rick Johnson to protect his privacy. Rick Johnson—the very epitome of a kind and gracious, caring soul. And yes, as a matter of fact, he was a big man.

Rick was perfectly positioned on the staff of Focus. His job was to establish relationships between the organization and people who made major donations to it. He offered his time and his service to make certain that the list of such donors assigned to him received anything in the way of personal attention Rick could deliver in return for their sizable contributions.

Rick also shared his family's church life in common with the Dobsons. In addition to his work at Focus and his active involvement in his local church, Rick Johnson provided an extraordinary and unique service to Dobson at a very sensitive moment in the life of the Dobson family. Late in her life Jim's mother was institutionalized in a nursing home nearby, where her mind and body were deteriorating in that excruciatingly painful process where we must say goodbye to our loved ones long before they actually die. She was increasingly confused about the identities of family members and could be found almost constantly curled up in a tight ball in her bed.

Dobson approached Johnson about becoming a caregiver to his

mother, a stand-in son if you will, due to Jim's schedule. And, as Rick told my wife and me over dinner one evening, because her constant need for attention irritated him. So it was that Rick visited the dying Mrs. Dobson on his way home from work, in the evenings after supper, and on weekends, offering whatever comfort and companionship a loving bear of a man could, so that Jim would be relieved of the uncomfortable feeling that his mother was dying alone.

Now, flash forward several months. Jim's mother has died and Rick no longer works at Focus on the Family. Among other things he is assisting retired individuals at the church he and Dobson attend as they manage their financial assets. Again, it was the kind of thing you would entrust to someone like Rick.

One day Dobson got a report from a couple of Rick's clients that they were concerned that Rick might be mishandling their funds. They were understandably fearful because they were on a fixed income and a major financial reversal, such as a trusted counselor absconding with funds, would be an irrecoverable setback.

Dobson swung immediately into his finest streetfighting mode. With all the weight of his corporation behind him he called Rick and his wife into his office, without any evidence of wrongdoing, and accused them of financial mismanagement. He told them he wasn't going to tolerate Rick's abuse of elderly, defenseless people and he was going to see to it that Rick never did it again. At one point he turned to Rick's wife and asked, "How old is your son now?" She told him. Jim said, "It would be a shame for him to have to grow up without a father. They put people in prison, you know, for what Rick has done." Notwithstanding Rick's explanation that the complainants were chronic malcontents and that their accusations were groundless, Jim instructed Rick to return to his office the next day with every check he'd written for the last year for further interrogation. Rick refused.

Dobson then used a reported $28,000 of Focus on the Family funds to secure an attorney to investigate Rick's financial dealings. The end result was the discovery of nothing fraudulent or illegal, just as Rick told him it would be. In the meantime, however, Rick was forced to spend thousands of dollars of his own limited resources to defend himself legally against Dobson's allegations.

Because the religious community the Johnsons shared with Dobson was so tightly knit, Rick's wife, who worked at a nearby Christian school, experienced additional fear for their livelihood. She recounts that the principal called her into the office and ominously asked her if the "Dobson problem" was going to become a problem for the school.

To add insult to injury, Dobson announced to Johnson that he didn't feel comfortable any longer worshiping with him at the same church.

Rick and his wife offered to leave the Christian community with which they had been identified their entire adult lives, and the only church home their son had ever known.

What is the common theme throughout the Reed, Woodbridge, Warner, and Johnson encounters with James Dobson? It is Jim's instinct to resort to confrontation rather than to civil, personal, one-on-one efforts to resolve a dispute—not the approach you would expect from a psychologist and a follower of Jesus Christ who has spent an immensely profitable career selling a message about respectful, productive human relationships. And to picture Dobson wielding national power is frightening. This is a man deprived of basic relational skills and a sense of fair play, someone who often feels threatened by illusionary enemies, who provokes fights when he's in a mood to punish; a man who responds to his own troubled spirit by throwing a fist, the first punch or the second—it doesn't matter to James Dobson.

NOTES

1. Ralph Reed, *Active Faith* (New York: The Free Press, 1996), p. 252.

2. Ibid.

3. Ibid., p. 251.

4. John D. Woodbridge, "Culture War Casualties," *Christianity Today,* April 24, 1995, p. 29.

5. Ibid.

6. James Dobson, "Why I Use Fighting Words," *Christianity Today,* June 1, 1995, p. 13.

7. Ibid.

8. John Woodbridge, "Why Words Matter," *Christianity Today,* December 19, 1995, p. 17.

9. Gary Warner, "Post-Reagan: It Could Be Even Worse," *EPA Liaison,* March-April 1988, p. 1.

8 🌿 Rewriting History

In April 1996, I noticed on Dobson's Internet site on America Online that he had chosen, as the subject for his regular monthly fund-raising letter, the story of how Focus on the Family began. The article caught my attention because, as you now know, I was there and I wondered how he would describe those events. In fact, I thought we'd use Jim's letter as a way of explaining a little more about Focus on the Family's history as well as Dobson's skill as an occasional spin doctor.

Jim wrote that a "nostalgic look at the past" might be beneficial to people who write to Focus on the Family each month for the first time." He put the number of first-time writers per month at twenty thousand. That means that his mailing list of over three million American households, with donor science saying that every household on a list represents 1.5 constituents, is growing by approximately a quarter of a million households every year.

Dobson also mentioned that, in addition to those writing, 350,000 members of America Online had recently visited Focus's new home page on that computerized information service. Again, you can easily see Dobson's potential for enlisting and mobilizing fresh recruits for the war.

Jim's letter then made the obligatory reference to his past connection to USC and the Children's Hospital of Los Angeles. Here we have one of those humorous aspects of Jim's mode of operation, as I've already mentioned—doing the work of a man of Christian ministry and public policy leadership but always reminding us that he is a behavioral scientist by credential.

Then came the requisite feature of any effective fund-raising letter, a crisis that threatens the reader and the related appeal that the continued funding of Focus on the Family makes it possible for the author to intervene on the constituent's behalf. Specifically, Jim wrote that he started Focus to address what he believed to be ". . . the approaching disintegration of the family." He indicated that, at the time, ". . . the initial signs of decay were evident everywhere." (Read: for a gift of fifteen dollars we might be able to stave off this decay of everything precious to you for perhaps one more month—until you get my next letter.) I don't mean to trivialize or joke about the good Focus on the Family does. But I do question the constant heavy alarmist tone in Jim's analysis of our society. And in response to his cry of "foul" when people suggest he's manipulating his mailing list with these tactics I say: "You are the author of this letter. No one else. And it is you, Jim, who are combining in the very same document a message of alarm and a request for support. The challenge that you may be using fear tactics to raise money is a challenge you have invited."

Dobson then told the story of how he raised the capital to fund the very first year of Focus on the Family—1977. It's the account of a $35,000 grant from a publisher of his books, Tyndale House of Carol Stream, Illinois. Jim had grown weary of the public speaking circuit and had decided, as a result, to include in the negotiations for his next book contract the request that the publisher give a grant to fund Jim's new nonprofit corporation. They did, for business reasons. Dobson's books were selling very well, but the proposed nonprofit corporation would sell even more of them by placing him before a larger public by means of a radio series.

The founder and president of Tyndale House, Ken Taylor, and the president of the Domain Advertising Agency where I worked, Doug Mains, were golfing partners. And so it was that Taylor agreed to give the grant that launched Focus on the Family and recommended to Dobson that our agency would be an excellent place to spend it on the professional skills and services Jim lacked.

A SLIGHT EXAGGERATION

Jim's letter recalls, ". . . we were totally unprepared for what was about to happen," sounding a little like we enjoyed instant success. Actually, we began small and we stayed that way for longer than pleased Jim. He would make guest appearances on other religious talk shows and return asking, "Why do I get more listener mail when I appear on someone else's program than my own?" In his frequent flashes of raw business competitiveness, he would ask, "So when do you think we'll be as big as John Jess or Chuck Swindoll [other, more successful religious broadcasters]?" Jim's exact quote in this recent fund-raising letter was, "Within a few months, we were reeling backwards under a barrage of mail, phone calls, speaking invitations and requests for counseling." Just a bit of hyperbole in those words, I'm afraid. Actually we were reeling backwards under a barrage of bills, wishing for letters and donations. I realize that Jim may be indulging in literary license here, compressing two years into one sentence. I just think a better way to tell the story would be this: that after several years of very hard work, we were finally discovered by the American public and became a hit.

Jim states that to keep up with this "barrage" he had to hire and train staff to help him handle it. To be more precise, there was no listener mail arriving at the Duarte Road office, so Jim needed no staff. Doug and Faith Mains, owners of the Domain Agency, agreed to open a Focus on the Family post office box in the Chicago suburb of Wheaton and Jim's listeners were invited to write him there. My secretary would open the "barrage" of five or six letters each morning before she began her other duties, as well as prepare a deposit for the Focus on the Family bank account in Wheaton, add the writer's name and address to Jim's small mailing list, and prepare whatever return mail was required. Building the California staff of Focus on the Family would come years later.

It is especially interesting to me that Dobson writes next of the first real financial crisis we faced as a new organization. He indicates that in the fall of 1979 the organization's payables were $30,000 more than its assets. Jim tells of a crisis prayer meeting where the problem was "given to the Lord" and that in the following month more than $60,000 was donated to Focus. It was at this time that a new publisher, Word, Inc., released a product that was to make Jim a personal fortune and bring Focus enormous exposure in the marketplace—an educational film series, also called *Focus on the Family,* rented by churches and eventually seen by over 70 million viewers in the years since.

I believe in prayer, but I also recall that our new business reached a turning point that fall whereby enough people were finally hearing about Focus on the Family, finding us on the dial, tuning in for the first time and the second time, beginning to donate, and providing us with word-of-mouth advertising, that we began to grow exponentially rather than by ones and twos. Prior to this point we were adding a new radio station and waiting for new listeners in that market to donate enough money to cover the cost of purchasing that air time. Then we would invest in the next market. But now, we had reached a point of exposure and acceptance in the marketplace whereby, in the case of one expensive Los Angeles radio station, we began recouping our investment in air time within three weeks of our first broadcast.

Another change unmentioned by Jim that brought on that fall's business expansion was the fact that the broadcast was so much better than in the early days of production. In addition to serving as the project manager for the Dobson account at Domain, which meant managing the day-to-day business aspects of the work of Focus on the Family, I was the radio broadcast's producer. When we chose a conversational format for the program, that meant we needed a co-host to dialogue with Jim. I hired a female announcer in the Chicago area named Flo Schmidt for that role. But the in-studio chemistry between Jim and Flo never worked. So uncomfortable was Jim that I recall recording sessions where he asked me to arrange the studio so that the announcer sat on the same side of the table as him, both facing me as I sat in the control room. Imagine two adults having what sounded to the listener like a dialogue about, say, sibling rivalry without ever looking at each other during their conversation. No wonder we were having trouble building an audience.

Toward the end of that first year of production, during a lunch meeting that included just Jim and myself, he asked me to move out of the control room and into the studio; to assume the role of the on-air announcer and co-host. He did so indicating that the kind of animated conversation we enjoyed during our lunch breaks was exactly what he craved but could not create in the studio. I agreed and, before long, a broadcast team was born whose chemistry was exceptional, or so we were told over and over again for the next seven years. I've now been off the air for more than ten years and yet I still have the experience of a stranger hearing my voice, looking at me quizzically, and then asking, "Are you Gil Moegerle from the Dobson program?" We were a hit. Jim couched that "hit" in religious language—namely, that the "blessing of God" produced the business success—but too much of such language leads to misunderstandings about why an equally valuable company or product may fail. I would prefer the explanation: "We were fortunate to do a lot of things right and blessed with talent that we worked to the bone. Furthermore, we created the right product for the right time and market." I get nervous around God talk that gives people the feeling that certain individuals have figured out how to wring out of God something so ephemeral as business success or that their business failure may have resulted from God's lack of blessing.

AND NOW, THE HEAVY ARTILLERY

Dobson turned next, in his explanation of the history of Focus on the Family, to the social issues that stand at the center of his political agenda. He wrote about what he called the "campaigns" to abort thousands of babies, to promote teen promiscuity, to legitimize and even legalize homosexual "marriage," to block parental rights, to murder the sick and the elderly, and to end religious expression in American public life.

As I've indicated, it serves a powerful purpose to use God language and crisis talk when raising money from people of faith. I do not question that Jim believes what he writes in this regard. But now that I'm so far removed from Focus, it's disturbing to observe that this type of language raises more questions than it answers. Dobson's choice of words has just put the fund-raising question to his constituents as follows: "Don't you want to donate to a company chosen of God? Don't you want to shore up the shaking foundations of a society that may collapse without us and your donation?" Risky language.

I spoke recently with a Jarrell McCracken, a retired executive who closely observed the birth and growth of Focus and did more than a little business with Jim during those early years. Jarrell founded the publishing house Word, Inc., which became the dominant publisher within the religious market I'm describing. He signed book contracts with such Christian luminaries as Billy Graham, Joyce Landorf, Charles Colson, James Dobson, and Chuck Swindoll. McCracken knows his business and his marketplace.

I indicated to McCracken that I thought most observers would assess the relative skills and strengths of James Dobson incorrectly, perhaps concluding that his number-one skill was that of a family advocate, with honors going first to his ability as a writer and speaker and, second, to his potent political instincts. But I suggested to McCracken that I would rate Jim's number-one ability to be sales and marketing. McCracken agreed and added that he thought Dobson had been a very "lucky" businessman in many ways, defining luck as being at the right place at the right time in the fluctuation of market demands. McCracken indicated that Dobson had clearly done a great deal of good. But we both agreed that at the root of the Dobson success story—his multimillion-dollar personal fortune, and his 100-million-dollar-per-year educational products and services business—were superb market research and great product development. You see, Mrs. Dobson had no children who were business fools.

Returning to Jim's April 1996 appeal letter, I was interested to see him review the primary Focus objectives. Dobson itemized the Focus goals as (1) helping what he called "the single mom in Ohio" to find the nerve to face another week—a little melodramatic perhaps, but Jim does offer a lot of encouragement to his listeners, and (2) helping Congress understand family issues. I'd say that's accurate for once, in contrast to Jim's constant attempt elsewhere to disguise the political side to his work. Here he gives it equal billing with developing and marketing family life products.

Unfortunately, Jim concluded his fund-raising letter with a distinct misrepresentation of the history of Focus on the Family. He told his readers, "It has never been our purpose to grow as a ministry." It is simply not true to suggest that we took a different approach to growth than any other business. In the years I worked side by side with Jim, there was never a single moment when it was Jim's objective to stand still or to reduce the size of our company. Anyone who knows Jim knows that he is nothing if not competitive, reaching, marching forward. Growth was always the clear and unmitigated agenda. Not reckless growth, but certainly becoming successfully large and influential.

There is nothing to apologize for, in my view, when a business has a growth agenda. Do you know any that don't? The only problem here is that Jim said this wasn't his objective. Again, there is so much about the Dobson mentality and manner of communication that requires an understanding of his religious perspective in order for you to assess it. That is where we're headed in the next chapter. For now, allow me to interpret this strange comment about growth being unwanted. First of all, in the world of conservative Protestants, leaders are perceived to be more religious, more pious and holy, if they present themselves as being unconcerned about growth, as being surprised by God's blessing, as Jim did. Behind that paradigm is the strange belief that God is everything and we are nothing; God blesses and their companies prosper, God curses and their businesses fail. In contrast, if religious leaders were to describe themselves as in charge, making the best plans humans can and setting a course to achieve those calculated ends using the best skills they can employ, they might appear to donors as pushing God out of the driver's seat and relegating him to the back of the bus. Mind you, I'm describing why Dobson talks this way, not why he runs his business this way. He doesn't. He plans and works hard and hires the best business minds he can find—just like everyone. It's interesting that he can't just say that.

In addition, false humility is a high virtue within Jim's subculture. To tell the history of your business in any way other than Jim just did would be to risk the appearance of arrogance. Again, at issue here is not what you are but what you say, which is unfortunate. One must not say words in this religious culture that could be construed as prideful, even though one may be justifiably proud of the human achievements represented by a company's success.

A publisher friend very close to Jim described him to me as suffering from two overriding failings, a compulsion to control and arrogance. If that's true, why would a very proud man write as if he and other co-workers had nothing to do with the success of his company? Furthermore, does his God take no pleasure in humans functioning at their highest capacity? Does He demand some false assessment that Dobson's annual $100 million comes mysteriously from Him, like the manna dropped on the Jewish people in Exodus? The answer is that Jim takes credit inside his head and behind closed doors for the great American business success story that is James Dobson and Focus on the Family. But, unfortunately, he often states the opposite publicly. For that reason Jim has a problem. When you read his materials, it's hard to know when he's saying what he means and when he's saying what he thinks you want to hear. As someone said, religion can be the strangest of human endeavors.

9 ❧ A Peculiar People

A large portion of the portrait I'm painting for you is that of a professional religious worker. Consequently, many of the colors on the canvas come from Dobson's religious roots, his denominational affiliation, and his beliefs. And what exactly are those beliefs? James Dobson is obviously a "Christian." That's the easy part. Now we have to figure out what kind of Christian.

Perhaps I can best answer that question by telling you what Dobson is not. He is not a Roman Catholic Christian, an Orthodox Christian, or a mainline Protestant Christian. By "mainline" I mean Methodist, Presbyterian, Lutheran, Episcopalian, Baptist or other historic, centrist American Christian denominations.

Dobson's religion is a mirror image of his theories of family life and his politics. He springs from an ultraconservative, sometimes extremist denomination known as the Church of the Nazarene. Jesus, you will recall, hailed from the Palestinian town of Nazareth, thus the group's name. And what do Nazarenes believe? For starters, Jim and his denomination believe that the answer to the following question will reveal whether or not you are headed for heaven: On what date, where, and under what circumstances were you born again? Nazarenes are part of that wing of Christendom who believe that instantaneous crisis religious experiences are very important, those rock-your-soul emotional happenings that are so dramatic you will never forget where and when they took place. Chuck Colson's famous book *Born Again* revolves around just such an occurrence in which, seated in his car in a friend's driveway, reviewing his life, he was overcome with certain religious feelings and insights. Nazarenes encourage adherents to "testify" to these crisis experiences when they meet together. They do so in a manner that can make you feel second class or even downright unredeemed if you have no hair-raising story to share.

We're talking about a frontier denomination with roots in stem winding camp meetings where members of the audience "walked the sawdust trail" from their pew to a railing in front of the preacher's podium called an "altar." There the evangelist often warned them of the sizzling fires of hell while the choir sang "Amazing grace that saved a wretch like me." At the altar, weighed down with remorse for your sins, you are encouraged to pray what you're told will be a dramatic, life-changing prayer on the order of, "I'll never sin again if you'll just save me." If you are sincere, you are born again. Nazarenes are distinguished from pentecostals or charismatics by virtue of avoiding and even criticizing dramatic displays, such as speaking in tongues or faith-healing crusades. By the way, I myself share many of these core beliefs, with several exceptions.

ETERNAL INSECURITY

For all their talk about "knowing God personally" and "having a personal relationship with Christ" and "knowing beyond doubt that I'm going to heaven when I die," members of Jim's religion are beset by epidemic proportions of eternal insecurity. Theirs is not a safe, restful religion. That's because Nazarenes can be "converted" one day and the very next day "fall from grace" and return to their former unredeemed state. And so, if you are Nazarene, you might have a dramatic testimony about the first time you were born again . . . and the second . . . and the third. This is a fascinating aspect of Nazarenes (assuming religion fascinates you) because this group is hypercritical of other expressions of the Christian faith whose doctrines add "good works" to "simple faith" to gain one's place in heaven. And yet, if you watch how they do religion, their uncertainty about losing their salvation leads them to engage in conduct that looks suspiciously like good works—just to make sure. For example, this group is compulsive about church attendance and daily Bible reading and praying and avoiding their particular list of taboos which, as with so many religions, seems to change from generation to generation. For example, Nazarenes in the nineteenth century, the era of Dobson's evangelist grandfather and great-grandfather, were noted for labeling the use of makeup and the wearing of jewelry as sinful. You can still find Nazarenes who will tell you that all makeup is from the pit. It goes without saying that dancing and motion pictures were demonic and that alcohol and smoking condemned the soul. As I indicated, many of these super sins survived well into the twentieth century. Some Nazarenes still believe that using wine for a church sacrament or going to the local theater to see the latest Disney animated feature are evidence of being out of union with God; of loving the flesh rather than the spirit. For these believers, when the New Testament story has Jesus turning water into wine, the writer meant to say grape juice.

Nazarenes rank their sins. Surprisingly, one could attend a hundred of their meetings without ever hearing religious arrogance, the type that causes them to view non-Nazarenes as lost, condemned, although we can safely assume that such an attitude is very offensive to God. On the contrary, religious pride almost seems to be encouraged. By that I mean one can detect among them a very strong aroma of "We are the true followers of Christ." But if pride isn't on the list, what is? Chief among Nazarene super sins is any activity related to your sexuality. Best to be a eunuch. You're in deep trouble not only if you sleep with someone other than your spouse but if you even think of doing such a thing. And God forbid that you should ever look at, touch, talk about, or fantasize about anything or anyone sexually other than the person to whom you are married. And if you're not married, sublimate!

You will find books published about America's ultraconservative Christian subculture carrying such titles as *Why Do We Shoot Our Own?* that decry the ugly manner in which this wing of the faith treats those whose sexual experience includes anything not on the approved conduct list. Have you had sex before marriage? Have you been seen going into a theater showing a sexy movie? Did you get pregnant out of wedlock? Have you had an affair, even a one-night stand? Do you masturbate? Do you enjoy explicit art? Do you have sexual fantasies? Are you divorced? Are you remarried? Unfortunately, if you answered yes to any of these questions, it is more likely that you will be judged than accepted and loved.

To aspire to leadership within this subculture, one must project an outward image of being ideal in all the above categories. Having knowledge to share or a desire to serve is not enough. It is vital that you display yourself as overcoming everything currently on the group's unacceptable conduct list and embodying everything on the group's list of things Jesus would do; including, or so it sometimes seems, voting Republican and picketing abortion clinics. When I say that this group likes its leaders perfect, if only in appearance, I mean that it is not attuned to the style of leadership Christian psychiatrist and author M. Scott Peck offers. Peck introduced himself, in a speech called "Addiction, the Sacred Disease," with words no self-respecting Nazarene would dare utter:

> I think it is important that you realize that the person talking to you is an addict, in particular an almost hopeless nicotine addict. I talk all about self-discipline and I don't even have the self-discipline to stop smoking. So it's important for you to realize that the person talking to you is a phony and a hypocrite.[1]

Peck clearly believes that leadership emanates from some authority other than perfection, while Dobson's sect would write Peck off as having nothing to say to them.

In a manner that is hard to describe but very relevant to your understanding of Dobson and the rest of this book, to say what Peck just said is to disqualify yourself from spiritual leadership in Jim's world. Authority flows from images, not from reality or candor. As this chapter continues, perhaps the reason for this unusual and unfortunate way of thinking will become clearer.

PECULIAR . . . AS IN NORMAL

I titled this chapter as I did because one of the oddities about Dobson's religious culture is that its members point with pride to a verse in the Bible (I Peter 2:9) that refers to followers of Christ as being "a peculiar people." The idea goes like this: If you stop following the sinful ways of your heart and begin obeying God, then you will stand out from the rest of the world because you will not do what filthy sinners do. This quality of "standing out" from the world is a very good thing. You are encouraged to make a show of how much you stand out. Don't just avoid smoking, point out to those who do smoke that you don't and let them know the error of their ways. And if criticized or, better yet, ridiculed for this quality of standing out, take it as a badge of courage. It is good to be different and it is very good to be seen as very different. Thus the pride in being "a peculiar people."

You are seeing here the origins of another distinctive feature of Dobson's religious group—a robust epidemic of judgmentalism. It is inevitable that any group that expends this much energy maintaining lists of acceptable and unacceptable behaviors, cultivating an outward appearance of abhorring one list and living by the other and taking pride in being different from society, will emit a strong odor of finding fault with others. Jay Kessler is one of my favorite conservative Protestants. For sixteen years he was the president of a Protestant youth organization called Youth for Christ and is now the head of a university within the same religious community. An extraordinary speaker, I've often heard him warn audiences that, from his perspective, children of orthodox religious groups are sometimes the most judgmental kids on the high school campus. He describes them as sometimes compulsive about finger pointing, as if it is clearly not enough in their faith to believe themselves right. Adherents are called on by a strange tenet picked up in their religious training to point out everyone else's wrongs, to set the whole world right. Kessler commented recently in letters we exchanged,

> Certainly not all children of [Christian] parents develop these unattractive symptoms but if parents operate out of a spirit of fear, intolerance, or inflexibility, it will take its toll. This is true of all orthodoxy if it displays a spirit of intolerance. This seems to be the challenge of culture today, to maintain convictions and yet insist on tolerance and civility.

I know an attorney whose license plate reads "Sue U All." Ultra-orthodox Christians might well display one that reads "Judge U All." If one's head is filled with the view that the issues of life are clear as a bell, black and white, right and wrong, then there are a hundred incidents in any day that will activate that paradigm in the mind. Did you hear him use that curse word? That was wrong, wasn't it? Did you notice how much cleavage her new dress shows? That's wrong, isn't it? Did you hear that the six of them got drunk after the game Friday night? The children of this group, and, as Kessler points out, of most ultra-orthodox religious movements, are often like Pavlov's dogs. The bell rings, they judge. These young people see conduct that's currently on the taboo list and their mind condemns it and the person doing it. They're dysfunctional in this regard because at the same time that one part of their brain is judging their fellows as sinners, another is viewing the conduct exactly as we all do. They, too, want to have a raucous good time after the game or feel the attention a low-cut dress elicits from the boys. In some ways, the offspring of the hyper-orthodox are the most nonintegrated, unhappy of children.

If I sound unkind, allow me to add that I'm describing myself in years gone by. This is my general religious heritage, although I did not grow up Nazarene. It is one of my highest current spiritual priorities to stop judging those whose values and beliefs are different than mine. Some days I think I've made progress. But then on others. . . .

WITHOUT SIN

Allow me to balance the picture I'm painting by adding that when I describe Dobson's religious orientation, I'm describing the general religious perspective you've seen presented with great dignity and beauty by Billy Graham. Although he has made some serious political mistakes, such as supporting Nixon and his Vietnam policy, Graham's presentation of his faith has, in my view, been inclusive and positive. However, extreme groups like the Nazarenes have harshly criticized his inclusivity. You've undoubtedly watched at least a few moments of Graham's televised "crusades" and listened as he's described Christ's loving death on the cross for needy humanity. You've seen him invite those wanting to become Christians to walk forward and dedicate their lives to Christ. Graham, Dobson, and virtually all conservative Protestants would hold that this "walking forward" or a similar moment of personal commitment represents that dramatic conversion experience I described earlier in more extreme terms.

With that as background, allow me to turn to one of the most unusual beliefs to which Dobson ascribes, one I believe to be highly relevant to an understanding of the man now leading the religious right. Nazarenes are part of what is called "The Holiness Movement," an approach to Christianity that includes several small denominations and which teaches that, subsequent to the dramatic altar experience of being born again, an adherent should have yet another dramatic crisis experience on yet another date and time that one remembers forever. This crisis is called "Entire Sanctification" or the "Second Work of Grace," and as a result of it one's ability to sin is eradicated—removed—exorcised by the instantaneous work of the Holy Spirit. James Dobson believes that he has been entirely sanctified, morally perfected, that he does not and cannot sin. Now you know why he and moralists like him make a life of condemning what he believes to be the sins of others. He is perfect.

I recall an incident early in my relationship with Jim in which this belief surfaced in the Focus on the Family radio studio in an unforgettable manner. We were recording a new radio broadcast on the importance of forgiveness in relationships, and at one point in the script I dropped into the conversation the remark, "Well, one thing for certain is that we are all sinners." Dobson shot me a disagreeing glance and immediately motioned to the engineer to stop the recorder. He proceeded to lecture me on the fact that "we are not all sinners," that it's possible to rise above that type of living, and that he had no intention of using his broadcast to encourage the notion that he sinned. I remember being shocked. The man actually believes, I thought to myself, that he cruises through his weeks and months without so much as a single lustful thought or a moment of excessive pride or a hostile reaction or desire for vengeance against his detractors or even what are called sins of omission—the failure to love God and our neighbor as we should. But for Jim, none of this applies and we were not going to suggest otherwise on the air.

I'm a little amused by the fact that Nazarenes and other holiness groups sometimes refer to this state of moral perfection as having received the gift of "Perfect Love." In other words, the reason Dobson never sins is because, in his belief system, God has given him a heart that loves everyone at all times. And loving everyone with a perfect love makes it impossible to do them wrong. Somehow, that's not quite how I would describe the James Dobson I have observed for the past twenty years.

As you might imagine, Jim's sect has a creative way of explaining away attitudes and actions they display which are clearly, to the rest of us, your basic corrupt humanity on parade; that dark side we all restrain and work on improving. When they lose their temper they explain that they didn't actually lose their temper. Yes, it did look as if they lost their temper, but what they were actually feeling on the inside was not the type of rage you and I experience in our unsanctified state; it was more like moral indignation or perhaps a state of strong irritation or agitation. This is intriguing because those who work closely with Jim or observe him for any length of time comment immediately on his anger and yet Jim denies that he is ever powerfully angry. In January of 1988, in a telephone conversation with current Dobson radio co-host Mike Trout, Mike warned me that Jim was livid with me for a critical observation I had made about him. A well-known author within Jim's community described him in a conversation we had several years ago as "a very angry man; very aggressive and abusive, someone who could easily slip over the line into misconduct." A radio guest once wrote a letter to Jim asking whether Focus would enter into negotiations with him to pay him a royalty for cassettes Dobson sold of the guest's interview. Jim responded by putting out the word to our broadcast staff that this particular guest was never to be invited to appear again, nor was his very popular program to be rebroadcast as was the custom with all our best interviews.

Attorney Sam Ericcson, former executive director of the Christian Legal Society, appeared several times on our broadcast to discuss the virtue of Christians resolving their differences through arbitration within the religious community rather than going to court. Dobson wholeheartedly endorsed the conciliation services of Ericcson's organization, urging upon his listening audience what he believed to be the biblical course of action for anyone calling themselves Christian. However, some time later when

Dobson found himself in a serious dispute with a fellow Christian, he refused to participate in a private conflict resolution process within the religious community and led by Ericcson. Sam, among others, criticized Jim for his decision. Jim responded by wiping Ericcson from the shelves at Focus on the Family: banning replays of Ericcson broadcasts, the sale of his tapes, and the distribution of literature authored by the attorney or anyone else at the Christian Legal Society. I would say the phrase "perfect love" is not the first one that enters my mind when I think of James Dobson.

HOLIER THAN THOU

I mention all of this not to randomly criticize Nazarenes but because I'm convinced that this holiness issue is pivotal to your understanding of James Dobson. It is part of the reason he is so fiercely disliked by those who differ with his politics, his view of society and moral issues. It is why widespread disdain for him manifests itself in phrases like "Dobson is a moral elitist. He is an intolerant do-gooder." It is why, for example, during the recent Proposition Two campaign in Jim's home state of Colorado, a move to ban laws protecting the rights of gay men and lesbians, bumper stickers appeared in Colorado Springs that read "Focus On Your Own Damn Family!" Americans instinctively distrust and dislike holier-than-thou moralists like Jim.

The years of soul searching I've experienced since leaving Focus on the Family—years of reflection that have led me to disavow many of the extreme things Dobson stands for—brought to mind over and over the question: Why did I once do religion like Jim? What was there inside me that identified with what I now disdain, that espoused what now disturbs me—the extremism, the intolerance, the judgmentalism, the anger at things in society that are simply different, not wrong? How did I become a cheerleader for a man and a cause I now question? The answer is that my background is very much like Jim's. My formative years were lived out in a similar social and religious setting.

Naturally, there are differences between Dobson's childhood and mine. He grew up in the South while I was raised in the North in the small steel milling town of Beaver Falls, outside Pittsburgh, Pennsylvania. Sports enthusiasts may know Beaver Falls as the hometown of the famed NFL quarterback Joe Namath. I went to high school with Joe, although we were not personal friends. I played trumpet in the Beaver Falls High School Tiger Marching Band that paraded up and down the football field at Geneva College just prior to Namath massacring every high school team in Beaver Valley.

Jim's youth in Texas and Louisiana included the exact same love of football and we enjoyed talking often about the game. But the real commonality between Dobson's youth and mine was that we grew up WASPs—conservative white Republicans in homes and families that were deeply religious. And both the Dobsons and the Moegerles were involved in denominations that were "Holiness."

EXPERIENCES I, TOO, HAVE SOUGHT

I remember as a boy going to holiness campgrounds across the state line in Ohio. I recall vividly sitting in the choir in those emotional, sweltering, summer camp meetings and being caught up in the frenzy of religion. I remember on more than one occasion responding to the evangelist's impassioned offer of "sanctification from all sin" and walking to the altar believing that if my heart was inclined a certain way, if I believed the right way, if my prayers included certain formulas of language, if my will was adequately bent toward the Almighty, then some magical, larger-than-life experience would follow.

I sat in those camp meetings throughout my adolescence and even during college at a holiness school, longing for that experience, wondering about it, questioning whether I might already possess it, or might obtain it that night, or maybe never grasp it. Later, the journeys of adulthood convinced me of the error of believing that any of us rise to absolute moral perfection this side of the changes that await us after death; that the orientation from which we live life cannot be one of attaining personal perfection but rather of maturing toward that goal. And I came to realize that believing otherwise was a short cut to the disaster of religious and moral arrogance. But Jim never changed.

Here's my point. There is an important link, I believe, between the James Dobson America now experiences as the most powerful man within the religious right—intolerant, holier-than-thou, moralizing, finger-pointing—and the young Jimmy Dobson who sat on the front pews of those tiny wood frame Nazarene churches in the South fifty years ago.

Pride makes for very poor national leadership and public policy. It's impossible for people like Dobson to engage in a dialogue with his political opponents on the basis that his side might be flawed or incomplete in some way. He does not ask himself, when working on the complex moral issues of the day, whether this might be a good time to work on his own failings, to do the personal work of becoming a more sensitive person, to confront his own attitude of prejudice, and to reach toward a higher level of maturity in controlling the immoral forces within himself; to evolve ever forward to become more sensitive and caring for people different than himself. In short, it's hard to be humble when you're perfect. But it's those in touch with their own humanity, with humility, those who can identify with the personal struggles we all share, who are able to build consensus solutions to major social issues, not those holier than thou. The latter are inclined to set people against each other rather than bring them together into strong community.

Dr. Scott Peck, one of my heroes, commented on this likelihood in his book *In Search of Stones*. He referred to the famed psychologist Carl Jung ascribing the root of human evil to the "refusal to meet the shadow." Peck defines our "shadow" as that part of us containing "traits we'd rather not own up to, that we're continually trying to hide not only from others but also from ourselves, that we're continually trying to sweep under the rug of our own consciousness."[2] Peck and Jung contend that every individual has a shadow side. And Peck writes, in a way pertinent to Dobson's self-proclaimed civil war of values:

> Wars tend to be started either by individuals or by groups lacking integrity or wholeness, who are out of touch with their own sins, who are filled with pride over their strengths but lack the humility to see their weaknesses and deal with their shadows.[3]

Have we not found the fountainhead of James Dobson's war on America?

The late Stan Mooneyham, former president of World Vision, the most highly regarded world relief organization within conservative Protestantism, once offered me one of the most striking assessments of Dobson ever spoken in my hearing. He said that he believed that, like televangelist Jimmy Swaggart, James Dobson was set for a personal moral collapse. He indicated that he believed it was inevitable because both men aggressively projected their own dark side onto others. Mooneyham speculated during a conversation we had at his home, "Dobson believes he has no dark side, he doesn't accept his shadow, which only means he has pushed it into the cellar and locked the door. But it will someday roar out and do him in."

This is a good place to add what a friend of mine once said of my personal failings, "Some day you're going to have to apologize to the nation for giving us James Dobson." As you now know, I was Jim's right-hand man for those critical first ten years, and part of what my friend meant by that comment was that if one were to search for the single methodology that Dobson has used in his rise to power and influence, one would conclude it has been radio, my speciality and my primary gift to Jim. As a result, I agree that I share responsibility for many of the problems represented by Dobson's rise to power that I write about in this book.

In many ways, I gave you James Dobson. Now I wish it were possible to take him back.

NOTES

1. M. Scott Peck, Ph.D., "Further Along the Road Less Traveled, Addiction, the Sacred Disease," in *The Road Less Traveled,* tape series, tape 1.

2. M. Scott Peck, M.D., *In Search of Stones* (New York: Hyperion, 1995), p. 261.

3. Ibid.

10 ❧ As I Say, Not As I Do

When I think back to some of the things I said and did during my years with Dobson, while caught up in what we called "Focus fever," I feel a little foolish. For example, I traveled for the organization, meeting in living rooms with small groups of donors to thank them for their contributions. During question-and-answer sessions I would invariably be asked by the quintessential fan, "What is Dr. Dobson really like?" And like an idiot I would respond with a sanitized, shrink-wrapped, pre-packaged answer designed to cause people who were already engaging in far too much hero worship to elevate Jim even closer to sainthood. The most common of my misguided responses was, "Well, one thing for certain, he is a man of integrity." To some extent that was true. Dobson always worked hard to ensure the organization's financial integrity, for example, as well as integrity in our mail answering system. But now that I've stepped back from the organization and can offer that objective look that is impossible when you're inside, that was an unhelpful way of describing Jim to his public. I believe in integrity. But there's a problem making a big deal about this virtue. That is, if integrity means that what you believe on the inside you practice on the outside, then none of us has complete or pure integrity. There are things I believe that I don't practice, starting with my conviction that there is value in exercising. I have absolutely no integrity when it comes to physical fitness. None. So am I a bad person? In that spirit I want to explain why I believe that Dobson has serious problems in the integrity department.

One of Dobson's glaring private departures from his lucrative public message is the fact that he maintains a runaway work schedule, but talks constantly as if he doesn't. He seems driven by an inner compulsion, almost an obsession, to burn both ends and the middle of the candle. His work habits, by virtually every criterion imaginable, are those of a classic, consummate, Type A, textbook workaholic. And yet if you read his writings he is constantly on a soapbox stating the opposite. In the years I worked with him I was not aware of any work weeks that were less than six- or even seven-day marathons for Dobson. Jim spoke with pride about the fact that he hadn't had a vacation for years. When he finally did take one at the demand of the board, he referred to it as a "working vacation," as if that somehow appeased some tyrant running his brain who refused to give him permission to completely shut down. One year Jim took his wife and children to England on a special summer trip. When he spoke of it on the air he felt the need to add that it was a combination work and pleasure trip during which he spent part of each day in a hotel room writing his next book while his family saw the sights without him. That made it all right. We could all breathe easier knowing Jim didn't spend the entire day sightseeing.

Jim's workdays are extremely long and hectic—by deliberate choice. He takes pleasure in the unreasonable demands he places on himself. If you have ever worked with someone who complains constantly about the pressure he's under and yet voluntarily elects to undertake every single obligation on his calendar, you have worked with James Dobson. It's as if he derives some dysfunctional pleasure from being so busy that he can complain about it; as if his own internal answer to the question, "Is your life significant?" requires the response, "Yes, I'm busy, aren't I?"

There is no single characteristic of the corporate culture around Dobson you will hear mentioned more often by those who know Jim and work with him than the pace at which everyone at Focus works. It's frantic. That's because Jim is frantic and companies reflect the temperament of their leaders. Jim often refers on air to the fact that there are sixty-two different projects underway at Focus. That's deliberate. Ten would simply not do. Sixty-two equals significance.

WORKIN' 5 TO 9

I remember the day Jim told us he'd reached the point where it was no longer possible for him to use a common briefcase to carry his unfinished paperwork home at night to complete after the family dinner. It seemed funny at the time, and still does, to think of the pride Jim took in outgrowing his briefcase. He announced he was switching to a large cardboard box instead of saying, as he should have, "This is absurd. I refuse to do this to myself and to my family."

My point would be meaningless, inappropriate criticism if I were describing Joe CEO, president of Widgets, International. But I'm painting a portrait of the head of "Focus on the Family." And a central tenet Focus sells to his customers in cassettes, books, and magazines is the necessity of slowing down the pace of life and reserving prime quantities of your time, effort, and energy for your family. Search through the complete works of James Dobson and you'll find this principle everywhere. Check out his book *What Wives Wish Their Husbands Knew about Women,* and listen as Jim wows the American homemaker—who buys his stuff by the boatload—with lines like, "The number-one enemy of the American family is the pace at which we live our lives." One wonders how Dobson keeps a straight face while saying that.

This inconsistency accidentally slipped into plain view one day on Jim's own carefully spun radio broadcast. The accidental disclosure of Jim's lack of integrity in this area occurred because Jim was absent from the studio. His co-host Mike Trout was interviewing his head of publishing, Rolf Zettersten, about a new book Rolf had just written on the key virtues by which Jim lives his life—things like integrity. As they opened the discussion they inadvertently stumbled into a dialogue about how common it was for Jim to call them at home, late at night, to discuss business. Wait a minute! James Dobson routinely works late at night instead of spending quality time with his wife and two children? And he commonly interrupts his vice presidents' quality time with their families in order to extend the work day? And these guys lead Focus on the Family?

Jim telegraphs to the world this "I'm very busy; therefore, I must be important" side of his disposition without even realizing it by the way he normally begins his personal correspondence. Again, it's a funny idiosyncrasy to which I'm sure Jim is partially blind. He began one of his most recent letters to me: "Dear Gilbert, Forgive me for this overdue response to your letter. I asked Paul Nelson to call and explain my impossible schedule. . . ." Another letter began, "Dear Gil, I am leaving for an eight-day trip, so I will quickly express a few thoughts in response to your recent letter." Yet another began, "Please forgive this delayed reply to your letter. As you know . . ." (right, he had been very busy). I told you the story of Jim's much publicized magazine exchange with historian John D. Woodbridge in chapter 7. Dobson's rebuttal article began with these words, "My first reaction was to decline [writing this rebuttal]. I didn't have time to reply."

Apparently this illness is catching. The last time Mike Trout wrote me he began, "Let me begin by explaining why it's taken so long to reply to your letter" (he had been very busy, too).

Tim Stafford observed in his *Christianity Today* profile of Dobson that many call Jim a workaholic and that he hates the label. He dislikes it because it contradicts his well-crafted public image. Nonetheless, Stafford was exactly right.

I'LL BE HOME SOON

I recall a meeting of the executive staff of Focus on the Family in which our frantic corporate pace came up. We were discussing the staffing needs of our burgeoning publications department. The specific issue on the table was a report from Ròlf Zettersten, head of publications, that one of our magazine editors, whom I will call Randy to protect his privacy, had been working overtime for three months to help us launch a new magazine and now that the magazine was up and running, he wanted to get back to normal hours. The time had come, according to Rolf, to hire another editor and divide the work. Dobson responded with a reasonable CEO-type question about whether there was a way to avoid the additional payroll expenditure. Rolf indicated that the current editor's work ethic was excellent, and there was no problem with his productivity, but he refused to work any more overtime, since he had done so for three months straight. Randy stated, we were told, that he had made a firm commitment to his wife to leave Focus on the Family at five o'clock and that his young boys could expect Dad in the back yard pitching ball with them by five-thirty every day.

Now, if you read Dobson's books or listen to his eloquent sermons on the need for American dads to reserve time for their families rather than focus solely on climbing the corporate ladder, you would assume that at that moment James Dobson would stand with moisture in his eyes, turn to us all, and say: "Rolf, that is one of the most inspiring reports a vice president could bring to the Focus on the Family boardroom table. I want to make a positive example out of Randy. I would like you to tell his story within our staff and in our magazine emphasizing that the CEO of this company said that Randy's values are exactly those by which he wants every single member of this staff to work. Spread the word, gentlemen, if we can't live this stuff here at home, we've got no business selling it to the world."

Sadly, Jim displayed nothing remotely resembling that attitude. His first response, upon hearing that this young father refused to work any further overtime, was, "Well, we'll just have to find someone who will!"

In other words, he suggested that we might have to terminate a man for focusing on his family. To Rolf's credit, he held his ground and made the case again that the proper solution to the staffing problem was to create a second editor's position within the publishing department. He prevailed, having battled Jim every step of the way.

On another occasion, Jim was away from the office on vacation (have no fear, it was a working trip). Our executive staff was holding its regular weekly meeting in his absence, carrying on the general work of the corporation, when the conversation turned to how tired each of us was due to the frantic pace that was a constant part of work at Focus on the Family. Several examples were offered by my colleagues of how weary they felt from our breakneck stride and of how their spouses were complaining about the long hours we kept and our lack of availability for family life.

As I sat there listening, I was suddenly struck by how stupid we all were regarding this issue. We were the senior executives of the company so we were the ones who established the to-do lists, the deadlines, and the expectations with which we burdened our middle managers and front line staff. In fact, everyone in the organization was frazzled because of us and we were, too. It struck me that those of us around that table were the culprits. I spoke up and said so. After offering the group the thought that we were creating the very environment we were complaining about, I made a concrete policy proposal. I suggested that it be made a matter of corporate procedure at Focus on the Family that no staff meeting in our divisions would remain in session beyond five-thirty, including our own cabinet meetings, which often lasted well into the night. If the work of any group was not complete by five-thirty, I proposed that the group would stop for the day, determine when they could reconvene, return to their desks, and prepare to go home to be with their families.

I further expressed the specific proposal that the men around that table make the black and white commitment to our spouses that we would not leave the office later than 6:00 P.M. each night. And I suggested that we invite our wives to hold us accountable to that commitment as a part of what it meant to be an executive at a company called Focus on the Family.

I recall a very strange atmosphere settling over the room when I stopped talking. It was as if I had introduced a subject of great awkwardness, spoken a sacred word that was never to be uttered lest we all die. After several moments of bulky, labored discussion, my policy recommendation was agreed to unanimously. I know the reason for the uncertainty and discomfort because obviously I knew those men well, having hired many of them and worked beside them for many years. The awkwardness had to do with one of the basic rules of corporate America: The boss sets the pace for how hard everyone works and it's your responsibility to study your boss's habits and to keep up with him or her. In other words, if you want to go somewhere in your career, work exactly like your boss works. This rule encompasses what time bosses arrive in the morning and what time they leave in the evening. It includes how much work they take home with them as opposed to leaving work at the office for the next day—not good. It includes things that you might hear them say directly or in an offhand fashion about working weekends, about unpaid overtime or traveling for the company. All such factors make up the company's policy about executive work styles. And every man around that Focus on the Family board room table knew that my proposal contradicted the policies each of us had observed coming straight from our boss. The discomfort revolved around a question no one had the nerve to voice: Were we prepared to contradict Dobson's own work style? Were we prepared to say no to Jim's expectation of routine after-6:00 P.M. workdays?

BUSINESS AS USUAL

The interesting part of this story is that when Mr. Turn-Your-Heart-Toward-Home (the name of one of his educational film series) returned from vacation and read the minutes of that meeting, he was *angry*. He said at our next meeting that he felt betrayed because we had raised the subject at a session he hadn't attended and had arrived at a new policy without his involvement. In fact, I recall Jim voicing the slightly paranoid thought that perhaps we had deliberately raised the subject in his absence in an attempt to "pull a fast one." Since I was the moving party relative to the new policy, and since I was one of the few members of the group who felt at ease opposing Jim, I spoke up. I stated first that the discussion could not have been an effort to bypass him because it was standard practice that minutes were taken that Jim read and approved if he missed a meeting. Secondly, I indicated that the subject came up spontaneously and that, notwithstanding his negative reaction, I thought it was the right thing to do. I attempted to make the same case to him that I had made in his absence. I remember saying to Jim that I thought his reaction to our setting a policy in his absence was strange since we were aware that there were frequent examples of him taking independent action without coming to the executive committee to discuss them.

I can still remember the look in Jim's eyes as he glared at me down the length of the great boardroom table. The look said, "Gil, you have crossed the line." It was a look I had seen often and it went with a stock oration of Jim's we called the "nipping-at-the-heels" speech. We had a member of our staff in the early days by the name of Judy for whom the "nipping-at-the-heels" lecture was first created by Jim. Judy had one of those "Question Authority" temperaments that was inclined toward offering management frequent gratis critiques of how the company was being run. She was very bright and I recall that most of her concerns were valid and worth the time and energy it took to listen to her. But her criticisms hit the executive office suite so often that I suppose we sometimes cringed when Judy walked through the doorway with her "we've got to talk" look. And so it was that Jim delivered his nipping-at-the-heels speech for the first time to Judy. His point, accompanied with the same glare now focused at me, was that he was not going to tolerate somebody constantly questioning the way he ran the company; that he found such people to be a nuisance and bothersome and that he had no intention of allowing such criticism. I lost the go-home-at-six argument. My policy was rescinded and we went back to business as usual. "Slow it down" is a message Dobson sells rather than lives.

Here are two final examples of the contradiction between the public messages by which Jim makes a personal fortune and how he conducts the private work style of his company.

One of my wife's closest colleagues when she worked at Focus on the Family, a woman named Marilyn, tells the story of deciding to apply for a management position in the company. During the interview, several routine questions were asked about her family. Yes, she replied, she had a husband and three children and her family life was very important to her. Obviously Marilyn not only responded truthfully, but she also assumed those sentiments were the ones an interviewer would hope to hear when selecting someone for leadership at Focus on the Family. To her surprise the response came back, "Well, you can forget about having time for your family if you get this position. This may be Focus on the Family, but that doesn't mean your family."

THE FOCUS IN HIS FAMILY

This aspect of Jim's modus operandi took on a particularly distasteful flavor at times in terms of how he related to his own wife. Jim had a pattern, for example, of misstating the reasons for his being delayed leaving the office at the end of the day. The pattern Jim repeated over and over again went like this: Like any executive team in a fast-growing corporation, our days at Focus were filled with meetings and working sessions, times with our individual staffs, and times together in the executive team developing the overall course of the corporation. And like any executive team, most of the calendar events of the day ended somewhere around 6:00 or 6:30 in the evening. On the third floor of the corporate headquarters building, which was occupied exclusively by those of us who were vice presidents, this late afternoon period took on a special characteristic. We worked hard all day, internal engines running a hundred miles an hour, and when we reached the end of the day there was a collective sigh that could almost be heard throughout the executive floor. We had gotten a lot done, and now it was quitting time—almost. As a physical manifestation of that corporate sigh of relief you would see, on any given afternoon, one or more vice presidents wander into the office of another vice president, sit down heavily in guest chairs and say either out loud or by their body language, "What a day." And then a review-the-day ritual would begin. There was a particular need to share extraordinary events of the day, maybe a call from the White House or a very large donation, as some type of ceremony of self-assurance or mutual warranty that all was well. Of all of the executives who practiced this end-of-day ritual, Dobson was king reviewer. If one or two vice presidents didn't wander in his direction by 6:30, he would go looking for them. He seemed to need constant reassurance that Focus on the Family was continuing on some spectacularly upward business spiral.

It was very common for me and my peers to swing around the corner of Jim's secretary's outer office, glance through the inner door into Dobson's plush CEO office, see him sitting at his desk working on his papers, and inquire whether he wanted to talk. Of course he wanted to talk. He wanted to hear everything—twice. An hour to an hour and a half of debriefing would follow. The conversations were sprinkled with phrases like, "You won't believe what happened this afternoon." Or, "Has anyone mentioned to you, Jim, the call we got from so and so?" Or, "Did you know that we had one of the largest income days in the history of the organization?" Or, "We got a report today that five more radio stations have added our show and that takes us over the two thousand station mark." It was clearly Jim's favorite time of the day. The atmosphere during such end-of-the-day hobnobbing was intoxicating; it was an adrenaline rush and we were all addicted.

In the middle of this ritual it was common for the private phone on Dobson's desk to ring. It was now perhaps 7:00 or 7:30 in the evening and that was supper time from the perspective of Jim's wife, Shirley. When he answered the phone on such occasions and we would listen to Jim explain to "Shirlzee" why he couldn't come home right then. The excuses he used are common to husbands around the world, I'm sure, and I don't repeat them here as though they represent some scandalous aspect of Dobson's character. But it was noteworthy to observe this guru of marriage and family doing exactly what other insensitive executives do every day: blowing off a wife in the interest of things they care about more than going home. He would say, "Yeah, Shirlzee, I know we're going out tonight and we still will, but I can't leave yet. Gil just walked in and we've got an emergency. I tell you what, I'll meet you at the restaurant, you go ahead and order for me." The painful truth was, on most such occasions there was no emergency, certainly nothing that couldn't hold until morning. We were simply overly driven male executives going through our "We're darn good at this, aren't we?" ritual. And we were. But we were often better at business than family.

11 ❧ An Unsuspected Millionaire

James Dobson consciously projects an outward image of being easy-going, loving, gentle, gracious, and highly respectful of others. But Dobson's management style is based on a very different set of attributes. Take, for example, a business concept to which Jim refers almost daily in his dealings with his staff. He calls this management precept "mutual accountability." Sounds good so far. A more accurate description, however, of how Jim runs things at Focus on the Family would be "management by suspicion," a very negative and unattractive way of viewing employees and one which certainly contradicts his highly spun public persona of being loving and trusting.

Jim began using the phrase "mutual accountability" during the early eighties, when Focus's growth was exponential rather than incremental. Looking back on that period I suspect that the feelings behind Jim's introduction of the concept were fear that he might lose control of his company, so fast was its expansion after the initial difficult years. At best, it represented the fact that he wanted Focus run by very tight controls—no surprises, no independent decisions, no loose cannons. At worst, however, it meant that Jim trusted no one but himself and needed a management system that ensured that he could micromanage his company.

He stated that every worker needed accountability. Employees tended to be less productive, he philosophized, when not monitored and more productive when more accountable. But these generally accepted management principles were then taken a step further into what was clearly a management system based on the premise that employees simply cannot be trusted. To Jim's way of thinking, managers must constantly and closely "police" subordinates if a company is to be well run.

Executive staff "cabinet" meetings were sometimes disrupted by disputes triggered by Dobson jumping to conclusions about a rumor he'd heard regarding what employees were doing in a certain department. His tendency was to believe anything he heard, overreact without investigation, and issue directives about how to fix things without consultation with the VP in charge of the department. It was management by suspicion.

He also referred frequently to what we will call a subtheory within the "mutual accountability" school of business management called "smoke smelling." Jim's theory was that someplace in every company at any given moment something was going wrong, some employee was screwing up. And according to Jim's theory of smoke smelling, it was the supreme daily responsibility of managers to move throughout the company sniffing the air for the smoke of employee misconduct.

NIGHT PATROL

One of the most irritating examples of James Dobson, chief smoke smeller, took place one day with the discovery on the part of our executive team that Jim would sometimes walk through the office late at night, when no one else was around, randomly opening employee's desk drawers looking for evidence of misconduct. If he found something that looked suspicious to him, say what appeared to be an unpaid bill lying in an accounting department desk, he would bring it to the next cabinet meeting and angrily display it as an example of why we must all continue to sniff for smoke in our daily rounds.

Jim's principle of mutual accountability held, in addition, that no single executive could make a decision by himself; decision making was to be done in teams—not a bad idea until you look more closely at Jim's actual meaning. We were all to submit to accountability to our peers as Focus executives, to check off before taking action, to ensure that nothing done at Focus would be a surprise. The inconsistency here, the hypocrisy in this particular aspect of Jim's work, had to do with the fact that Jim didn't obey his own rule; Jim himself was not part of the "mutual." The CEO who invented the system of accountability repeatedly acted on his own, taking action that surprised the rest of us when we later learned of it, frequently making himself unaccountable. Jim made it clear by his conduct that his management system was meant to make sure that everyone was accountable to him but he was accountable only if and when he wanted to be. Jim trusted Jim but no one else.

Dobson would obviously protest this description of himself, responding, as he frequently does in public, that he has a boss like everyone at Focus, the Focus on the Family board of directors. And he would argue that he is fully accountable to that boss. But that is simply not accurate. You will learn, as you read on, that there is overwhelming evidence that Jim is unaccountable in ways and to degrees that warrant serious concerns about the way Focus on the Family is run. And with regard to his specific relationship with his board, it is a joke to suggest that they hold him accountable in anything more than a token fashion.

I was a founding member of the Focus board of directors along with Jim and Shirley, Mike Roberts, Bobb Biehl, Mac McQuiston, and Peb Jackson. I was present at every board meeting for the first ten years of the organization's history and participated in every conversation about starting and building the board. The Focus board was created in the image of its management team, not the other way around. The process used to form and add to the board is one reason I contend that any claim by Jim that he is accountable to the board is questionable. Early in our history Jim verbalized to senior staff members his vision of good and bad board members. The ideal candidate was a person who would not rock the boat, who would not question too strongly what Jim wanted to do with the organization. Dobson often stated that boards of directors could, in his view, become a great nuisance to the entrepreneur who had the original vision for the company. If a board was made up of people who were independently minded then, according to Jim, it became unwieldy in its tendency to control management.

OUR SORT-OF INDEPENDENT, SORT-OF SELF-PERPETUATING BOARD

From a historical standpoint, the board of directors came into existence and then progressed from one class of board members to the next at Jim's discretion. To describe the Focus on the Family board as self-perpetuating would be erroneous. The first step in adding a board member was that Jim commissioned vice president Peb Jackson to look for new candidates in his executive role as Jim's traveling ambassador to the wealthy and influential. In fact, those were two of the primary criteria for being nominated—wealth and influence. When Peb returned from his many journeys across the land with such a recommendation, he would bring that nominee's name to the cabinet and we would discuss whether the person

Peb recommended would be a good candidate for the board. Prominent in any such discussion was Dobson's concern regarding whether the person had an independent temperament or would "go with the flow." Finally, if nominees passed this management review, then their name would be presented to the board for a rubber stamp approval. This was a board created in the CEO's image. So it was that in the entire decade that I was on the board and senior staff, we enjoyed a gracious, harmonious, socially pleasant combination of board personalities who gathered together two or three times a year to hear glowing management reports and to praise us and God for the glorious progress of the organization. It was a group that virtually never challenged us.

In all fairness, there were two instances in that decade in which the board said or did something that could be characterized as independent scrutiny—twice in ten years. The amount of time these two incidents consumed represented a grand total of fifteen minutes. On one occasion the organization was experiencing great difficulty answering its mail in a timely fashion. There was a backlog of unanswered correspondence so great that if you had written Focus on the Family at that time you might have waited a month or two to receive a receipt for your contribution or the book you requested in return for that donation. A board member asked whether, when facing an administrative crisis like this one, we executives planned to roll up our sleeves, and read and process the mail ourselves. The answer was no. It was an attractive moment of tough questions, but it was just that—a moment followed by no action.

The second incident revolved around a decision Jim had made, without board knowledge, to take $100,000 that had been contributed for Focus on the Family programs and to send it instead to another nonprofit organization by the name of the Urban Alternative. It was Jim's view that Focus should support an organization that was struggling for funding. When the next board meeting took place and Jim mentioned the $100,000 in a manner devoid of any sense of seeking board consensus or approval, his action was challenged by one board member. Jim agreed, somewhat embarrassed that he should be more accountable to the board. Then, after the board left town, he expressed anger over the entire episode.

In short, Dobson runs his organization not on the basis of an objective principle of mutual accountability, but in a style that would be best characterized as a one man show. A much more subtle example of Dobson's lack of accountability has to do with an issue not easily researched by reporters and others who attempt to analyze Dobson.

Jim often boasts during fund-raising appeals that he does not take a salary from Focus on the Family and never has. As with so much of what he says, that statement is not what it seems to be. The self-caricature Jim tries to create regarding his compensation package is that his service to Focus and its customers is sacrificial and without self-interest; witness the fact that he receives no remuneration for his long and burdensome hours of service to God and country. It's an inspiring picture to be sure: Jim exiting the back door of his building each evening, cardboard box under his arm, several of the fifteen hours of his work day still ahead of him, and never with a paycheck tucked in his pocket. How does that work?

For starters, Dobson forgoes a salary not for sacrificial reasons but so that he will be free of the customary accountability that accompanies a paycheck. If the company doesn't pay Jim the net result is that the company is indebted to him, giving him much more control than a regular CEO would have. How can the board question vigorously or terminate someone who works for free? How could the board demand that the company turn left at the next fork in the road when its no-cost CEO wants to turn right? In human relationships, wherever debt is created, that's where power lies and one thing that Jim has mastered is the creation and use of power. He has structured an employment relationship at Focus where he has power in excess. When Jim tells his audience he takes no salary honesty dictates that he should add that he likes it that way because the balance of power is in his favor. What he leaves out of the picture is that he and Shirley have become multimillionaires under this "sacrificial" arrangement with the ministry. He has lost nothing and gained a great deal. This is a fabulous compensation package.

THE MONEY MACHINE

How is Dobson's compensation arrangement with Focus so lucrative if he draws no salary? It is enormously profitable by virtue of the fact that Focus on the Family is essentially a publicity-generating machine for Jim. Three million households receive positive advertising impressions of James Dobson weekly—James Dobson the writer of books, the maker of educational films, and the seller of audiocassette albums—all of which are available at your local religious bookstore, where Jim is always in the top ten authors category.

For example, Dobson's November 1996 fund-raising letter[1] announced to his donors a new Focus on the Family venture: youth rallies in major cities across North America called "LOTE" or "Life on the Edge." Dobson said of this new enterprise: "The first [rally] of its kind was held in Cincinnati on October 5. Some 3,200 teenagers and their parents spent all day listening to [a variety of youth speakers, including members of the Focus staff]. From all the reports we've received, the seminar was wonderfully successful. We had to turn away hundreds in Cincinnati. If resources permit, it is our plan to take this program to fifty or more cities in the next couple of years."

On the surface, the observer sees nothing in such an announcement other than James Dobson, care provider to the nation's youth. But when one looks more closely, one sees a national event strategy into which hundreds of thousands of dollars will be poured, creating immense visibility and market interest in "Life on the Edge," which is more than the name of the event; it is the title of Dobson's latest book as well as of a video and film series, all Dobson's personal property, from which he earns immense royalties.

Jim does not donate the income from his books and many of his communications products to his nonprofit corporation, as do many heads of ministries. He retains control of the revenues they generate, and foremost among all who benefit from the massive marketing and publicity generated daily by Focus on the Family is James Dobson himself. Furthermore, since a guest spot on the Dobson program turns other authors into instant best-sellers, his promotional power puts him in a position to demand higher-than-normal personal advances and royalty percentages from publishers of his own books.

Another way of explaining the difference between Jim's public and private approach to the issue of taking a salary would be to describe to you the way Billy Graham has handled the same issue with his nonprofit corporation. I'm told that early in his work, Reverend Graham stated to his board of directors that he was concerned about the problems with power that heads of successful privately controlled nonprofit corporations often encounter and that he was intent on avoiding the abuse of power in his career. He observed that one such pitfall was the mishandling of money. He asked his board of directors to conduct a survey of the average income of American pastors and then to pay him whatever that figure was. For that story to have meaning you need to understand that, commercially, Billy Graham is one of the best-selling authors in the country. His many books, including his classic *Peace with God,* have sold in the millions of copies and would have made him and his family a fortune had he kept the proceeds. But Graham included in the compensation arrangement he made with his nonprofit a plan whereby all royalties from his books would go to the organization rather than to him. One of the results was that the control and the balance of power between him and his organization rests with the corporation and its board of directors, not with Graham.

Dobson has chosen the opposite path. By the way, Jim and Shirley are major donors to Focus, in specific recognition that Jim is the primary beneficiary of its enormous capacity to promote the sales of his private product lines and to generate the related royalties. Their contributions are, of course, tax-deductible. So they offer him yet another financial advantage.

One of the ways Jim benefits financially from Focus on the Family is the relationship he has established between the ministry and his private for-profit corporation, JDI, or James Dobson, Incorporated. For example, JDI owns the copyright to all "Focus on the Family" broadcasts as intellectual property. Then Jim donates them back to Focus on the Family for a tax deduction. Dobson thus uses program material developed for the Focus broadcast for the production of his own products, such as books, cassettes, videos and films, contracts he negotiates and owns privately. Let me add that James Dobson is the only person at Focus on the Family with proprietary rights over the material developed and used by the organization. Guests on the broadcast sign over to the organization ownership of the content of their interviews. Dobson's co-hosts, myself included, retain no intellectual property rights to the ideas they bring to the table. In some ways, Focus on the Family is Jim's personal product factory, including perhaps the most powerful marketing research system in existence. When Jim takes an idea first developed at Focus, either by him or a guest, and walks across the hall to JDI to prepare a new profit-making product, he and the publisher know before one sentence of their new contract is written that they are creating a runaway best-seller. The jury is already in about market demand, because Focus has received 40,000 letters responding to the broadcast where the idea was floated as a trial balloon.

In short, Jim Dobson is an extremely shrewd businessman, for which he should be congratulated. He has taken advantage of every business benefit legally available to him at Focus and has skillfully maximized the relationship between his high-profile role in his successful nonprofit enterprise and his closely connected and highly profitable private company. In the process, he has structured a job for himself that gives him unprecedented personal freedoms. Nice work if you can get it.

JUST DO AS I SAY

The point of the previous chapter and this one has been that there are some fairly significant differences between what Jim says publicly and the realities of how he lives and works. One final example of this reality and then we'll move on.

A friend of my wife, a woman we will call Suzanne to protect her privacy, told my wife one day how she listened with fascination to a recent Focus on the Family radio broadcast. The subject was education. Dobson had in the studio with him a group of teachers and was attempting to solicit from them ideas on how parents could be more supportive of their children's teachers. One teacher told of the stress created when parents needlessly criticized them, mentioning, as an example, the cruel notes that teachers sometimes receive from parents. Jim responded with marked disapproval, telling the listening audience that rather than criticism, what teachers really needed was the parent's prayer support. Suzanne said she laughed out loud at Dobson's on-air comment. "I used to teach Dr. Dobson's children," she explained. "Never in my entire teaching career did I receive notes from a parent that were nastier than those I received from him."

Yes, sir, just do as I say, not as I do.

NOTE

1. Dr. Dobson's letter, Focus on the Family home page, America Online, November 1990.

12 🌿 Edited, Brushed, and Spun

There is nothing more important to Jim than his own image and that of his organization. And by "image" I mean just that—how things appear to be regardless of how they are in fact. Jim is, without any question, compulsive and obsessive about the way he's seen, about what people think of him. As long as I've known Jim, appearances have been as or more important than reality. At times this obsession caused me to feel like saying, "Jim, what are you so afraid of? Why is the mere possibility that someone will form a false perception of you, one that cannot possibly be backed up by reality, so threatening to you? After all, a false perception is, by definition, 'false'; it is not the real "you." But somehow, inside the Dobson mindset, damage to one's image is as serious as damage to one's person. There was little difference in his system of thought between the public falsely believing Jim was having an affair and Jim actually having one. They were essentially the same in terms of the power Jim invested in false perceptions.

I observed two general problems with this way of thinking during my experience with Dobson. First, by elevating perception to a level higher than reality, Jim began manipulating his constituents' perceptions, essentially misrepresenting the facts, because he thought he was dealing with something as important as reality. Conversely, by equating reality with the lower level of perception, Jim cheapened reality; he rendered almost meaningless, at times, that which had the highest level of meaning—reality itself.

Let's use as an example a very personal and somewhat painful story. You will read in detail in chapter 27 the rather dramatic account of how

Jim and I parted company after ten years of close association. For now, it's important that you understand two key turning points. First, in 1985 Jim decided to discontinue using me as his radio co-host when my wife announced her decision to end our marriage; second, in 1987 Jim decided to discontinue my employment altogether when I announced my decision to marry a staff member. Both decisions revolved entirely around perceptions. Neither had the slightest thing to do with reality.

WE NO LONGER NEED YOUR SERVICES

Like too much of the Dobson public presentations, the on-air announcement of my departure from the radio program in 1985, after seven years as co-host, was not an accurate reflection of reality, it was designed to address perceptions. Dobson explained to our listening audience that my family was going through a period of stress (true) and that I had asked for a less demanding assignment (false). The reality was that Dobson simply did not want a divorced man as co-host and he, not I, made the decision to remove me. So why did he use such contorted language to announce my departure? When perceptions are elevated to reality, one begins manipulating perceptions because they're just as important. Let's recap to make the absurdity of all this abundantly clear.

REALITIES: WHEN I LEFT THE BROADCAST

- My wife announced that she wanted a divorce, after years of marriage counseling and hard work by us both to try to save the relationship.
- There were no scandals or breaches of the marital vows on the part of either one of us.
- Before my wife's decision I believed in and worked hard to achieve a "lifelong marriage," a core Focus belief. After my wife's decision I still believed in lifelong marriage.
- There were people working at Focus in all stages of relationships—single, married, separated, divorced, remarried. There was no policy against being employed at Focus if you lost your "lifelong marriage," just against believing in easy, casual divorce or being unfaithful during your marriage.

PERCEPTIONS: WHEN I LEFT THE BROADCAST

- Jim worried that the audience might conclude that if his teachings on lifelong marriage couldn't save his own co-host from divorce, what value were they to his customers?
- Dobson was concerned that false rumors might start that I had not been faithful to my marriage.
- Jim was worried that someone might conclude that he was soft on divorce if he permitted a divorced man to remain in the studio.

It's fascinating isn't it, the mental contortions that arise from the belief that public perception is as important as reality? And we're dealing here with something far more important than a philosophical point. How can your public determine whether what they are being told is something designed to create a certain perception or simply what is real if you yourself are a slave to the "perception is reality" doctrine?

WE NO LONGER NEED YOUR SERVICES, THE SEQUEL

In 1987, Carolyn Alexander, a Focus on the Family employee, and I decided to marry. Immediately Jim terminated her employment and mine. Again, you're going to hear the details later in this book due to their relevance to any critique of Dobson, but for now let's run through another Dobson reality check.

REALITIES: WHEN WE LEFT FOCUS ON THE FAMILY

- Carolyn and I had never met prior to my first wife announcing our divorce and physically separating from me.
- From the beginning of the romance with Carolyn, I informed Dobson of the relationship and openly discussed with him issues such as whether Carolyn should transfer out of my department and into another.
- There was nothing about the marriage, according to Jim's written and verbal assessment, that violated Focus beliefs or policies.

- Focus employed divorced and remarried board members, vice presidents, middle managers, and front line staff.
- When we announced our plans to marry, Jim, the cabinet, and the board required that we resign immediately.

PERCEPTIONS: WHEN WE LEFT FOCUS ON THE FAMILY

- In a written report to his board and in public remarks to our staff Jim announced that we had done nothing in violation of Focus's beliefs or policies; however, Focus was worried about the damage that *might* be caused because a false rumor *might* start that the relationship with Carolyn broke up my first marriage.
- No public announcement about the terminations was made because such an announcement might create a problematic public perception of Focus, i.e., that it terminated people for fear of a false rumor, or that it discriminated against divorced and remarried people.

One footnote to this personal example of how Jim handles perceptions and realities. Five months after Carolyn and I were terminated, I had lunch with Jim. In the course of our luncheon, Jim, who had heard that I was unemployed, asked how my search for a new job was going. I responded that it was my belief that one of my difficulties finding work within our small industry had to do with the fact that no announcement had been made of my departure from Focus. I reminded him that there were only two likely scenarios going through the minds of prospective employers: (1) I was still at Focus and not in need of a new job. This was likely, I said, because he was still airing repeat broadcasts with my voice on them. Or (2) prospective employers thought that I had been fired for good reason, in which case I was not a desirable candidate for a new position.

Dobson responded, "I made no announcement because the very best thing for Focus would be if our constituents thought you were still in your old department making films." Dobson believed that nurturing a false perception among donors was superior to reality. Is the point made?

I'm able to speak of these two painful stories somewhat lightly now, but, as you can imagine, they were difficult to live through. For that reason, and because of the special responsibility of publicly funded organizations to be forthright with their donors, I argue that equating perception with reality is a very serious problem. And yet there are many more examples, humorous and significant, of James Dobson's obsession with images and perceptions.

MY GOD, I'M GOING BALD

One of the great illustrations of Jim's compulsiveness about his image has to do with the fact that he prohibits photographers from taking his picture from his right side where his dramatically receding hairline can be seen. On a scale of importance, Jim's obsession with his hair is rather benign, but it does serve to illustrate how "image" is pervasive in his life. An enormous part of Jim's morning routine is devoted to swirling long hairs growing on the back side of his scalp forward and across his forehead to create the appearance of a fairly full head of hair. The reality behind the perception is that he has a garden-variety, half head of hair, as I and so many men our age do.

I recall that this particular concern for his image surfaced during the early days of Jim's involvement in politics. He had the heady experience of being invited into the White House Cabinet room, where he was seated opposite President Ronald Reagan for a meeting between the president and other religious leaders. As is customary in such situations, a photograph of the session was taken for the benefit of those attending. Jim returned from Washington filled with pride about the powerful symbolism of that photograph: James Dobson, seated at the Cabinet table, a man with access to the president. Surely, Jim pointed out, our constituents would want to see such a picture. The problem Jim had, as our publishing department prepared the picture for the Focus on the Family magazine, was that the White House photographer had made the nasty mistake of standing directly behind Jim and shooting across his head into the face of Ronald Reagan. As a result, the camera's flashbulb illuminated exactly how bald Jim Dobson is. The piercing light of the strobe shot right through Jim's thinning hair and bounced off his lily white scalp, reflecting back into the lens far too much skin and far too little hair for Jim's taste.

No problem, though, in the highly imaged world of Jim Dobson. He instructed our editor to airbrush the photo. This may be commonplace in Manhattan advertising agencies or Hollywood's touch-up studios, but in the world of conservative religion it's a little out of character.

THE NAME IS "DOCTOR" DOBSON, THANK YOU

From the earliest days of the broadcast, Dobson's obsession with his image took a somewhat less benign form by way of a fixation on his professional title, a preoccupation which, I believe, has served him very poorly over the long haul. He insisted that everyone in the studio, including our guests, address him as Doctor during the taping of radio programs. He, on the other hand, always addressed me and our studio guests by our first names. If you review the tapes of my years with him you will find remarkably few examples of Jim being called "Jim" on the broadcast. His explanation was plausible enough, as is the case any time he tries to argue for his eccentricities. He stated that he was in the business of offering advice. And if his advice was to be perceived as worth listening to and applying to the listener's family, it should be made clear that it was backed up with a Ph.D. from USC. Additionally, because of the significantly greater esteem Jim felt our culture confers on medical doctors than on Ph.Ds, he wanted to capitalize on that subtle inference in our listeners' minds when they heard the title "Doctor." I noticed that most psychologists do not force their titles into conversations quite as Jim does. In fact, the titling protocol of professional publications such as the *Wall Street Journal* calls for the reference "Doctor" to be applied only to those with an M.D.; in other words, only to medical doctors. The *Journal* would refer to Jim as Mr. Dobson. But we dared not.

LIFE IN THE EDIT BAY

This constant imaging, or what we sometimes hear referred to as spin doctoring in the political arena, is very much on display in the making of the daily "Focus on the Family" radio broadcast. You cannot conceive, no matter how knowledgeable you may be about the production of radio and television, how much editing goes into the production of a spontaneous-sounding "Focus on the Family" talk show. Once again, the contrast between perception and reality is enormous.

The average thirty-minute "Focus on the Family" radio broadcast takes approximately two hours of in-studio recording work plus another hour or two of editing to complete. Sometimes more. The process used during the recording session is exactly like the making of a motion picture. One short scene is shot and then another and then another. For example, at the end of a session a short illustration might be recorded for insertion at the beginning of the broadcast. Then these various pieces of short "takes" are placed in the hands of a professional editor who splices them together to create the final impression that the program was one spontaneous stream of eloquent conversation. During the final editing, if needed, a word or even a breath might be borrowed from someplace else on the tape, or even from a different tape, in order to create the illusion that the conversation happened as you hear it.

Our routine approach to the recording session was that Jim would arrive in the studio with a handwritten outline for our broadcast conversation. He would hand me a photocopy to review as he seated himself opposite me at the six-foot studio table. Beside us was a large, thick studio window looking into a control room filled with electronic equipment where our engineer was seated, ready to operate and monitor the technical aspect of the recording. The program outline included several questions Dobson wanted me to ask him and notes for himself of what he wanted to say. One of my roles was to express appropriate awe in response to Jim's answers. In fact, the outline Jim handed me often included the very words "Appropriate Awe" or their abbreviation "AA" next to my name. Each question, each answer, and each appropriate response was delivered to tape as if no script existed and Jim and I were just talking.

The massaging, crafting, and subtle acoustical manipulations that are employed to allow Jim to start and stop, to say something, revise it, try to say it better, throw it out, think of something more humorous, walk back into his office and look for another illustration, and start over, are so pervasive that, as I said, it would be difficult for you to conceive of how highly edited the Focus broadcast is by listening to it.

My point is that Jim goes to unnatural lengths in virtually all aspects of his work to appear one way when actually he is functioning in another. There's certainly nothing wrong with editing a broadcast per se. But the net effect of the editing of every other aspect of Dobson's presentation of himself has been the creation of a public persona different from the private man. Perhaps one more example will suffice.

JIM DOESN'T DO EXTEMPORANEOUS

If you hear Jim deliver a public speech, you will again witness a perception of spontaneity so important to the Dobson style of communication, but not necessarily real. Jim presents himself in an offhand, casual, folksy manner in person, giving the impression that he just strolled to the podium and spoke off the top of his head out of a vast wealth of wisdom and wit. When it's over, you would be left with the impression that this is one of the great speaking talents of our time. You might not even be conscious of the great symmetry and rhythm of his speech, so effective would Jim have been at appearing spontaneous. And you would certainly be conscious of having been moved, entertained, and informed by James Dobson.

But you would be incorrect to interpret the presentation as spontaneous. You were watching a man work harder than any public speaker you know, but not wanting you to know it. Jim's practice of speech preparation will offer you additional insight into how this artificial spontaneity is created. He works first in the privacy of his office or home for however long it takes to craft a specific speech. He does not accept invitations to speak extemporaneously. Perhaps a particular speech will take weeks or even months to design and prepare. Next, Jim will plan many small speaking situations during which he will try out the pace and content of a new presentation and steadily refine it. Dobson delivers these mini-speeches over and over again, watching for places where humor should be added or information deleted.

Finally the day arrives when he delivers this particular speech before either a very large crowd or a very important one. When that moment comes, James Dobson will perform like a well-rehearsed actor delivering his lines after six months of rehearsal.

This practice sequence presents an interesting dilemma, however, for a highly imaged communicator like Jim Dobson. In delivering his practice speeches, he says virtually the same words over and over again, so much so that if people in the audience were to hear repeated deliveries of the same speech, they would likely conclude there is an element of phoniness in some of Jim's mannerisms and inflections. Identical, seemingly offhand gestures and comments, maybe even a break in the voice and perhaps the appearance of a tear at the exact same spot in a speech, would suddenly be recognized as not spontaneous at all, but would take on the air of manipulation.

How does Dobson resolve this dilemma? He orders his staff not to attend his public speaking engagements after they have heard a speech once. Repeatedly during my ten-year association with him, he would say to me and others, "Gil, I'm uncomfortable with you coming to Friday night's presentation because it makes me self-conscious to have you in the audience knowing exactly what comes next."

The story is told of a best-selling author and speaker named Joyce Landorf, who often shared the stage with Jim at family life workshops during the seventies. Joking innocently with Jim one day, she said, "I've heard your speech so often I think I could deliver it myself." It was a common, everyday, harmless wisecrack, but Jim was offended by it and reacted angrily. He was the Ph.D., he had crafted that speech and honed its perfect timing and rhythm. How dare she suggest she could do better with his material?

The issue here is balance. Editing a radio program is a good thing. But where is the line between delivering a very enjoyable and substantive audio product to market and creating a false image? Air brushing a photograph is innocent enough by anyone's standards. But there are steps a high-tech company can take which, before one realizes what has happened, carry that company out of the real and into the murky world of crafted perceptions. Someplace there is a line between perception and reality and it's an important distinction. It is not, in my view, a line that Jim respects.

13 ✿ Weird Science

In his extensive *Christianity Today* profile of Dobson, Tim Stafford makes an observation that few outsiders have pinpointed, but which is supported by my inside experience with Jim. Stafford suggests that, notwithstanding the enormous pains to which Jim goes to project his professional status as a practicing, perhaps even clinical, behavioral scientist with a Ph.D. and the related psychologist and M.F.C.C. licensing, he does not function as a scientist or a therapist as society defines those professions. It would be more accurate to think of him as having a background in educational psychology, including a graduate degree plus some limited experience in the field of teaching.

Stafford reports that one of his interviewees for his article, psychologist James Alsdurf, Ph.D., told him that during his doctoral training at Fuller School of Psychology, the leading institution of its type within Dobson's religious world, he never once heard Dobson's work evaluated or critiqued. Stafford describes Dobson's books with phrases like "a melange of Scriptural principles, traditional American values, and common sense."[1] He adds, "Dobson is a generalist and a popularist."[2] Understand, there is clearly nothing untoward about being a Mark Twain, a gifted communicator with a knack for restating the common wisdom a culture has held to for two hundred years in a way that updates the traditionalist perspective. And if one can make a fortune in the process, we should applaud yet another example of American capitalism at work. The issue I raise is simply another example of whether the image and perception, that of a religious Benjamin Spock, matches the reality of a religious Mark Twain. Stafford suggests, interestingly, that being a successful popularist and a serious scientist may be mutually exclusive; that one of the proofs that Jim's work has little depth, either religiously or psychologically, is the very fact that it sells so widely. He writes, "If Dobson were more qualified in his assertions, if he developed careful theological arguments or if he marshaled psychological data for his positions, it is doubtful that he would sell millions of books. . . . It is certain that he would not be James Dobson." And Stafford rightly points out that when Jim is asked, "What has been the greatest influence on your thinking?" his response makes no reference to academia or the field of psychology. Jim answers, "My father." Dobson's father was an evangelist who, later in life, taught art.

The only question here is one of verbal integrity. The role of a popularist is an honored one in American tradition. But Jim would angrily deny that he is merely a purveyor of "Scriptural principles and traditional American common sense" with a gift of gab. He insists that he is a scientist in the best traditions of the field of psychology. In contrast, Stafford observes, "Dobson's books contain almost no references to the vast psychological literature." And, "Dobson resigned from the American Psychological Association some years ago feeling they were worlds apart from him."

NOT YOUR FAMILY THERAPIST

It may surprise you most to learn, as Stafford also observed, that Dobson's behavioral science background was limited mainly to administering a large research grant, which, by the way, he apparently did very well. But, as Stafford points out, "He has little actual practice as a family psychologist. A reader of his books will note that he draws more from his years teaching school, a requirement of the educational psychology program he followed, than from professional counseling experiences."[3] James Dobson is not a clinical family counselor, he's an educational psychologist by training. And even at that, he appears estranged from his own profession, especially when you notice how often he bashes the field in his writings and broadcasts. Take, for example, a comment he made in his September 1996 fundraising letter. He spoke of attending a continuing education class on the treatment of drug abuse in order to renew his psychologist license. At one point in the lecture the instructor told the story of using the word "prostitute" in a conversation with a professional colleague and being chided in return that such individuals should be referred to instead as "sex workers."

Dobson went on to say, "Her point is a familiar one among the culturally elite—that value judgments are offensive. In this case, the word 'prostitute' implies there is something wrong or immoral about that 'line of work.' We have no right to make that assumption. Who are we to say that providing sex for hire is less desirable than any other profession?"[4]

But the dissonance here is broader than just his particular discipline. Jim seems generally to be more at home in the world of business, politics, and populist communication than in the world of the sciences. One of the most obvious examples of Jim's nonscientific approach to his work, one that you observe working with him daily, is the fact that he is not a reader, one of the common denominators among people of science. Make no mistake, Jim loves books. But to accurately understand him you have to look closely at the titles and take note of how he finds out what's between the covers.

Dobson's favorite reading material is political and military. His favorite characters are those historical figures who dominate the landscape of their time (is there a Freudian message here?). And his preferred (and only) way of consuming a book is by ordering it on tape and listening to it as he goes about his activities at home or drives to work. He's one of the best customers the Books on Tape company has, ordering a steady stream of their products, listening through the rented cassettes and then returning them for another set. If he finds an exciting book, say the life of Churchill or the memoirs of Douglas MacArthur, then all of us in the executive suite hear about the day's listening blow by blow. In fact, Jim solicits listening partners who want to hear each tape in a series after he does and before they're returned to the renter. And so, at any given time, you could discover five or six VPs going through World War II with Dobson via audiotape. To say that Jim showed a fascination and enthusiasm for the Battle of the Bulge that he never demonstrated for the literature of his profession is an understatement. He never even talked about the literature. But I recall him saying that there were times when he would arrive in our parking lot and could not get out of his car for fifteen minutes because Churchill was speaking to Parliament and the emotion of it all was so compelling to him.

I WAS DEEPLY MOVED

In fact, emotion is a key to the Dobson school of communication, much more than the scientific emphasis on rationality. In his view it is more important what you feel than what you think. And appealing to the emotions of an audience is, without question, the single highest goal of his writing and speaking. In this regard Jim would frequently lament that the nation's schools, specifically its Christian seminaries, were inept at preparing communicators because they failed to understand the essence of powerful communication, which was to appeal to emotion. He would explain his own approach to preparing a speech as an example of how ignorant trainers of ministers were. Step one is to be an astute observer of the human drama taking place all around us daily. Watch and listen for those occurrences you come across that make great human interest stories for a later speech, he would often advise.

Step two is to capture and preserve those stories so they don't get away from you. I recall once telling Jim in the hallway of our offices a very funny thing that had happened to me the previous night. I had noticed my young son standing on a box at the window, part of the drape behind him so that just his little legs were showing as he looked out the window. As I quietly walked toward him I suddenly heard him say, "I gotta get outa here." The attractions of the outside world had captured his attention and convinced him that being indoors was much like being in prison. So my boy was feeling the need to escape. I learned later that Jim went back to his desk and wrote down my story. Later still he came back to me and asked my permission to include it in a new book.

Step three in Jim's science of communication is to string together such stories in a sequence that makes logical sense, that moves in a straight line. This step includes the process of answering the question, "What point does this story illustrate?" It was here that Jim would become the most vocal in criticizing the training philosophies of seminaries. He would exclaim in frustration that future preachers are taught to dissect the Bible instead of telling stories. Then they are told to throw a few illustrations into their outline just to hold interest. The Dobson approach is to search for illustrations and then to throw in a few points just to ensure minimum rationality.

You can see the problem. If one wants to be a Mark Twain to one's society, then this approach is perfect. But if one wants to be taken seriously as a scientist, then telling stories with an occasional point probably doesn't get the job done.

Tears of Whatever

Another aspect of Jim's preoccupation with emotion over reason was even more bizarre: his view of crying. Tears, whether his own or his audience's, was the surest sign possible in Jim's theory of verbal or written interaction that the highest possible level of communication had taken place. There was no higher test that could be applied to a speech, not richness of content, not originality of thinking, not structure, not effectiveness of delivery, than the test of whether someone teared up. Jim would sometimes pray before a speech, "Lord, do it again." What he meant by this prayer was that the previous time he had given this particular speech a wave of emotion had hit him and his audience, resulting in such deep feelings that tears flowed. He was asking God for more tears this night.

If you're thinking that this concept of communication sounds a lot like stereotypical southern conservative Christian preaching, I agree. I suspect that Jim grew up being told by his religious community that weeping meant that "God was moving" through the congregation and thus weeping meant God. You might hear Jim pray at the end of speech, "Lord, I feel your presence in this place." The meaning is the same.

I'm reminded of an incident that took place in my career prior to meeting Jim. I was directing the videotaping of three identical Sunday morning services at a church for later editing and rebroadcast. At the first of the three services a southern gospel singing family was introduced as guest musicians for the day. I was hard at work directing camera shots and audio levels when the daughter began to cry as she introduced the group's next number. It was a very touching moment that I was sure would be captivating to the television viewer. An hour later we were taping the same group performing the same numbers before a second audience when the daughter broke into tears at exactly the same point. Something in the back of my head wondered if we were being duped by someone who had learned that emotion sells. Third service. Same daughter. Same introduction. Same tears. I never saw Jim contrive tears in quite so manipulative a manner, but he certainly communicated out of that same southern religious tradition. Emotion means God.

Again, the point here is not that the work of a communicator is discredited by an overt appeal to emotion. Rather, it is that this approach is not consistent with what our culture defines as the work of science. And of emotion, James Dobson is a great communicator.

A RELIGION OF THE HEART

Southern religious traditions bequeathed to Dobson yet another aspect of his nonscientific approach to his work. Conservative American Protestantism has struggled for centuries with an anti-intellectual bias that one sees reflected in Jim's style. Science has been suspect to this group. It is often viewed as an effort to replace faith with reason and to replace God with man. You find within some sectors of this community a fear of science, even a scorn for thinking. For example, you can still find churches, here on the eve of the twenty-first century, where sentiments out of the Dark Ages are repeated: "Beware the university. Beware higher education. Beware of sending your sons and daughters to these godless places." Even when referring to conservative Christian colleges and seminaries you can still find preachers who will proclaim, "I have seen more than one fine man, filled with the Spirit of God, on fire to serve God, who went away to Bible college and came back worthless, cold, speaking without certainty and conviction."

At issue here is the constant tug of war between faith and reason, between the seen and the unseen. In Dobson's tradition, seeing is not believing. In fact, his people would say with excitement, "Believing is seeing." So Jim is caught between two worlds: the science of human behavior, which, like any science, needs to examine, to hypothesize, to test, and then to announce truth, and that of religion, which announces truth that is already revealed in the Bible and needs no testing. Unfortunately for Jim's integrity, he declares citizenship in the world of science but functions almost entirely in the world of religion. His presentation of himself would be stronger if he decided on which side he wanted to function.

It was faith and his view of biblical sexuality that led Jim to claim Ted Bundy as Exhibit A in his fight against pornography. The scientific fact that Bundy was a pathological liar and therefore could not, by definition, serve as the foundation for any theory, did not dissuade Jim. When ABC News reporter John Hockenberry brought up the Bundy incident in a broadcast profile, Jim said as much:

Hockenberry to viewers: Paranoia about being lured into some dark sexual world was also the theme of this unusual instructional video about pornography, the final death row interview with serial killer Ted Bundy the day before he was electrocuted.

Video excerpt, Dobson to Bundy: You really feel that hard core pornography and the doorway to it, soft core pornography, is doing untold damage.

Bundy to Dobson: Pornography can reach out and snatch a kid out of any house. . . .

Hockenberry to Dobson: Why should we believe Ted Bundy?

Dobson to Hockenberry: Why not? I'm telling you, John, we get mail in here every day from women whose husbands are addicted to that stuff. They have lost interest in marital sex, they want their wives to do the kinds of crazy stuff they see on video. That stuff is a curse and Ted Bundy knew it.

Hockenberry to viewers: Nevertheless, after he was criticized publicly for capitalizing on a serial killer, Dobson gave away the proceeds from the video [almost one million dollars] and no longer distributes it.

Observers could not believe that a trained psychologist, a Ph.D. from USC, would latch onto Ted Bundy as a case study to prove a theory of pornography—Dobson's "slippery slope" theory of morality. And they were stunned that this "doctor" would say to the same ABC News reporter that he believes participation in university women's study programs leads to lesbianism.

Hockenberry to viewers: Some of Dobson's political ideas are . . . bizarre. Like his warnings to mothers in this recent fund-raising letter that their college-age daughters may go away to school and come home with lesbian lovers.

The implication in the literature was that university education causes girls to become lesbians.

Dobson to Hockenberry: I said it once, let me say it again. I didn't say university education, I said women's study programs have that flavor to it.

Hockenberry: But can it cause lesbianism?

Dobson: I think it can encourage it, yeah.[5]

But in their shock reporters sometimes misunderstand that Jim's true role is not that of a psychologist but of a religious worker.

Dobson has two primary theories of human and social morality by which most of his writings and his aggressive lobbying work on Capitol Hill can be properly interpreted and understood. The first, the "slippery slope theory," mentioned above, which you may also refer to as Jim's "domino theory," holds that when a person becomes involved in whatever happens to be on Jim's list of Top Ten Vices at the moment, let's say gambling, that person will become caught up in an irreversible downward spiral of destructive immoral behaviors. Dobson announced in the fall of 1996 that he had agreed to serve on a new government commission to study the gambling problem in America and to make recommendations to the Congress to help save America from the evils of power ball. Count on it, the results of the commission's work, at least from Jim's perspective, will include evidence of this theory. He will announce that betting on your state's lottery places one foot on this slippery downward slope. And then you slide, uncontrollably, toward the urge to go to the nearest race track where you wager more than you ever dared spend on the lottery. While at the race track the thought will cross your mind that you've never been to Las Vegas. And so it will go until your family finds you living in a cardboard box over a hot air grate. If you murder several people along the way, Jim will make a video of your story as one of his case studies.

His second theory is the "I've fallen morally and I can't get up without new legislation" theory, which holds that as individuals and cultures slide down these slippery slopes (or as the dominos fall uncontrollably against each other), they cannot right their own course. They can't see the danger they're in, so how can they protect themselves? That's one of Jim's roles, to tell society where its troubles lie. Americans are blind but Jim is not. He calls out to us warning that we are sliding precipitously down, down, down toward the pit of personal and social destruction. His companion role is to alert Congress to our plight on the slope and to convince them to enact morality measures that will halt our slide. Since we cannot see ourselves sliding and since we cannot stop ourselves, the answer is Congress. A new law will save us.

WE'VE GOT TO HELP THESE PEOPLE

I listened to the radio broadcast in which Dobson announced his appointment to the new Congressional Commission on Gambling and was struck by the insulting and patronizing elements in his argument. He spoke of driving past a casino at four o'clock in the morning and looking with amazement at a parking lot full of cars. He said that at midnight the next night he was returning on the same highway and the lot was still full. Somehow he seemed to be able to tell that the cars were the same ones he'd seen twenty hours earlier because he commented on the "fact" that those customers had been gambling for that entire period! And then came his punch line. He spoke of his loving concern for those troubled individuals and their families, his worry that money was being spent that their families might need. That was why he, James Clayton Dobson, was on his way to Washington to help the poor people who owned those cars. As he spoke of his new mission, you could almost hear the strains of "America the Beautiful" playing soulfully in the background.

Seriously, the people inside that casino were, in his eyes, on a slippery slope to destruction and he had to save them from themselves. The answer was the legislative recommendations his commission would make that would reach out and stop those poor souls from hurting themselves. The same theory and social strategy applies to pornography, according to Jim. The problem with *Playboy* being for sale at the local 7–11 is the slippery slope. You read it and you want more explicit stuff. You can't control yourself. Soon you are buying illegal child pornography and before you know it—bingo—you're a serial rapist. Again, two aspects of your collapse define Jim's function: First, it's his job to tell us what we otherwise would never know about ourselves. Second, it's his job to save us from ourselves.

What's wrong with this picture? It is the factor, so prevalent in the Dobson approach to political activism, that we don't need Dobson's view of morality to help us determine a healthy and positive life for ourselves. We certainly don't need a new law to help us off the slippery slope or, more accurately, to force us to approach morality as Jim does. In this land of the free, we prefer to be free, thank you very much, to make such moral choices for ourselves.

What do we have here? James Dobson influential political activist and moral reformer? Yes. James Dobson popular religious broadcaster? Yes. James Dobson successful writer and speaker? Yes. James Dobson behavioral scientist? If so, we're talking weird science.

Notes

1. Tim Stafford, "His Father's Son," *Christianity Today,* March 1988, p. 17
2. Ibid.
3. Ibid.
4. Focus on the Family home page, America Online, September 1996.
5. "Day One," ABC News, October 18, 1995.

14 ✻ Sexism

One of the reasons why James Dobson, public policy maker, concerns me, while James Dobson, family advisor, does not, is the evidence I saw during my years with Jim of several very problematic views he holds, views that would have a very negative impact on society were he to gain even more political power. For example, there is his sexism, latent and otherwise.

It seems to me that projecting sexism into American public policy formation in Washington represents a much more serious problem for a society than merely projecting it into the creation of one's books and talk shows. The former can affect the rights and freedoms of millions of citizens by way of a single piece of legislation that Dobson and his foot soldiers might push through Congress, while the latter falls into the category of "Let the buyer beware." If consumers want to purchase products that include a sexist viewpoint, they have that right. But since Dobson wants power in Washington to create a society that is based on a sexist viewpoint, I'm inclined to speak out in opposition.

Let's start with the evidence I observed of latent sexism, by which I mean Dobson's less visible, unspoken attitudes about women. If you were to work side by side with Jim, as I did, you would not notice open hostility toward or abuse of women. To the contrary, you would observe a great deal written and spoken by Jim that honors and reveres women, in particular those who have chosen the more traditional role of becoming wives and mothers. But you would see, in between the lines, clear elements of sexism. Allow me to explain how the two can co-exist.

Jim spoke often as CEO about his belief that it almost always proved

143

successful to place a man in charge of a department of the company, even if that department was composed primarily of women. He believed that it was almost always a problem, on the other hand, to put a woman in charge of a department if it was primarily staffed with women. There was a distinguishable difference in his mind between men and women in leadership, which I believe was rooted in a sexist perspective. He believed that there was some strange workplace chemistry present when women led women that generated greater instability and tension within a work group. He clearly inferred a genetic tendency among women to degenerate into "cat fights"—bickering, petty, and emotional rather than rational patterns—when they worked together. Jim believed that men, by contrast, were largely free of this cat-fighting tendency. Because of this, in the Dobson view of the sexes, men made better leaders. He believed this even though, in my experience, I observed in Jim more pettiness, gossiping, unwarranted combativeness, and interpersonal warring than I have ever observed in any female supervisor for whom I've had the pleasure of working. I refer, for example, to attempts by Dobson to dictate to independent publishers which authors they should publish, attempts to dictate to independent professional associations whether their executive directors can write political editorials in that association's journals, wiping from the Focus warehouse shelves all resources for sale by a particular author merely because the person wrote Jim and challenged a decision he had made, and dictating to the Republican party whether or not that party could express tolerance of views different from Jim's in its 1996 platform. It would appear that internal sparring among female employees is a gender deficiency, from Dobson's perspective, but external macho power plays are perfectly consistent with Dobson's view of maturity and civility.

Dobson's belief that women are predisposed by gender to certain social maladjustments such as "bitching" is rarely expressed in public by this hero to millions of female listeners and book buyers. It surfaced most commonly in the all-male closed-door environment of executive staff meetings. On those rare occasions when it did appear in public it gave rise to a behind-the-back label given Dobson by a number of women in his organization, "Dr. Jekyll and Mr. Dobson." One such public display came in 1986 when employment concerns emanating from an almost all-female mail processing department caused Dobson to make one of his rare appearances in that part of the corporation. Reports of the sexist disrespect he exhibited in response to the issues raised by the staff that day are legendary. According to those present, including a close friend, Dobson made little effort to mask his contempt for the staff's complaints that they were the lowest-paid employees in the corporation (roughly five dollars per hour); their concern that the large number of letters they had to process every hour was leading to serious job stress and poor constituent service; and the fact that the management of Focus on the Family, including Dobson, was fostering a class structure within the organization that was unhealthy and demeaning to them. With each question Dobson became more upset and disdainful of the group, injecting sarcasm and using increasing numbers of inappropriate gender references in his responses such as, "You women clearly don't realize how good you have it here."

On the issue of classism a woman stood up and informed Dobson that her supervisor had instructed the entire group not to go up to the executive floor of the building, because that was where important radio guests might be found and Dobson did not want members of this group mixing with important guests. The staff member asked respectfully if that instruction accurately represented Dobson's personal feelings towards them. He responded coldly, displaying no sensitivity to the elitism expressed by that policy, that the restriction was indeed his policy. A newcomer to the staff rose and began a question falteringly, "I'm new here and I'm not sure exactly how I should address you." Dobson, by now clearly hostile, snapped back, "Dr. Dobson will be just fine!"

Friends who attended that meeting use the most extreme language imaginable to describe the atmosphere of disrespect in the room. They refer to a number of staff members who spoke of resigning when Dobson left the room, and to their belief that they had seen a facet of Dobson's personality they could only describe as evil.

THE GLASS CEILING

It is true that Jim has promoted women to lower and middle management positions. But it is also true that only recently Focus on the Family got its first female senior executive, Diane Passuo, executive vice president for mail processing. Dobson consciously resisted the elevation of women to the inner circle of senior leadership during the entire decade I worked with him.

Our executive team was exclusively white and male and Jim spoke openly about the exclusion of women from that group. My wife, Carolyn, had an interesting exchange of letters with Dobson challenging this aspect of his work during the summer of 1988. She objected to the exclusion of women from the senior management team from the beginning of the organization to that point in time. In Jim's response he defended himself by pointing out that he had permitted a woman from the banking industry to be a candidate for the position of executive vice president and chief financial officer, which, he argued, proved his lack of bias toward women in senior leadership. The funny part of that statement is that, although a qualified candidate, the woman was not hired precisely because she was a woman, thus proving Carolyn's point.

I was given responsibility for that particular executive search. I solicited résumés, conducted the initial telephone and in-person screenings, and checked candidate references. And then I presented a candidate list to Jim. In other words, I have first-hand knowledge of the story to which Jim referred. And I recall in detail Jim's reaction when I presented a set of finalists, one of whom was the female banking executive in question. He did not respond with blatant or crass sexism, questioning why a woman made the list. But in the end, he drew a conclusion, voicing it openly to me and our entire executive team, that the addition of a woman would be more of a problem than an asset. We eventually hired another white male, Paul Nelson, for that post. Jim explained his negative conclusion with classic "old boy" concerns such as this: The informal atmosphere the all-male cabinet enjoyed while traveling on long trips together would be negatively impacted by the inclusion of a woman in the van we rode in. And Jim foresaw problems once we reached retreat sites. Afternoons were customarily spent playing basketball at an athletic club, leading Jim to speculate that it might become problematic if we invited a female colleague to play and it might be equally uncomfortable if we didn't invite her to play. In addition, late at night we normally hung out at Jim's resort condominium talking into the night about company business. How would it look, Jim asked, if eight married men and one single woman were seen "hanging out" together?

There was no sexually explicit conversation or other unprofessional conduct in that Focus van or at the Dobson condo. It was Jim's sense of all-male camaraderie that was endangered and he decided, as a result, to preserve his exclusionary approach to the cabinet at the expense of a highly qualified female candidate for the post of CFO and the enrichment all diversity brings to the leadership process. That approach is clearly an illustration of what the women's movement means by the phrase "the glass ceiling."

IT WAS WHAT HE DIDN'T SAY

I worked so closely with Dobson, attending every senior policy discussion during that first decade of Focus on the Family's history, that I was able to observe not only what he said on this subject but also what he did not say or do. In this regard, it is of concern to me that never once in ten years did Jim discuss with his board or senior staff any interest in or vision for gender or ethnic diversity in the seniormost management of our corporation. And he often ridiculed the women's movement as well as various civil rights movements for related positions. It never seemed to occur to Jim that he was taking very strong positions about what various individuals did or did not need from society, such as a woman's right to an abortion, even though the issues were not his. Jim frequently made an impassioned speech to his executives that women really don't need greater justice in the workplace, based on his male experience. He would argue fervently the view that new legislation minorities claimed they needed was not, in fact, necessary—this despite the fact that Jim's experience of life in this society is that of a privileged, powerful Caucasian, a member of the elite. A more humble observer of society might say, "I have not personally experienced the discrimination that gave rise to this bill but I worry that it might be the wrong approach." Jim, on the other hand, seldom displays such humility, stating instead, "There has been no discrimination. There is no need."

This lack of sensitivity and vision for inclusion, specifically for the value of including women in the workplace decision-making process, is, in my view, a significant piece of evidence in evaluating Dobson's sexism. We have here an old-fashioned, male traditionalist who simply believes in masculine leadership, as have men with power throughout history. He overtly advocates male leadership with regard to the Christian family and he functions in exactly the same way with regard to the office, as if he believes there is a divine order in which men are ordained to lead corporations.

But latent sexism is only the beginning of the story. There were also overt actions by Jim that raised serious questions about his attitude toward women.

The senior staff often met in Jim's large office on the third floor of our headquarters building, which looked north across Foothill Boulevard in Arcadia, California. Directly across the street was another set of office buildings used by Focus on the Family. It was commonplace for us to be holding meetings in midafternoon at coffee break time. When that happened our discussions would be interrupted by the sound of our large workforce exiting the offices for their break. A popular hangout was a cluster of fast food facilities located two blocks to the east, including an ice cream parlor and a McDonald's. As employees spilled onto the sidewalk, a frequent Dobson wisecrack would be, "There go our staff, beating a path of crushed concrete down to Baskin-Robbins." The reference to crushed concrete related to a number of women who were overweight. Since the issue here is sexism, it's important to point out that Jim did not make similar jokes about overweight men on the staff.

THE POWER OF NAMING

Yet another example of this aspect of Jim's value system was brought to my attention by my wife, Carolyn, based on her experience processing listener mail at Focus. One day she told me of a correspondence policy that Focus on the Family used regarding how we addressed female constituents when we wrote back to them.

Members of Carolyn's department were instructed by policy that if married women wrote to Focus on the Family, regardless of how they signed their name, if their donation check, their stationery, their return address, or the body of the text gave us the name of their husband, our return letter was to be addressed to "Mrs. (husband's first name) (husband's last name)." This meant that if Mrs. Deborah Smith wrote to us and if it was clear she was married to Mr. John Smith, then our staff was to address her return letter to "Mrs. John Smith," not "Mrs. Deborah Smith" and certainly not "Ms. Deborah Smith." Carolyn pointed out to me the dilemmas created by this policy, not only the general disrespect it can sometimes convey but several specific problems that seemed extremely insensitive. I was shown a letter, for example, from a woman who wrote Focus on the Family asking for advice and encouraging books or tapes we might be able to send back to help her through the painful experience of her husband recently leaving her for another woman. Our staff was forced by Focus policy to address that woman by her husband's first and last name.

BREATHING TOO DEEPLY

I recall vividly the moment when I presented this problem to our weekly executive staff meeting and made the recommendation that we change our naming policy. It became one of several moments toward the end of my working relationship with Jim where a silent alarm sounded deep in my consciousness signaling that my ability to work with James Dobson was coming to an end. In my presentation I told my fellow executives the story that I had learned from Carolyn. I expected concern and support for the woman abandoned by her husband who would be addressed by that man's name when we wrote back to her. To my surprise, no one in the room supported my concern. Not one Focus leader.

Jim personally led the opposition. There was an aggressive edge to Jim's voice as he opposed Carolyn's perspective on women. He was upset with my critique of a naming protocol that he himself had established. Jim attempted to explain why addressing women by their husband's name was a traditional and acceptable concept and that he was opposed to the effort by the women's movement to discredit that tradition. Clearly, it had never crossed his mind whether, if traditional roles were reversed, he might be uncomfortable being addressed as "Dear Mr. Shirley Deere." Included in Jim's remarks that afternoon was his routine opposition to titling women "Ms." It was clear that the extreme example I had offered—an abandoned woman being addressed by her husband's name—made no impression on Jim whatsoever. He concluded his forceful rejection of my recommendation by taking a disrespectful swipe at the woman who was to become my wife. "Don't breath that stuff too deeply, Gil," he warned. The look in his eye and the tone of his voice made it clear that Jim was warning me about departing from "the Focus way."

Jim expressed an even more overt attitude of sexism on those numerous occasions when he would be talking stream of consciousness with those of us close to him, about the relative difficulty of the work day for someone like him compared to a housewife. His public statements of reverence for homemakers notwithstanding, Jim expressed candidly his belief that women whose sole responsibility was to care for children and a home had an easy life, and that their day's work was not to be compared to the rigors of an executive like himself. "How hard can it be, guys," he would say, "to make a shopping list, to go to the grocery store, and fix a meal?" The speed at which he had to work and the tremendous weight of the responsibility he had to carry would, in his view, crush the typical woman.

MOM FOR A DAY

In his habit of publicly expressing views that were designed more for their marketing benefits than to convey his true beliefs, Jim told the story in one of his books of a time when he had to serve as the homemaker for several days while his wife was temporarily incapacitated. Employing his immense skills as an entertaining communicator he crafted a delightful tale about how his young son almost drove him crazy with early morning questions about when breakfast would be ready and why Daddy didn't know how to do it like Mommy. It was wonderful story telling that endeared Jim to the centerpiece of his market—conservative homemakers. The only problem was that the sentiments he expressed publicly were not matched by the observations he often made during all-male venting sessions in the office of the president of Focus on the Family.

In studying Dobson one realizes that his public praise of women is actually praise of a certain stereotypical woman whom Jim wants to reward for her subservience. He genuinely likes women—who know their place in his cultural view. He applauds women—who stay home and support their men. Of other women he speaks with disingenuous tolerance, stating that if a woman wants to pursue a career outside the home or to bypass motherhood, that is her choice, but he is working to ensure that society supports women who do stay home and raise the next generation. Such comments can hardly be viewed as either supporting a woman's full range of lifestyle options nor can they be viewed as egalitarian. Their very nature is to pass judgment on the choices women make about their lives and their careers.

One of the most dramatic places in Jim's writing and broadcasts where you see this view of women can be found in a story he often tells about how he proposed marriage to his wife, Shirley. The story serves, for example, as a centerpiece of the thinking about relationships expressed in his book *Love Must Be Tough*. It is as sexist as any slice of Dobson's thinking.

The two had dated for a period, but Jim perceived a crisis point building where each would have to decide whether to become serious about the other or to end their relationship. Shirley, for example, had been seeing other men, a fact that troubled Jim because she acted as if such multiple relationships were acceptable. And so Jim tells of planning a showdown. He describes this meeting as an example of how one needs to respect oneself and not allow one's partner to "cross the line" from mutual respect into taking you for granted. Actually, it's much more an example of Jim's differing view of men and women. At the end of one particular date Jim told Shirley that he had something important to discuss just before they parted for the night. He felt their relationship had reached a crossroads; she needed to decide between him and the other guys she had been seeing. Jim described how he saw his life unfolding: his dreams for his future, the fact that he was "going someplace exciting," and he hoped she would come along, which he would like very much. If Shirley wanted to be with another man that was fine. She simply needed to choose.

SHARING POWER

You've already noticed the problem here. Independence and self-confidence are good things and we all agree that strong relationships are not built on groveling, self-deprecation, or appeasement. But where is it written that the essential proposal of a marriage is one in which the man announces his dreams for himself and asks if the woman wants to "go along on his exciting journey"? Isn't her journey exactly the same as his? Doesn't she have gifts, skills, talents, and dreams that lead to her own fulfillment? Isn't marriage based on the proposition that two individuals will journey together toward both of their dreams, supporting each other's ambitions, helping the other become all he or she can be as the result of the magical support of a lover?

My wife has often remarked that you can tell a lot about people's value system by how the person shares power. If you see someone at ease with the sharing of power between the sexes you are probably viewing someone who is able to see both of God's children, man and woman, as equal. If you see someone who distributes corporate power primarily to men and whose marriage revolves primarily around his own goals and purposes, you may well be looking at a sexist.

15 🍃 Racism

Another reason James Dobson, public policy maker, concerns me, while James Dobson, family advisor, does not, is the evidence of racism I saw while working with Jim. As in the previous chapter, allow me to take you on a tour through the more latent as well as the more overt and highly abhorrent examples.

There were no people of color in senior leadership at Focus during the decade I worked with Dobson. Nor were there people of color in middle management. In all those years there had been only a handful of minorities scattered throughout the entire staff. No matter what department you might have strolled into, from broadcasting to publishing, accounting to information technology, correspondence to counseling, personnel to political affairs, video, warehousing, or general office services, you would have found only Caucasians in leadership roles, all of them answering to Caucasians like myself who occupied the vice presidential positions and surrounded Dobson. The Focus board of directors was also all white.

Of greater significance, there was not a single comment made by Jim during my ten years of work with him regarding the beauty or value of diversity in the workplace; about the fact that by bringing into our leadership the diverse perspectives of the ethnic groups in our constituency, we might have served that constituency better. There was no vision at the top at Focus on the Family for an integrated workplace. But the problem was not so much the absence of vision as the presence of prejudice. For that reason, one of the concerns I've experienced as I've watched Jim Dobson's star rise above the political landscape has been the threat he represents to the evolution of civil rights that this and every society needs to experience. There was clear evidence that Jim had a deep-seated, visceral objection to the entire concept of expanding the civil rights of minorities. He treated this political issue exactly like the stereotypical image of the southern white male who opposed emancipation during the 1800s or the northern male who opposed the suffrage movement in the next century. Imagine such a person sitting by a pot belly stove in the middle of an old frontier barber shop lamenting with his buddies why slaves had to raise such a fuss about their lack of rights or why women were causing such a stir about not having a vote. You are picturing what Jim Dobson looked and sounded like as he fussed and fumed in our offices over all civil rights movements—women, minorities, or gays. In his view, society had no need to wrestle with such matters; to extend the American dream that we should all be truly equal. Jim would say, "We are equal! We have no real rights problems, just imagined ones." He was oblivious to the danger that he was the least likely American to "get it" because he was white, male, wealthy, and powerful. Everything's just fine with James Dobson's personal experience with American civil rights. So everything's just fine with America.

LET'S HEAR IT FOR SEGREGATION

Jim is distinctly uncomfortable around those of other ethnic and cultural backgrounds. As a result I saw evidence in Jim that he may still believe that the solution to interracial conflict is the segregation of the races.

Jim spoke openly of his discomfort with the increasingly mixed racial environment of the Los Angeles area when Focus was based here. He often complained about seeing more and more foreigners when he stopped by the cleaners. I recall him stating that with each passing year more Asians, Hispanics, and Middle Easterners were moving into the area, a fact he found unsettling. His complaint was that nonwhites brought with them cultural ideas and religions foreign to the traditional American view of life which Jim defined as Western and Christian. He clearly wished for an America that was just like him.

You'll recall that when I met Jim Dobson, he was living in a predominantly white, affluent northeastern suburb of Los Angeles called Arcadia, next door to Pasadena. He established his first office in that community and when Focus on the Family came into existence in the late 1970s, we placed its offices in Arcadia as well. It was a suburb in which Jim felt comfortable because everywhere he looked he saw people like himself.

As time passed, and we grew, we faced the inevitable question of where to find adequate new office space. Initially we occupied multiple buildings in different parts of Arcadia. But the desire to have our staff under one roof was very strong, and because Arcadia was a fully developed community we began to look elsewhere. As the cabinet discussed relocating I began to notice that all of the communities that Jim talked about were pervasively white: Seattle, Raleigh-Durham, Colorado Springs. Jim never spoke of a vision for placing Focus on the Family in a well-mixed ethnic community for the purpose of drawing a staff from a mixture of groups that matched our customers. If you are creating an organization that serves all families regardless of ethnicity, you could easily imagine the CEO speaking of the need to have such groups represented liberally throughout the staff of writers, editors, engineers, artists, researchers and media strategists who create the organization's products. Jim's vision for relocating Focus was devoid of any statements about diversity, and, in fact, he specifically aimed the corporation in the opposite direction. He was looking for a lily white community where he could be with his kind.

True, a temporary relocation took place that might seem to disprove this observation. When, among others, Jim's wife balked at leaving southern California, the organization found a beautiful office complex nearby in the Los Angeles suburb of Pomona. And Pomona is, without question, an aggressively racially mixed community. But two things are important to understand about that move: first, the ethnicity of Pomona was not a positive factor in the decision to move there, it was a large problem in Jim's mind. After the move, for example, Jim gave instructions that all VIP guests being transported from the airport to the Focus offices were to be taken by the long route that approached the office from the west, where a university was located, rather than the short route to the east through a low-income black and Hispanic neighborhood. And the move was short term. Focus didn't stay. The organization moved on quickly to its permanent campus in Colorado Springs. Nineteen ninety-five statistics reveal Pomona to be 54 percent Latino, 25 percent white, 12 percent black, and 8 percent Asian. Colorado Springs population statistics for 1995 show it to be 86 percent white, 7.2 percent black, 2.5 percent Asian, and .08 percent American Indian. So Jim moved from a community that was 25 percent white to one that was 86 percent white.

A MOMENT OF INFAMY

The defining moment in my experience with Dobson relative to the issue of racism struck like a flash of California high desert lightning—unannounced, dramatic, powerful, unforgettable—one November day in 1986. About a year after my departure from Focus on the Family, I told the story of that explosive moment to Scott Fagerstrom, a religious news reporter, for inclusion in a larger, yet unpublished piece on which he was working, from which I quote here:

They called themselves "The Cabinet."

They met behind closed doors every Wednesday afternoon, in an executive conference room adorned with reminders of their growing power and influence: Photographs of politicians and celebrities. Awards from international religious organizations. Commendations from the White House.

They thought of themselves as generals in an undeclared war—a war against pornography, permissiveness and perversion—and on this particular Wednesday afternoon, in the waning days of 1986, they seemed to be winning.

Their leader, Christian psychologist and radio preacher James Dobson, had recently returned from Washington, D.C., where he'd served as a panelist with the U.S. Attorney General's Commission on Pornography. Thanks in large part to Dobson's influence, the commission—an arm of the most powerful government on earth—had officially entered the war on smut, declaring that adult-oriented magazines and movies lead inevitably to violence against women. It was a virtual endorsement of censorship, and to members of the Cabinet, who'd been saying the same thing for years, it represented a spectacular victory.

But Dobson wasn't feeling especially victorious.

From coast to coast, the conservative psychologist fumed, academics, scientists and media analysts were on the attack. Where was the evidence, critics demanded, for the Meese Commission's conclusion that pornography was dangerous? Where were the statistics? The polls? The psychological profiles of the criminal mind?

Alone with his trusted advisers, in the windowless conference room where he could freely speak his mind, Dobson admitted that the critics had a point. The Meese Commission couldn't come up with hard facts, he said, because no such evidence existed.

But that didn't mean pornography was harmless, Dobson insisted, his forehead creased with frustration. It only proved that no one had bothered to do the research. And why not? Because most behavioral scientists, he charged, were secular liberals, with little interest in any sort of experiments that might buttress Judeo-Christian, "pro-family" values. As long as liberals were in charge of America's scientific purse strings, he lamented, they could suppress any research on the impact of adult entertainment, then use the lack of evidence as an argument against censorship.

Around the room, heads nodded in agreement. This was familiar territory for the half-dozen conservatives who assembled on Wednesday afternoons. Dobson often waxed philosophical—sometimes for hours on end—about the conspiracies of leading liberals in government, science and the media.

The lack of research on pornography wasn't the only instance of liberal bias in the scientific community, Dobson added, leaning forward in his large executive chair. Consider the American Negro, for instance: Weren't the many differences between blacks and whites visible to the naked eye? Weren't black Americans the descendants of slaves, who were bred for physical strength? Wasn't that why blacks excel at sports? And didn't it make sense that as blacks had become physically superior, they had also become intellectually inferior?

All of it could easily be proven, Dobson said, gazing intently around the room, but the bias of most scientists against anything that smacked of racism meant the research would probably never be conducted.

As Dobson paused for a moment to let this sink in, Rolf Zettersten, the group's vice president of publications, noted that the discussion had brought to mind an old joke:

There was this teacher in a black neighborhood, Zettersten said, imitating an inner-city black accent. The teacher asked several little children to spell the word "before." Two got it wrong; finally, the third got it right.

The third student was asked to use the word in a sentence. So the little black boy replied, "Two plus two be-FO!"

A thunderclap of laughter exploded across the room. Dobson leaned back in his chair and howled. The Cabinet meeting, ordinarily the most sober of gatherings, dissolved into chaos. There were serious items remaining on the agenda, but the struggle against sin would just have to wait another week.

WHEN IS BENEVOLENCE NOT BENEVOLENT?

One final observation about James Dobson and racism. As is the case with sexism, you can find in people like Jim a confusing set of behaviors that mask true attitudes. I'm referring to a condescension that produces dramatic outward manifestations of concern and benevolence but whose inner quality remains bigoted.

Those who would scurry to the defense of Dobson, in response to any charge of racism, would point to the fact that he is generous toward needy people—minorities and the poor in developing nations of the world. Friends would make the point that surely these kinds of gestures remove any question about Jim's inner views toward fellow human beings of other races. But often within charity can be found the very seeds of racism. If you examine people's gift giving it's possible that the reason for giving a gift is that they have concluded that this poor, sorry group of beneficiaries are in their needy state precisely because they are inferior while the benefactor stands tall in his affluence and power, capable of being a benefactor precisely because he is superior. Those in society who are successful, intelligent, skilled, and wealthy have an obligation, do they not, to be benevolent toward those who are . . . needy (or was the word inferior?). The gift giving I observed in Dobson, including his generosity toward Third World missionary efforts, struck me much like the spirit of the colonial British as they "gave" political leadership and military defense to, say, India or Singapore. Their actions had the appearance of benevolence. But historians and cultural commentators have exposed the ugly demon of racism in British colonialism. England ruled the seas and the world. Why? Because it was blessed by God; it was white; it was . . . superior. And so, in his mind, is Jim Dobson.

16 ❧ Homophobia

Still another reason James Dobson, public policy maker, concerns me is the evidence I saw of his homophobia, his prejudice against gays and lesbians.

I am embarrassed to tell you that it's only been about a year since I became friends for the first time with a gay person. I consider that odd and regrettable. Perhaps if I explain a little about how a person like me reaches middle age without a single gay friend, you will understand better the homophobia I witnessed inside the world of James Dobson.

I've described two pieces of this puzzle in earlier chapters: first, the fact that young people growing up ultra-orthodox Christian in America are taught that one of the central issues of life is a constant vigilance regarding right and wrong, that which God approves and that which He does not, that which we should applaud in ourselves and others and that which we should not. This intense fixation with whether activities and people are right or wrong—judgmentalism we call it—becomes so powerful by late adolescence that it intrudes into our consciousness and emotions more than we can imagine. Even those of us who are not vocally judgmental transmit a subtle negative energy to those around us. My first problem establishing friendships with people unlike myself was that I was judging their lifestyle and they didn't like the negative energy I generated toward them. It's remarkable, as I think back, how clearly people communicated to me that, as a young ultra-orthodox Christian, I made them feel uncomfortable. I recall, for example, working on the staff of a television station in Lexington, Kentucky, early in my career in broadcasting. One of my colleagues had a reputation for heavy drinking on the weekends, conduct that I judged as sinful and irresponsible. Never mind that his drinking was none of my business, or that I knew nothing about the personal story behind the drinking. Everyone's conduct *was* my business.

One night we were getting ready to broadcast the late news when my co-worker stumbled into the station. He was in one of those states where he was both highly entertaining and truly pathetic. He vacillated from doing things that made it almost impossible for our on-air people to keep a straight face in front of the cameras to moments in which he would talk in an uncomfortably open way about his personal problems. During one of those down swings in his mood that night he turned to me and said, "I know, Gil, I'm just a lousy sinner going to hell. I know. I know."

I was shocked and heartbroken. I had not befriended him because he wasn't "like me." But I had never once verbally condemned his drinking or any other conduct that I did not approve of. I didn't need to. He knew. I dislike that part of the Gil Moegerle of those days. I was not my colleague's judge and I had no business acting as if I were. And part of my disservice to him was that his heavy drinking might have meant that what he needed was a friend to help with some pain he was experiencing. If so, I lost my opportunity to support him by being too busy judging him.

THE VERY WORST KIND OF PERSON

The second explanation for my avoidance of gays was this: Of all the behaviors that my religious background trained me to judge harshly, the top of the list, A-1 candidate for condemnation was any sexual conduct other than sex between a married man and woman.

Sex before marriage? How dare you! Subscribe to *Playboy*? My God! Rent R-rated videos? You poor soul, it won't surprise me when they lock you up for molestation! Sleeping around? I can only pray for you, except that's hard because your lifestyle disgusts me! Adultery? I can't believe it!

If sexual conduct triggers the greatest levels of judgmentalism within the ultraconservative, then the specific sexual practice that heads that category of wrong conduct is homosexual behavior. How completely foul, I would say to myself, that a person would have sex with someone of his or her own gender. And this overwhelming emotional reaction against people engaged in homosexuality short-circuits the capacity not only for friendship but even for whatever rationality the ultra-orthodox person may be capable of. To demonstrate, allow me to simulate an interview with a person of Dobson's persuasion, with a little sarcasm thrown in if you don't mind. My main point here is the lack of logic in the stereotypical responses I've heard from Jim and members of his religious community.

Question: I notice you don't have any friends who are homosexuals. Do they make you uncomfortable? How do you feel when you meet a homosexual?

Answer: Their conduct is aberrant. I become sick to my stomach when I think about that lifestyle. I can't stand to to be near them.

Q: Really? I can easily understand someone having a difference of opinion with someone else regarding their sexual choices, but I'm not sure I understand why you would become sick to your stomach.

A: Everyone knows what those people do. It's unnatural. It is disgusting.

Q: Perhaps a simple solution is for you to avoid becoming a homosexual because the lifestyle disgusts you. But why do you have such difficulty allowing others to be and to do as they please?

A: Because their choices threaten our society and our children. They're depraved and corrupting. And they know it. Homosexuals could choose the straight life. They just refuse to do so.

Q: You're a heterosexual telling homosexuals what their innermost thoughts and feelings are, what their desires and motives are. Isn't that a little absurd, not to mention judgmental? Homosexuals say that they don't voluntarily choose to feel homosexual, to find their own gender sexually attractive rather than the opposite sex. They say they "discover" these feelings within themselves; perhaps even fight against them for a long time before recognizing them as their identity, usually at a great personal price. They say that they are no more destructive to themselves and their partners than are any two heterosexuals who fall in love and live together. They argue that heterosexual Americans are not exclusively responsible for America's strengths. Both groups have stable and unstable partnerships, they would say. Both groups include irresponsibly promiscuous members. Both groups contain members who weaken and destroy other people's partnerships by encouraging unfaithfulness. There is enough sexual sin in America, they would argue, to keep every heterosexual and homosexual American humble about who's to blame.

A: We're talking about my personal beliefs. That's all. I believe that God's plan is for men to be with women and women with men.

Q: That I understand. You have religious convictions. And convictions should be respected. Fair enough. But homosexuals have convictions. Do they warrant your respect, just as you demand theirs? We come back to your first reaction. Why do your powerful negative reactions against the beliefs of others cause you to avoid them, to make no friends among them? If the subject is the challenge America faces managing sexuality in a positive and constructive way, don't you think some of those challenges are yours?

My point in offering you a conversation that could have easily taken place between Jim and me is not to suggest that resolving society's sexual issues is as simple as respecting everyone's individual viewpoints. Obviously, society has a legitimate need to distinguish between constructive and destructive expressions of sexuality by its members through such means as defining marriage, controlling prostitution and obscenity, punishing sexual abuse, and so on.

The pathway to resolving differences of opinion and building consensus on this or any issue does not pass through contempt and deception. We're going to have to proceed on the basis of dialogue and civility. And we're going to have to be friends or the journey will not be possible. Toward that end, I'm afraid we'll receive no help from James Dobson.

BROKEN DREAMS, BROKEN WINDOWS

There was a reference to the hostility between the religious right and gays and lesbians in Marc Fisher's profile of Dobson in the *Washington Post.* He told of touring the chapel on the Focus campus. His guide pointed to cathedral windows that had been shattered by homosexual activists opposed to Focus's support of an anti-gay rights amendment in Colorado. "We've had bomb threats, we had bricks thrown through a window in our bookstore," Focus vice president Paul Hetrick told Fisher. "Still, we bear the brunt of being called war-mongering haters. Which way is the hate flowing?"[1] I'd like to try my hand at answering Hetrick's question.

Think about the feelings and the thoughts responsible homosexuals in this society are trying desperately to bring to the attention of those of us who are heterosexual and particularly those of us who are in power. They are made to feel like second-class citizens, disenfranchised. They feel sometimes as if all the rest of us possess and enjoy a wonderful package of rights that are guaranteed to us and are enforced vigorously by society—rights to life, liberty, and the pursuit of happiness, rights to privacy and fair work opportunities, to be treated equally and without discrimination when we seek loans and housing and the American dream. But when they look inside their package of rights, they feel shorted. Their voices call out to us saying that they have experienced real discrimination.

People like Dobson often respond to such voices by saying that gays are not deprived of any rights, that they are demanding special rights. He claims they are not experiencing any reduction in rights; instead, they are inventing this entire social disruption to impose on the rest of us something we don't want.

As with other aspects of his work on public policy, I'm amazed by the sight of Dobson telling homosexuals what their experiences in society really are and what they should want and not want for themselves. How does he know? Why is it his business? Here, then, is my answer to Paul Hetrick: You and Jim are concentrating so hard on your own needs and your own perspectives, on what you as heterosexuals in this society want and feel, that you have no capacity to hear the voices of your homosexual neighbors. You're right, there's no justification for throwing a brick through your window, but there's also no justification for being as deaf as you are to the voices that asked for equality with you before frustration overwhelmed them and they tossed that brick—assuming it was a gay person who tossed the brick. The problem here is not your broken window, it's the unheard voice of someone who is having a decidedly different experience in this society than you are. You don't have to agree with their views and they don't have to accept yours. But somehow, we have to hear each other and fashion a society based on mutual respect. And half of that mutuality is your responsibility.

DOMA AND ENDA

During the summer and fall of 1996 two historic bills related to homosexual rights moved through the United States Senate focusing attention once again on the battle raging between the gay movement and the right. The Defense of Marriage Act (DOMA) and the Employment Non-Discrimination Act (ENDA) gave us yet another opportunity to take measure of the kind of America Dobson would give us if we gave him increased political power. It was not a pretty sight.

Dobson called up his troops by means of his radio talk show, indicating that his ongoing war on America had entered yet another period of battle. Lesbian lovers in Hawaii, he explained, had filed suit contesting that the state's law against same-sex marriage was unconstitutional. As a result, a state court had ordered Hawaii to make a compelling argument before it regarding why gays couldn't marry. That trial began in September and made history in December 1996 by striking down the law and opening the door to

marriage between gays and lesbians. In advance, conservatives had fashioned DOMA to protect other states from being forced by the Constitution
to recognize Hawaiian same-sex marriages. DOMA passed handily. But
before the vote, Senator Ted Kennedy attached an amendment to it that outlawed discrimination against gays in the workplace. In other words, if you
voted for the defense of marriage you got gay employment rights as well.

You don't need a scorecard to recognize which position on the court
Dobson was playing. He was the one in favor of DOMA and passionately opposed to ENDA. So much so that his battle order to the troops was this: They
were to call their senator and announce that ENDA must be stripped from
DOMA so that a vote for one was not a vote for the other. Their senator was
to vote against ENDA and for DOMA. But here's the fascinating part: Dobson told his listeners to tell their representative that if the two bills could not
be separated, senators were to vote *against* the defense of marriage.

Exactly what aspect of ENDA was so repulsive and repugnant that
Dobson would rather see DOMA lose, and see Hawaiian marriages
spread like wildfire across the continental United States, than to see
ENDA win? What horrific disaster did he see befalling our land's work-
places if Ted Kennedy got his way? Actually, what ENDA offered, the
17,000 employees I work with at Edison International already have.
Allow me to quote from our handbook:

> Employees shall not discriminate against anyone on any unlawful basis,
> including sex, race, religion, color, national origin, *sexual orientation,* age,
> medical condition, physical or mental disability, HIV or AIDS condition,
> marital status, veteran status, or family leave status.[2] (Emphasis added)

There it is in all its scary detail. ENDA would have added "sexual orientation" to other aspects of people's background and personal circumstances that cannot be used as a reason to treat them differently than other
Americans. Nineteen ninety-six polls showed that four out of five Americans favored ENDA, that, as a group, we believe homosexuals should
have the same employment rights as heterosexuals. The bottom-line issue
here is whether the package of rights gays carry around includes one in
your package and in mine—the right to any job for which they are qualified, the right to earn a meaningful wage, to support themselves, to pay
the bills. It's a right to fairness and equality that, if denied to me, over and
over, might conceivably cause this peace-loving white boy from Pennsylvania to at least think about pitching a brick through the window of a
company that said to me, "Gil, you already have that right. All you ever
do is demand special rights." ENDA lost by a vote of 50 to 49, but supporters predicted it would pass during a future session of Congress.

Dobson's positions on such matters seem to overlook the complexities of state-sponsored morality. They appear naïve, simplistic and theocratic, out of step with the hard work a democracy must do to address its evolving needs on the basis not of one religion's view of morality but of the moral consensus. For example, Carol Moseley-Braun (D-Ill.), the only black woman in the Senate, reminded her colleagues during the ENDA/DOMA debate that when she was a girl one of her relatives was married to a white person, an act that was then illegal in sixteen states. "As a child that did not make any sense to me," Braun said, adding that such laws were finally overthrown by a 1967 Supreme Court ruling. "That kind of restriction may seem unbelievable today but it was a reality of life only decades ago." She continued, "And now the exact same moral arguments are being made against domestic relations of another order." It was once thought moral to own slaves and to deprive blacks and women of the vote. Now such social positions are an unthinkable type of morality. Can we really hunker down in the late 1990s and take the position Dobson advocates, that all the work of building a just and moral society is behind us, and that Washington is now to preserve the past and the status quo?

Consider also the fact that a distinguished Christian voted in favor of ENDA, while Dobson equated it with the moral ruin of the nation. Senator Mark Hatfield of Oregon, long recognized as a leader within the religious world of American conservative Christians, voted for full employment rights for gays. And yet part of Dobson's argument against the legislation was based firmly on the fact that it was, according to him, "an unbiblical view."

PROTESTER ON THE LAWN

During July of 1994 an extraordinary scene unfolded not far from where the brick sailed through the Focus window, which spoke volumes about that brick. One of the best-known writers in Dobson's religious community, a creative dynamo named Mel White, sat down on the front lawn of Dobson's headquarters and began a protest. The issue being protested? James Dobson, gay basher. The drama behind that scene, apart from the spectacle of a sit-in protest on Focus on the Family property, was the fact that Mel White, who had written numerous best-selling books and other creative materials for such luminaries as Jerry Falwell, had come out of the closet a year earlier, publicly declaring himself to be gay. With him at the sit-in was his male life partner. The media noticed.

Mel's protest was not merely over the philosophical issues of equality and discrimination that I've raised here. White, speaking from within the gay community, called out from his campsite for Dobson to stop killing homosexuals. He said in a letter he delivered to Focus's front door, which later appeared on several Internet pages:

> Jim Dobson is not an evil man. Focus on the Family is not an evil organization. In their misunderstanding of gay and lesbian people, they are victims of superstition and prejudice that have been passed down to them over the ages. We need to give them time to come to an understanding of us. But in the meantime, whether his motives are good or bad, we cannot remain silent in the face of Dobson's anti-gay rhetoric and his national anti-gay political campaign. His words and actions lead directly to the suffering and death of innocent and loving gay, lesbian, bisexual, and transgendered Americans.

White's reference to the suffering and death of gays was based on his conclusion that hate crimes against gays in various parts of the country, some leading to the death of their victims, were often incited and fueled by the strident anti-gay language Dobson and others within the religious right use.

It was interesting to me that Jim's letter of response, hand carried onto the lawn by a Focus vice president, conveyed the same streetfighter arrogance that characterizes so much of his behind-the-scenes persona. Jim wrote:

> It is clear from your manipulation of the press that your purpose in this campaign is to capitalize on the visibility of Focus on the Family to publicize your book and to promote yourself. What we have here is an elaborate publicity campaign wrapped in the cloak of human rights.

Nice touch, Jim. So much for listening, for dialoguing with, or at least befriending those different than yourself.

I learned during an October 1996 conversation with Mel White that the only reason White had gone to Colorado Springs and staged a public confrontation was that Dobson had refused numerous requests to engage in a private exchange of letters about the inflammatory, violence-generating rhetoric he uses against gays.

Mel offered me specific examples of direct quotes he had collected from Dobson's writings and broadcasts. He indicated that he had been trying to persuade Jim that his language was inaccurate and endangered the lives and well-beings of gays and lesbians. He mentioned the following examples:

- Dobson asks his constituents broad, fear-inspiring questions without defining the precise meaning of his terms, such as "Would you object if your children were routinely indoctrinated in homosexual ideology in the public schools?

- Dobson poses absurdly hypothetical questions, unrelated to the true gay concerns of the day, that suggest that the "homosexual agenda" is unacceptably radical, such as "Would you object to the state telling your pastor or priest what he can say from the pulpit about Sodom and Gomorrah?" Dobson reports untruths as facts about the gay agenda: "Homosexuals see the traditional family as a barrier to the social engineering they hope to accomplish."

- Dobson portrays homosexuals as perverse and degenerate and thereby trivializes their social concerns with statements like, "There are people in our society who find sexual satisfaction in engaging in intercourse with animals. Would we suggest that these groups deserve special protection, too?" or, "Communities do not let prostitutes, pedophiles, voyeurs, adulterers, and those who sexually prefer animals to publicly celebrate their lifestyles, so why should homosexuals get such privileges?"

- Dobson continually showcases on his broadcast and quotes in his published materials individuals such as Eugene Antonio, Randall Terry, and Wil Perkins, who spread inflammatory and misleading rhetoric about gay issues.

MAKE FRIENDS NOT WAR

Dan Johnson and I worked in the same department of our electric utility. Early in our friendship, Dan was sitting in my office one day telling me about National AIDS Awareness Day. He did so not only as a gay man and an activist of sorts, but because, he revealed, he had been diagnosed as HIV positive. I felt an immediate pain at the thought that this man whom I was coming to enjoy so much as a professional colleague—with a great personality, tremendous skill at what we did every day, a variety of talents that were fun to watch in action—had a death sentence hanging over his head. I asked him how he maintained such a positive outlook, how he dealt with the tragedy of being infected with an incurable disease. Dan's characteristic style at a moment like that is to shrug off any suggestion that perhaps he's brave or displays special courage. He indicated that it was merely part of life and that one of the challenges we all face is to manage problems and pain.

I felt such sadness at the thought of what it must be like to face what Dan was confronting that as he was leaving my office I stood up, walked around my desk and embraced him. And my eyes overflowed.

I knew that most people in our department knew that Dan was gay and I was conscious that the door of my office was open and other workers might see the two of us embracing. Somehow, I didn't care. The message I wanted to deliver at that moment was, "Dan, on this National AIDS Awareness Day, the gift I give you is that I touch you, I place myself in contact with you. I realize this is merely symbolic, but I will hold you for a moment nonetheless and in so doing say to you that you are as important a human as I am. I do not ask you to be like me and I do not wish to be like you. But I do care about you."

As I drove home that night I cried. Not for Dan but for me. The tears were not from the pain I felt knowing that this good friend may someday call in sick and never return to work. These were tears of joy that I had somehow become a different person, one who could feel affection for someone whose life choices were so different from my own.

NOTES

1. Marc Fisher, "The GOP, Facing a Dobson's Choice," *Washington Post,* July 2, 1996.

2. *Business Conduct Guide,* Southern California Edison, 1996–1997.

17 🌿 Abuse of Power

When I first met Jim during the 1970s, when his speaking and writing careers were blossoming, there was another writer and speaker within Jim's niche market whose career was also blossoming. Her name was Joyce Landorf. Joyce had an extraordinary talent for words and ideas. In many ways she was identical to Jim—a superb communicator whether through the spoken or the written word. She was quick-witted, and she had an excellent sense of the needs and interests of her market and how to speak to those needs in a manner that people found helpful. Her products and services were in great demand, as were Jim's. Her speaking engagements were jammed and her audiences enthusiastic. Her books were consistent best-sellers, just as Jim's were. In fact, during the seventies, after each had been on the speaking circuit for years, these two writer-speakers sometimes teamed up, offering joint seminars on the family.

Needless to say, Jim and Joyce developed a very special professional relationship based on a common bond of religious perspective and target markets, as well as business and professional interests. So it was natural that, when we began producing Focus on the Family radio programs in March of 1977, Jim indicated that one of the first guests he wanted to interview on his new series was his friend Joyce Landorf.

I remember that first meeting with Joyce and her recording session very well because the communicative talent she unleashed in the studio lit it up as if someone had set off a fireworks display. I had an intense interest in finding communicators and developing broadcast products with such talent. That interest produced a kind of inner radar, constantly scanning the horizon for the sound of a great relater of ideas. And that day an enormous blip hit my radar scope. "Joyce Landorf has a great gift," I said to myself.

A GIFT OF COMMUNICATION

Joyce is the type of person about whom you would say, "I could listen to her all day long." She presented herself with the requisite humility of a great communicator—the attractive sense that she does not take herself too seriously, which allows listeners to receive her ideas without being turned off by any arrogance. She had an innate sense of what was worth talking about. And she had that special quality of being able to tell a story about the most common experiences of everyday family life in an entertaining and suspenseful manner that made you hang on every word wishing it would never end, taking you inside the characters of the story and witnessing their traumas or triumphs. I remember, for example, her oft-repeated story about the ritual she and her first husband, Dick, enacted when locking up their home each night before retiring. Joyce described, with a twinkle in her eye that promised you this verbal journey would be worth the ride, how annoying it was that after she had checked to make sure the house was locked and climbed into bed, her husband would invariably ask her if she was absolutely certain she had completed this chore. Joyce would offer the ritualistic yes only to watch Dick get out of bed and circle the house one more time. Joyce would describe the sound of her husband going down the hall, rattling the back and front doorknobs, and then returning to bed. I cannot do justice here to the humor of the story because Joyce's comedic abilities were so strong that just the look on her face as she described the sound of the doors shaking under the weight of Dick's inspection made you laugh. And then came the punch line—not a comedic jab for the sake of laughter but an educational punch line intended to help Joyce's audience do the work of family. Joyce would say that one night as she lay in bed contemplating kicking her husband in some appropriate part of his anatomy for this seeming act of disrespect for her efforts, it suddenly struck her that she was observing a demonstration of a strength, not a weakness, in her mate, a quality that made Dick successful in his job. Her husband was a banker and, she went on, one of the elements of temperament bankers must have if they are to remain in business is that of checking and double checking, of adding the numbers and then re-adding them, of checking an applicant's qualification for a loan and then checking it again. She suddenly saw Dick in a different light: not as a husband doubting her word but as a man double checking their safety because he was, by gift and temperament, a "checker."

Again, the capacity of this talented communicator to do what Dobson did so well, to tell a story and then make a point that encouraged listeners with their marriage or their children, was superior. And it seemed to me as I met Joyce that day in the studio that these two communicators were not only alike, but they had benefited from their mutual association. I could imagine the marketing power of having Joyce participate often in the work of Focus on the Family.

I provide this background in order to explain exactly how shocking it was to observe the collapse of the friendship between Jim and Joyce as a result of conduct by Jim that I can only imagine a judge and jury would find to be not only abusive but illegal. I must assume this only because Joyce has chosen not to prosecute Jim for the events I'm about to describe.

The falling out began with a problem in the marriage between Joyce and Dick. None of us who were their friends knows the details. I say that as a very pointed and important part of telling you this story. Speaking as a divorced person myself, if you ever hear someone say that they know exactly what happened in the demise of a marriage, I authorize you to think of them as a fool. Only a fool assumes that an outsider can assess the complex breakdown of a private relationship between two people who went from loving each other intensely to disliking each other. That's why I say none of us who were friends of Joyce and Dick knows what happened other than the obvious: They encountered painful differences they were not able to overcome despite the fact that both tried to do so. Joyce and her husband sought marital counseling, a fact that figures prominently in this story.

Joyce turned to a professional counseling clinic in southern California, Associated Psychological Services, that was run by two psychologists, Neil Warren and Cliff Penner, who were Jim's close friends. Neil is a very distinguished leader within Jim's religious community, having written a number of books, appeared on the "Focus on the Family" radio show often, and spoken across the country. In addition, Neil served as dean of the School of Psychology at Fuller Theological Seminary, the graduate school some think of as the premier educational institution within Jim's community. Cliff's career was almost identical to Neil's with the exception of Neil's work at Fuller.

MAY I HAVE A REFERRAL?

Neil and Cliff's offices were located just minutes from Focus on the Family in Pasadena, California. Because of that proximity as well as the close friendship among the three men, a powerful financial partnership developed between Jim and Associated Psychological Services that represents yet another key element of this story. It was speculated that, at times, 75 percent of the counseling customers the clinic obtained came from referrals by Jim and Focus on the Family. In other words, Neil and Cliff were indebted to Jim and dependent on him for a significant portion of their livelihood.

This referral link had its roots in the fact that Jim was known nationally as one of the most trusted figures in a field that conservative Protestant Christians didn't trust very much—psychology. To grasp this you need to understand that there is a strong "trust Jesus only" mentality within this group. Its preachers and teachers speak out loudly against entrusting one's inner well-being, one's spiritual development, to mere men. In many circles, the science of psychology is treated exactly as is the field of astrology—a bogus endeavor from the pit. The emphasis is on "giving one's problems to God" and "trusting Christ to provide the answers to your needs." The idea of looking to the methods of psychotherapy to address what are thought to be spiritual problems, such as depression, loneliness, fear, addictions and obsessions, inferiority, or other such concerns, is treated as sin.

One positive way of assessing the Dobson legacy is that he may well be the man most responsible for conservative American Christians opening their minds to the simple premise that if going to a doctor with an infection is not sinful, then going to a psychologist with a pathology isn't sinful either. Stafford's profile of Dobson in *Christianity Today* touched on this point: "Dobson has brought a secular vocation to a Christian cause. Dobson has grafted the scientific authority of doctors and psychologists onto the emotive moral force of an evangelist."[1] I think that's accurate, and what we must add is that the vast majority of conservative American Christians decried any such grafting prior to Dobson's influence in the 1980s and 1990s.

So when I say that Warren and Penner depended on Dobson for a large percentage of their livelihood, I mean that, as conservative Christian therapists, they were struggling in a market where the customer was extremely reluctant to see a therapist. Dobson eased that reluctance and then specifically told listeners and correspondents that there were two counselors in Pasadena who could be trusted to help them save their marriage or "fix" their teenager while still trusting Christ. The debt Neil and Cliff owed Jim was immense and Jim found a way to collect.

I was told by Dobson and a Focus vice president and close personal friend of Joyce's therapist that Landorf was having marital problems and that she was seeing Cliff Penner for counseling. It seems that our suspicious, smoke-smelling family advisor, who routinely prowled the offices of his staff at night, nose in the air sniffing out their misdeeds, had turned his insatiable appetite for gossip toward his friend and professional competitor Joyce Landorf. Looking back on it, the fact that I was even told by Dobson or vice president Peb Jackson that Joyce was in counseling with Dr. Penner is itself a disturbing part of this story. The staff of Focus should not have known. And whoever on our staff first learned this very private piece of information, whether Jim or Peb, should not have repeated it within our offices.

WORD OF MOUTH

The general comment repeated at Focus on the Family during this period was that Joyce was having marital difficulties and was in counseling. But two more specific and alarming pieces of information were also circulating that make it clear that somewhere in the relationship between Focus on the Family and Associated Psychological Services the privacy of patients was being violated. First, we were told that a conflict had arisen between Jim and Cliff and that Jim had temporarily suspended all referrals to Dr. Penner. The cause of the conflict was twofold. Jim disapproved of the way Cliff was counseling Joyce. Apparently Penner was supporting the idea of a possible divorce. For Dobson, no marriage should ever be terminated, period. Secondly, Jim had received word that Cliff was counseling some of his patients that abortion might be acceptable in certain circumstances. Like marriage, no pregnancy should be terminated in Dobson's view. He reacted strongly and negatively, cutting off the flow of business from Focus to Penner. When Penner learned his referrals had dried up, he pled with Dobson to reconsider. Penner and Dobson met, they made a deal, and Penner was reinstated.

Several years after I left the organization, Joyce revealed that Penner had talked to her in a counseling session about Dobson removing him from the referral list because of the way he was counseling her. He told her he'd met with Jim and he was back on the referral list. But he never revealed the nature of the agreement that got him reinstatement. Joyce said that soon thereafter, the specific content of counseling sessions began filtering back to her from mutual friends of Dobson. I learned as well that Penner had spoken openly to her about my own family's therapy which was being handled by Penner's colleague at the clinic, Neil Warren. At the end of one of her sessions, Penner told her, for example, not to go out a certain door because "Gil Moegerle's waiting to see Neil and, boy, is his marriage a mess. It's not going to survive, either."

By now Jim had begun making regular reports to our executive staff during our weekly meetings, stating among other things that Joyce's counseling was not going well and her marriage might end in divorce. Again, the questions raised by such comments are obvious and alarming: How did Jim know the status of Joyce's counseling and why would a licensed psychologist, trained in doctor-patient confidentiality, make it public?

The Worst Is Yet to Come

Some time after word reached us that Joyce's first marriage had indeed ended, the most startling chapter of this story took place. Dobson had long since pulled even the memory of Joyce Landorf from the shelves of Focus on the Family. She had once graced the cover of our monthly magazine. No more. Not a single Landorf book remained in our warehouse. No past broadcasts featuring Joyce were to be re-aired regardless of their popularity. And no new ones would ever be scheduled. No references to Joyce were to be made in our materials and anyone writing and inquiring about her was to be given the most limited amount of information possible. But that was all preamble. As these events unfolded during 1985, Jim told our senior staff that he had spoken with his and Joyce's publishing house, Word, Inc., and that fellow best-selling Word author Chuck Swindoll had traveled to that publisher's office, both men delivering the ultimatum that either Word cease publishing Joyce or they would take their valuable contracts to a competitor. The publisher buckled and discontinued all business dealings with Joyce Landorf.

It was not Dobson's first venture into attempting to coerce an independent publishing company to stop doing business with people whose personal lives he disliked. Jim copied me his handwritten note to the same publisher regarding their decision to publish Stanley Mooneyham: "I'm disappointed that you would publish Stan Mooneyham's book. There are times when I think I am spiritually in harmony with you and times when

I think not. This is one of those concerned moments." The meaning of those words was crystal clear: Jim was thinking of taking his business elsewhere. And since he was, at times, the number-one revenue producer for that publisher, you could accurately interpret such a note as coercion of the crassest kind. It is made all the more obscene when you realize that, according to Stan, Jim had never even met Mooneyham before writing that note. He had heard rumors, he had drawn his conclusions from gossip. And in true Dobson style, Jim was prepared to interfere with Stan's publishing business when he heard Stan was divorced and remarried.

Jim saw it as his business to assess the private lives of people and decide if they merited a book contract by his publisher or not.

NOTES

1. Tim Stafford, "His Father's Son," *Christianity Today,* March 1988.
2. Joyce Landorf Heatherley, *Special Words* (Nashville, Tenn.: Moorings, 1996).

18 ❧ Misuse of Funds

Allow me one additional reason James-Dobson-public-policy-maker concerns me: his misuse of publicly donated funds. Whenever reporters interview me about my years with Dobson they always ask about money. Did I ever see Jim misuse Focus funds? In the years immediately after I left Focus on the Family I would quickly answer no, explaining that while I disagreed with Dobson on many things, the one absolute regarding Focus was the integrity of its fund-raising and spending practices.

Jim, like any leader, brought to the organization certain individual passions, and one of these was how money should be handled. Donors were to receive a prompt receipt. Vendors were to be paid within thirty days. Revenues were to be accounted for in a manner consistent with the highest levels of accounting practices. Our books were to be audited on a regular basis. Reporting was to be thorough and timely. Jim's rhetoric about this aspect of the company was impressive. He spoke often of donations as "blood money" and demanded that we remember that the revenue of the company, now over 100 million dollars annually, was made up of individual $15 and $20 donations, often from low-income contributors who could barely afford their gift. In response, our expenditures were to be frugal and circumspect.

Furthermore, Jim's philosophy of raising money was exemplary. He rejected the use of canned, formulaic fund-raising strategies from consultants, those who travel around telling nonprofits how to squeeze the most out of their mailing lists. Instead, Dobson relied on his own personal instinct for how to write fund-raising letters and voice on-air appeals. The stories of those who were less circumspect were legend.

A Planned Crisis

Chuck Colson, a close Dobson friend and also a fund raiser, because his organization, "Prison Fellowship," depends on public donations, told us once of a professional fund-raising consultant who visited him to pitch for his account. The services available included ghost writing Colson's "personal" letters to his list, strategically "segmenting" the mailing list into names that should be "purged" because they were not productive financially and those that should receive extra appeals because they showed promise of doubling or tripling their contributions, and designing special donor campaigns such as drives to build new buildings or develop large new enterprises. (Focus uses such consultants but in a more limited way.) The consultant displayed for Colson a chart showing the number of times per year he proposed sending appeals to the Colson list. The idea, he explained, was to appeal enough times to gain the maximum revenue possible without "burning out" the donor.

As Colson studied the chart he noticed that three times during the year the consultant had penciled in a mailing he called a "crisis letter." Such a letter had as its theme, he was told, the concern that the organization was experiencing a serious shortfall in donations and needed emergency help from its friends lest it have to close its doors. Colson asked how such "emergencies" could be placed on a long-range planning chart in advance. The answer illustrated the manipulation and corruption that is sometimes found in the religious fund-raising industry. The consultant responded that, obviously, he didn't know when slumps in donations would take place but that it was important to tell constituents that a slump had occurred, even if it hadn't, since response to crisis letters was always better than to other types of letters. Colson did not hire the service.

Dobson never contrived financial emergencies or engaged in crass manipulations of his donor list. He never even sold the names and addresses to direct mail advertisers, which is generally considered ethical. For that and other reasons, I always gave him an A+ when asked by reporters about his handling of money.

But with the passage of time, I've begun to question whether the Focus story is indeed pristine in this area. Allow me to list a few questions that illustrate my concern.

Question #1: Why doesn't Dobson accept a salary and the accountability that goes with it?

I raised this issue earlier, so I will only touch on it here. As I indicated, Jim brags publicly that he doesn't take a salary as an act of sacrifice and benevolence. But his motive, from all I could determine, was to avoid placing himself in the traditional accountability relationship with his board that is true of any CEO, one in which his board of directors pays him and then holds him accountable for his time and conduct. No matter what Jim and his board say publicly, the fact remains that the board cannot challenge the direction in which Dobson takes the company as it would under more normal circumstances. I believe one of several reasons the Focus board is a largely passive group and Focus is a personality-dominated corporation is due to this very strange compensation arrangement.

Question #2: Why doesn't Dobson donate the proceeds of his books, tapes, and films to his corporation, as do Billy Graham and other religious leaders who head nonprofits?

This is the flip side of the first issue. Jim personally controls the revenue from his books, tapes, and films, some of them created on Focus on the Family time and using Focus resources, for his own profit. He refuses to give up all royalties because he is unwilling to entrust the issue of his personal income to someone else. As a result, in real world terms, he is accountable to no one.

Question #3: Why are Focus on the Family buildings much more expensively designed and furnished than is typical of donor-supported, nonprofit organizations?

Jim and Shirley's personal tastes run in a more lavish, upscale direction than is generally considered appropriate for publicly funded organizations where donors are paying the bills. Often, nonprofits are characterized as austere in terms of the facilities they occupy. For the typical donor to drive a Ford but the CEO of the charity they support to drive a Mercedes is generally thought to be out of balance. At the very least, it is traditionally believed that a publicly funded organization should spend no more on its physical plant and overhead than is essential. But this is not the standard used by Jim. Were you to take the daily guest tour of Focus on the Family, you would be jolted by the rich decor that, in so many instances, goes far beyond an approach to architecture and interior decorating that would be termed modest or basic. In Marc Fisher's 1996 *Washington Post* profile of Dobson he wrote of Jim's office buildings: "If Nordstroms [an upscale department store chain] were to branch out into selling the Word [of God], their operations might look something like the Constituent Services Building at Focus on the Family."

James Dobson likes nice stuff. His self-image is that a Ph.D. who should dress well, drive a Mercedes, and own a house and office representative of society's best. Many other rationalizations are used by Focus, but that's where you'll find the fountainhead of Focus spending on lush facilities—Jim and Shirley's uptown tastes.

Question #4: When Focus executives travel, why do some of them stay in four-star hotels?

One of the ongoing debates within the cabinet when I was part of Focus on the Family was why Dobson's executive with the assignment of courting wealthy and powerful friends of the organization was staying at four-star hotels rather than more mid-range accommodations. The executive to whom I refer was Peb Jackson and the argument that he used for this practice, one which Dobson supported, never quite made sense. He contended that if you are visiting Washington, D.C., on assignment from Dobson to befriend the powerful, you can't stay at the local Holiday Inn. If you're in Denver to meet and court one of the wealthiest oil men in the West, you can't use a Best Western for your housing. On several occasions cabinet members asked, "Why not?" And the detailed and helpful answer always came back, from either Peb or Jim, "Because you can't associate with the wealthy without eating where they eat and sleeping where they sleep." It always seemed to me that this line of reasoning raised a disturbing question. Can you build a nonprofit on an average donation of eighteen dollars from lower- to middle-class donors and justify spending those donations on restaurants and hotels they themselves cannot afford?

Question #5: Is Jim accountable for how he spends Focus money? How much power does he have over the organization's expenditures and how independent is that power of real checks and balances?

On December 28, 1988, Dobson was sitting on the witness stand in family law court in Los Angeles County answering questions by an attorney regarding why he was routinely sending fairly large amounts of Focus money to a divorcee.

As Jim testified that day, he began by acknowledging that he had personally directed that Focus on the Family funds be sent to the woman. He indicated that the first check sent had been for $1,000 on April 23 of the previous year.

Question: If I indicated to you, Mr. Dobson, that there has been some $17,200 that have been advanced to [woman's name] since April of 1987 would you say that is approximately correct?

Answer: To the best of my knowledge, yes.

Q.: The decisions in regard to the money that has been directed to [woman's name] have all been at your direction; is that correct?

A.: I was certainly aware of them, yes.

Q.: Do you know, Dr. Dobson, of any single instance where Focus on the Family has contributed sums of this magnitude to one individual?

A.: No.

Q.: Dr. Dobson, I direct you to Exhibit 1, payable April 22, 1988, and I ask you to read the reason [shown in the check request form filled out by a Dobson associate].

A.: This is something Jim has asked me to do.[1]

There are two aspects to this story that raise questions regarding how Dobson handles donations. First, he personally donated to Focus some of the $17,000 given this woman, directing his CFO to send a check in an equivalent amount to the woman. Officers of nonprofits, or 501(c)3 charities, as the IRS calls them, cannot use their own charities to grant tax-deductible receipts to themselves for donations they then direct to a friend.

The second concern this story raises is why Dobson used donor money, contributions raised by means of the expressed appeal that they would be used to strengthen marriages and families, in support of a personal friend who admittedly divorced her husband simply because of "irreconcilable differences."

The story told earlier in chapter 6, about Jim's use of $28,000 of donor money to secure legal services to hound Rick Johnson, whom he falsely accused of mismanaging retirement accounts unrelated to Focus, is an even more potent example of this concern. And that story pales in comparison with one that is still to come, the account of Jim's misappropriation of hundreds of thousands of donor contributions to litigate a fair labor practices dispute after an employee had repeatedly asked him to resolve the claim by means of a free one-day arbitration process within their religious community. Is Jim too independent in his control of donor funds? That is the question.

NOTE

1. Court record, Los Angeles Superior Court, December 28, 1988.

19 ❧ Physician, Heal Thyself

My father's general approach to the medical profession was one of skepticism and a strategy of avoidance at all costs. Illness, to my father, was a challenge much like making that next sale. And Dad was a great salesman. He realized that if you were just persistent and hard working, the percentages were with you. He seemed to approach medicine just that way. If your leg hurt the chances were that if you just kept walking on it the problem, whatever it was, would yield to the persistence of your will. And when it came to personal problems that were not medical but emotional or psychological, his approach was exactly the same. If a person was depressed the answer was—just keep moving forward. The problem would sort itself out under the pressure of your will. Perseverance combined with faith in God was Dad's way.

When my first marriage began to fail, my marital problems hurt my father a great deal. His response was wonderfully and irrationally comforting. Dad would say that he just couldn't understand why my wife acted as she did and why she didn't fix the problems he perceived she alone was creating in our home. Never once did he suggest that I played any part in the breakup. Talking to Dad was one experience during those terribly painful days that guaranteed me an escape from the tougher and more realistic accountability questions of my therapist like, "So, Gil, what are you going to do about your unhelpful responses to what you perceive to be your wife's wrongful conduct?"

When I would talk to my father about my experiences with our marriage counselor, his response would always be, "Gil, do you really think that helps?" To Dad, the solution lay in my will and that of my wife. Life

183

was simply a matter of moving forward, putting your weight down on the part that hurt, and knowing that somehow, by the perseverance of your will, all would be well.

Dad died in 1985 of prostate cancer that was diagnosed too late because he didn't like doctors. Between the diagnosis and that heart-breaking moment that he drew his last breath with all of us standing around him, Dad's will did not save him. As he died he learned one of life's great lessons: all of the answers aren't here inside; we must entrust to others enough of ourselves so that they can help us where we cannot help ourselves.

A Personal Assessment

I've come to appreciate the aid available from professional counseling not only in times of personal crisis but also in the general business of self-dis-covery and personal growth. For example, I've benefited from several pro-files of myself done by psychologists as I've attempted to determine which direction to take in my career. I recall one "Psychological Assessment Re-port" done in 1980, involving filling out several questionnaires and a per-sonal interview. The final analysis read: "A man of varied talents and lively, albeit not consistent energy, Gil certainly has the versatility to handle posi-tions involving different arrays of duties. Has leadership gifts, and could convey a caring, warmly supportive attitude toward those he directed." My reaction to reading this part of the assessment was that psychology is a wonderful thing and people who write such words should be honored and respected. Then I read on: "Is not likely to be a firm supervisor, however, or one who would discipline and correct others effectively." At this point I switched back to my father's point of view—this is a waste of time. Seri-ously, I find it amazing that a psychological assessment form can ask you 150 questions and then an analyst can look at the boxes you check and make comments which are precisely on target. The assessment was right: I love managing work teams but in many ways I'm a less effective manager because of the very lack of firmness this 1980 analysis pinpointed.

I don't know if Jim has ever submitted himself to such an assessment. But I have often speculated that if a psychologist were to professionally analyze the language Dobson uses in his writings and broadcasting for the purpose of writing a psychological profile of James Dobson, the result would be a report showing that Jim's perceptions of the world are, to some degree, skewed. Not being a professional in that field I have no idea what categories or degrees of skew would result nor whether such an analysis would label any of Dobson's idiosyncrasies as pathological, substantial, or dysfunctional. But there is no question in this layman's mind that the world James Dobson sees through his spectacles is at least somewhat different than the world you and I see each day.

CONSPIRACIES EVERYWHERE

I refer, for example, to the vast quantity of conspiratorial language in Dobson's work by which he describes a world where evil coalitions of enemies meet regularly and conspire to create an orchestrated, unified attack on ideas Jim holds dear.

Actually, Jim's conspiratorial thinking goes beyond the bizarre into the truly humorous. According to him, there exists a large and powerful association of liberals who are united in their position on the various social issues of the day and who are funded in such massive proportions that they can do whatever they please, whenever they please: hire staff, distribute mass mailings, purchase print and electronic ads, lobby Congress, and "buy" legislators with campaign contributions. Their pockets give new definition to the word "deep." Furthermore, this corrupt cabal is united in the evil that permeates their hearts and motivates their actions. These are bad people who just don't care—about America, about children, about families, about God.

If you are a communicator like Dobson, it certainly simplifies your work load if everyone in your society can be described as either good or bad, for you or against you, and if you know the difference simply by where they stand on certain select political issues. No gray areas here. No "on the one hand . . . but on the other hand." This is litmus test politics at its best. In fact I recall a conversation between Dobson and a friend in which the friend was trying to help Jim understand a shockingly simple political reality: there are devout followers of Christ who are pro-choice. If you can imagine the scene, Dobson refused throughout the discussion to agree to that elementary argument. He held tenaciously to the position that a true Christian cannot, by definition, be pro-choice. Finally, when the friend's debating skills began to overtake Jim's position the friend was able to gain the following massive yet amazing concession. One could almost hear a mighty redwood fall as Dobson murmured, "All right, a person could be a Christian and be pro-choice but we're talking about a Christian who is misinformed and misguided."

The humor in Jim's warped view of the imaginary conspiracy arrayed against him was highlighted for my wife and me several months ago when we attended a meeting at a Jewish synagogue at which Barry Lynn spoke. We had heard so many scathing attacks on Lynn, former representative of the ACLU, whom Dobson calls "the enemies of God." In a question-and-answer session at the end of Lynn's talk a woman asked, "How are we to oppose the attacks by the religious right on the religious freedoms of those who believe differently? They are so well organized, so well funded, so unified. We are almost defenseless by comparison." Is that comment as fascinating to you as it is to me? I've heard Dobson use precisely those words about Lynn and the people in that room.

There is no monolithic organization on the right or on the left. James Dobson is barely on speaking terms with Ralph Reed and Reed is in the same religious camp. Dan Rather of CBS News does not consult with Planned Parenthood executives or Harvard liberals before deciding how to read the evening news to us. There are, however, fear mongers in both camps who provide their troops with phony political intelligence, often for the purpose of raising money to support their campaign against their imagined monolithic foe—people like Dobson, who, in his radio broadcasts, magazine articles, books, and monthly fund-raising letters, overwhelms his constituents with statements like the following:

> Two sides with vastly differing and incompatible world views are locked in a bitter conflict. I believe a winner will emerge and the loser will fade from memory.

> Secular humanists easily embrace abortion, infanticide and euthanasia when convenience demands.

> The resources available to secular humanists throughout society are almost unlimited in scope, and they are breaking new ground every day.

> The beleaguered, exhausted, oppressed, and overtaxed family now stands unprotected against a mighty foe.

> I will not take the time here to list or describe the specific attempts by secular humanists to weaken the institution of the family and the church, but they are legion.

> Our opponents are highly motivated, well funded, deeply committed, and armed to the teeth.

> Many Christians have . . . bought the notion, propagated by the secular press and their liberal friends, that it violates the separation of church and state for believers to take a position on controversial social concerns.

We are ordinary people trying to deal with incredibly powerful and dangerous institutions. We are often outgunned and undermanned.

We are witnessing an unprecedented campaign to secularize our society and demoralize our institutions from the top down. Having turned the culture upside-down, the secularists appear now to have agreed upon three specific mechanisms to complete the task of immobilizing and silencing conservative Christians: deny America's Judeo-Christian roots, label politically active Christians as violating church-state separation, and ultimately silence politically active Christians.

DEMONIZING

And closely akin to lumping together all one's perceived foes into a giant conspiracy is the psychological dysfunction so prevalent in Jim's work of demonizing that foe's intentions: jumping to the most extreme and negative conclusions possible about the hidden motives behind another person's conduct. Jim has perfected this form of warped ruminating. Here again is a sampling from his broadcasting and print materials:

> Once again, the majority of our congressmen have made it clear that they couldn't care less about mothers at home.

> Our representatives ignored their constituencies and voted with the special-interest groups. But whoever said the Congress was fair?

> Dan Rather, Tom Brokaw, and CNN will not tell you this story.

> We have seen a concerted effort to distort the truth about what this legislation does to church-based child-care facilities.

> The anti-family, anti-religious politicians and bureaucrats in this country have become bolder and far more aggressive in recent years.

> This transformation is occurring by the will of our elected representatives and by liberal judges who seem determined to recast society in their own image.

PARANOIA

Furthermore, the language of Dobson materials projects what appears to this observer to be feelings of paranoia. The attacks by his monolithic enemy are not mere differences of opinion over the issues of the day, but personal attacks on him.

You will recall the story I told in chapter 7 about the historian who criticized Jim in an article about Dobson's ill-advised use of war language. Do you recall the hints of paranoia that made their way into Jim's response? Also there was the earlier story of Gary Warner critiquing the religious right, only to have Dobson take it personally and try to muzzle Warner.

Several months after I left Dobson's organization, I became aware of this type of behavior by Jim toward me personally. I made a decision that I recognized to be controversial: to write a letter to fellow members of the Focus on the Family board of directors and to inform them of management problems inside the organization that needed correcting. I considered the letter to be constructive in its objectives and respectful in its tone. The letter Jim wrote me in response goes a long way toward explaining why I would raise here the question of Jim's possible paranoia: "No one has *ever* [his emphasis] set out to hurt me," he wrote, "quite like you did. That is unconscionable. Furthermore, no one has ever written such blatant lies to our board of directors in an obvious attempt to drive a wedge between us. It is obvious that you wrote the board with the purpose of making us look harsh. To accomplish this you played fast and loose with the truth. [However] I forgive you for hurting me. [Do not] use my name or the name of Focus on the Family in any more of [your professional] literature."

I draw your attention to two aspects of Jim's language. Notice Jim's compulsion to attach evil motives to his critics. If someone's response to a letter of criticism, prior to any dialogue with the writer, is to label his critic's words as "lies" and their motives as "harsh" and designed to "hurt," he has probably revealed far more about his own psyche than his critic's.

Jim has spoken recently of his belief that he may some day be martyred for the political causes he espouses, so strong are his feelings that his enemies are out to "get him."

ANXIETY

At what point in a psychological profile would a professional label a patient's anxieties "abnormally high" or "pathological"? In Dobson's case, he appears obsessed with fear of the future, and dread of society's impending doom. Here are still more examples of Dobsonisms:

The spiritual concepts on which [America] was built are being superseded now by philosophies and judgments that are rooted in atheism.
The God of the Bible has been removed from every vestige of public
life, as though He were a cancerous growth that threatened the life of
the organism.

How rapidly we are tumbling down the slippery slope.

Obscenity abounds everywhere, our values and symbols are mocked
incessantly on television, our children are corrupted by movies and
MTV, and our Congressional leaders are steadily encroaching upon our
constitutional freedoms.

Social engineers hope to destroy the Judeo-Christian system of values.

We are seeing vicious assaults every day on biblical morality and the
institution of the family.

It has become extremely difficult for Christian families to shepherd
their children through the teen years without having them victimized by
the wickedness of television, videos, MTV, movies, illicit drugs, safe-
sex ideology, and the rock music culture.

Eternal standards are disintegrating in western nations. Moral relativism
now permeates the universities, the public schools, the Congress, the
entertainment industry, the news media, the professions and the courts.

None of the leading parties dealt with the great moral issues facing our
nation [during the 1996 campaign season]. Instead, the political parties
bragged about their newfound "tolerance" and "inclusiveness."

The vacuity that I sense in each political party is a distillate of our
[national] moral confusion and uncertainty. That is the point I made during the trial of O. J. Simpson. The judicial system can be no more ethical than the society it serves.

Kids are dying from sexually transmitted diseases and our entire value
system is disintegrating before our eyes.

Sometimes Dobson speaks not of the state of things "out there" but
from inside his personal world of thoughts and feelings. The picture is
very telling:

I feel overwhelmed at times by what might be called "protest fatigue."

A person can become exhausted while trying to defend the principles of
righteousness on so many fronts.

The world of the Christian activist can be a very lonely place. War is
always tough on those who are called to fight it.

Is there a price to pay for taking the offensive? Very likely! It cost Jesus and most of His disciples their lives.

REPRESSION AND PROJECTION

I mentioned in chapter 9 that one of the toughest critiques of James Dobson came from the past president of World Vision. The late Stan Mooneyham stated that he saw within Dobson's demeanor signs of what psychology calls "projection," where the mind works so hard to repress feelings it finds unattractive in itself that it begins imagining the very same characteristics in everyone with whom it comes in contact. Mooneyham said in a conversation with me in his home: "James Dobson scares the hell out of me. Like Swaggart he is set for a fall. It is inevitable, 100 percent predictable. Swaggart's preaching was an exact duplicate. He ranted against pornography. His ranting made it clear he was either involved in pornography or wished that he was and was trying to throw that part of himself away. Men like that must get beyond self justification before they can be whole. They must face themselves. Dobson's religious world is built on a phony base. And he is a counterfeit."

FEAR OF INTIMACY

No more bewildering aspect of the Dobson psyche exists than the contradiction between the fact that we have here a man who has made a fortune advising people on how to succeed at human relationships while he himself maintains few normal friendships and exhibits an exploiting, utilitarian approach to the relationships he does have.

If you asked me to name the three or four greatest shocks I experienced in my ten years of work with Jim, one I would describe was an experience that took place during the months after I parted company with Focus on the Family. We said goodbye to each other in April 1987. It was September before Jim and I spoke again, and that was because I called his secretary and asked if he had any free time for lunch on his calendar. We met at a favorite restaurant to catch up on the preceding five months. It was painfully clear to me during that conversation that our friendship had, for Jim, been little more than one of utility. He had no time for an ongoing friendship. Which means that we had never been what I thought we were, friends who enjoyed camaraderie based on the essence of what we were, not on what we did together.

I remember talking with a mutual friend of Jim's at dinner one evening in our home. Joey Paul, an executive at Dobson's publisher, had known Jim for many years, and had worked closely with him on many business ventures. I told him how shocked I was by this experience. Joey responded that it didn't surprise him a bit. He said he'd seen it in Jim for years, and he was convinced that even Dobson's relationship with his wife was utilitarian.

The Stafford profile touches on Jim's difficulty achieving true intimacy with friends. He wrote, "Many of James Dobson's friends, though they genuinely love him, seem intimidated by him." And you will recall what Jim's "friend" Mike Williamson said of him, "I realized that the only way we would work together was if I let him be the pilot of the ship."

The point I'm making, as a layman, is that while I don't know how such elements of behavior would be labeled in a formal psychological profile of Jim, they appear to me to represent aberrant conduct.

These seemingly abnormal dimensions of the Dobson psyche are yet another of the surprising inconsistencies between the James Dobson you see and the one you don't. Here is a so-called man of faith who has little or no faith in his fellow human beings. He lives and leads by suspicion. He is a man for whom no religious phrase means more than that of "trusting in Christ," and yet he conducts himself as if he cannot trust in Christ or anyone else other than himself, whether the need is protection from his enemies or care for his beloved company and nation. Instead, he must control everything lest events go astray. He is a man who speaks out against the dangers of arrogance and self-importance in others and yet is described by every close observer willing to be candid as manifesting gigantic levels of pride. Here is a man who espouses an extraordinary religious doctrine of "moral perfection" and "perfect love," but who is plagued by unseemly hostilities and mean-spiritedness. He is a man concerned more about outward appearance than inner realities; a man who calls out to the men of his culture to slow down the pace of their lives and focus on their families, all the while climbing the steps of his own life three at a time.

James Dobson is a man for whom the phrase "personal integrity" is a mantra with which he divides those qualified to lead from those he dismisses, and yet the contradictions between his own inner and outer selves are clear to all who watch him closely. He offers us his services as a candidate for national moral doctor, yet is himself in need of healing.

20 ❦ The Dobson Agenda

One of the mistakes Bob Dole probably made during his 1996 bid for the presidency was to use a phrase in his nomination acceptance speech that provided Bill Clinton with one of those openings for a retort that is every politician's dream. Dole characterized himself has a "bridge to the past," trying to appeal to the fear of many that America has lost touch with its roots. And, astute politician that he is, Clinton came right back and offered himself to America as a "bridge to the future."

That conceptual tug of war serves as an excellent illustration of one of the primary issues on Dobson's master agenda for America—to take us back to the past.

Dobson wrote in a recent fund-raising letter that he thinks fondly of the 1950s, a time, he said, when America was a simpler and a better place. (Has he forgotten that in the fifties we were busy reaffirming the attitudes and actions that gave rise to the sixties, one of the most troubled decades in our history?) Jim provided us with his personal view of the fifties, a period when he was in high school, in his book *Parenting Isn't for Cowards*. He wrote that he was not aware of anyone at his high school taking drugs; that alcohol was not a problem; that there was some sexual experimentation, but "the girls who did were considered 'loose' and were not respected" (no mention here of whether the boys who played around were respected); virginity was "in style" and girls who became pregnant were "packed off in a hurry and I never knew where they went"; homosexuals were considered to be "very weird and unusual people"; and, Dobson recalls, "Most of my friends respected their parents, went to church on Sunday, studied hard enough to get by and lived a fairly clean life." This

was James Dobson's "norm" growing up. And James Dobson, political
activist, is searching for a way back to that personal norm.

I'd like to offer you one layperson's take on people who glamorize
the past and long to return to it. I cannot imagine that life in America in
the 1950s was the Disneyland Jim remembers it to be. A man like Dobson has so much at stake in reaching for evidence of his theories that he's
likely to invent false images of the past. Furthermore, the children of
ultra-orthodox families live such sheltered lives that we have every reason to ask, "What did Jim know about the real world of the fifties?" I
don't trust Dobson's basic social theory—the belief that culture invariably and inevitably runs downhill and therefore, by definition, any comparison of two points on the calendar begins with the assumption that the
earlier period was better and the later period worse.

In the interviews I conducted for this book I asked this question: "Do
you think our society is better or worse than in years past?" Barry Lynn's
reaction was the common one:

Gil: What is your overall assessment of the present state of our society?
According to Dobson we are in a moral "free fall." And the reason for
the free fall is that we've abandoned Christian principles in Washington.
We've taken God out of our schools, courts, and public squares.

Barry: Well I think, not only are we not a faithless society, we are a
country that is growing in its quest for spiritual understanding [notice
right off how Barry's evil atheistic tendencies show through—as Jim
predicted]. I think to answer your question you must look at specific
parts of our experience one at a time. If you look at drug use, for example, this is a country in vastly worse shape than it was fifty years ago.
But what's the status of African Americans now compared to fifty years
ago? The answer is, it's better. What's the status of women? It's better.
What is the level of freedom that we have in the country to express our
opinions? It's better. What is the public school system offering children? I'd say in most cases much more than they offered me, or than
they probably offered you if you went to public schools. When I went
to public schools they were boring places. I'm surprised I even got
through them, that I didn't lose all interest in studying. Now when I go
to my son's or my daughter's schools these are exciting times. Not just
exciting because they've got computers, but exciting because they have
teachers who, in my experience, are providing children with opportunities to learn that I didn't have, and that make it possible to be excited
about school. There's a lower dropout rate now than there was thirty
years ago. It's just that we become convinced that everything is bad and
can't see the improvements.

When I do talk radio, which I've done off and on for the last fifteen years, including two years opposite Pat Buchanan on "Crossfire," I talk to people with this deteriorating view of society. I don't know how they can get up in the morning. Every institution is their enemy. The schools are against them. The media is against them. These sinister forces are out there trying to destroy their family and their faith. I don't believe that's an accurate description of what's going on but if you wake up every morning assuming that's true, then it is going to be very difficult to see anything positive about your circumstances because you're so worried about who's trying to destroy you.

This paranoia is fed by the idea that everything is deteriorating, that we're in a free fall. In a free fall there is no way not to hit the bottom, which is a bleak way of looking at life, whether your own or our life together as a society. To call our condition a free fall makes people think we can't do anything. Free fall says that it requires a nearly divine intervention in order to stop the impending crash. That type of thinking leads to the belief that we must somehow elect divinely supported people to Congress so that they'll fix society for us. I don't think that the government ever fixes moral problems. It provides a framework for individuals to work out a moral consensus. But it doesn't solve our problems. We do that individually and in community with each other. I love government programs that simply provide people with a chance to be on the same playing field as other people. That is doable; to remove injustice and inequity.

I think, on balance, this country is vastly better than it was fifty years ago by most important standards of measurement of moral responsibility. The challenge is to look at its progress through many different measurements, not just those Dobson or Robertson selectively flash before our eyes in what I often think is a trivialization of the term "moral crisis."

Notice that two of Lynn's examples of culture rising rather than sinking were the improved status of women and of minorities. Here's my concern: If Jim doesn't believe women and minorities actually have civil rights problems—issues the society needs to resolve—might he overlook those categories of assessment altogether when evaluating American social change? And if he overlooks such facts, might his conclusions be skewed?

KEEP A LIGHT IN THE WINDOW

Dobson's chief political assistant is Gary Bauer, head of Focus's lobbying arm, the Family Research Council. I was surprised to read how Bauer expressed this take-us-to-the-past element of the Dobson agenda in his book *Our Hopes Our Dreams.* He wrote, describing the America Dobson and he were working to create: "The flickering light that shines from the windows of our nation's houses at night would more often be from the hearth, where 'family fireside chats' are taking place, and less often from the drone of television sets. Families would spend more time being real families, not watching artificial ones."[1]

By talking about his desire to see families turn off the tube, turn on the gas jet that runs between their lava rocks, and have a good old-fashioned family talk, Bauer makes it clear that it is social change itself that he's battling, not just evil. Bauer and Dobson are working hard to move America backward in time, believing that America's better days are behind her and that part of the objective of Focus on the Family and the Family Research Council, as we turn toward a new century, is to revisit past ways of addressing social issues. Dobson and Bauer believe that there is no current social thinking that rises to the height of past wisdom; that current legislators lack the moral fortitude and grasp of significant social issues that was second nature to our founding fathers; that today's judges are no match for those of a hundred years ago; that the Constitution and the men who framed it (they were all white males, like Gary and Jim, weren't they?) were unique in their ability to conceptualize the needs of the nation and translate those needs into law.

Bauer and Dobson glorify the past, its leaders and its ideas, in a manner that is a disservice to our contemporary social challenges and an insult to the men and women who struggle each day in our state and national legislatures, executive branches, and courts to address unique new needs and find exciting new answers.

CONSERVATIVES AND LIBERALS

The problem here is the classic division between conservative and liberal perspectives. I grew up conservative with a capital "C." I've always voted Republican, as did my parents and their parents, that is, until 1996, when I voted a split ticket largely due to concern about the rising power of the religious right over the Republican party.

It came as an awakening when, in college, I met my first Christian Democrat. After I got past stage one of our friendship, doubting his political sincerity, and past stage two, doubting his salvation, I slowly and with difficulty began to let go of the belief that political ideology and religious faith march hand in hand. I abandoned the notion that conservatives are close to the heart of God and liberals dangle perilously over the fires of hell.

It was about this time that someone told me that I could find within the very labels used by the two dominant political movements in America this understanding: each represents a strength and a weakness.

Generally, conservatives favor preserving the existing order. They treat proposals for change with distrust. They are cautious and traditional in manner. Liberals favor progress and reform, freedom of individuals to act or express themselves in a manner of their own choosing, even if untraditional. They are tolerant of the ideas or behaviors of others. Clearly, one of these broad ways of thinking is more likely to fixate on the past and feel a need to preserve it while the other is more likely to fixate on the future and feel the need to prepare for it.

Perhaps the conservative viewpoint provides society with the great service of preserving the best of our history. Our forefathers came here to be free. Immigrants still step off planes and ships and weep as they breathe the freest political air in the world. Let no progressive liberal concept ever replace our traditional love of freedom.

Perhaps the liberal viewpoint provides society with the great service of adjusting to accommodate needs unforeseen by the past. It approaches each new challenge with a free-thinking, open-minded creativity that says, "What new idea will resolve this new social concern in a way that moves society forward in its endless evolution through the generations?" Jefferson and Franklin didn't give us detailed leadership relative to the challenges we face in the area of free speech in cyberspace. For you or me to tell Martin Luther King, Jr., or Malcolm X or Rosa Parks that all they needed do to resolve their social concerns was to read the writings of the founding fathers would have made Letterman's Top Ten List of Stupid Human Ideas. The notion so prevalent among conservatives that the founding fathers are to be worshiped and obeyed and that contemporary judges are evil if they depart from "the intent of the founders," is trash talking.

HOW DO WE DECIDE THIS ONE?

What, then, are the downsides to these two great philosophical and political perspectives? From my experience, they are that conservatives tend to hold too tightly to the past and liberals tend to let go of it too quickly.

Since the focus of this book is the hyperconservative James Dobson, let's look at an example of a conservative holding on too tightly.

One of the greatest creative challenges we face at this time is resolving the issues surrounding the needs and requests of homosexuals. With respect to gay rights, Dobson is opposed even to the dialogue, as I explained in chapter 16. The conservative view? No changes needed. Preserve the past. And what was the past? In Jim's words, it was when "homosexuals were considered to be weird and unusual people."

Actually, this is another of society's milestones where a new challenge has surfaced and new laws are needed. Those with their hands in the air are saying exactly what minorities and women have observed about our society in the past: that in certain situations and places they do not experience the full freedoms and liberties promised all Americans and they want to. It is not, as Jim suggests in his demonizing responses, that they demand special rights. They simply want regular rights to work and rent and serve in the military as any other group would.

I described in chapter 16 the legislative battle over the gay rights employment initiative called ENDA authored by the liberal Ted Kennedy. As mentioned, one of the forty-nine senators who supported ENDA was the now retired Mark Hatfield of Oregon. Notice the balance of conserving the best of the past but changing to meet the future that surfaces in the following remarks by the honorable Mr. Hatfield as he spoke on the floor of the Senate on September 10, 1996, in support of ENDA:

> Throughout my career in public service, amounting to over four decades now, I have fought to end discrimination and advance the ideal of equal opportunity in society. These efforts have often taken the form of extending protection from discrimination in the workplace. Over the years, we have focused on discrimination on the basis of race, gender, national origin, age, religion and disability. These laws are based on a simple premise: employees should be judged on the work they do. The time has arrived to take the next logical step toward equality of opportunity in the workplace. Senate bill 2056, which would prohibit discrimination in employment on the basis of sexual orientation, is such a step.
>
> The Employment Nondiscrimination Act focuses on a group of citizens who have been victimized and vilified like few other minority groups in this nation's history. One prominent example took place in Medford, Oregon, last year where two women were murdered. Their murderer confessed that he killed them because of his hate for homosexuals. While we will not be able to wash this type of deep-seated hatred from our society merely by enacting a federal statute, employment relations is narrowly focused and appropriate for a federal statement of national policy, as we have demonstrated many times. It does not create special protections, preferences or hiring quotas for gay people.
>
> Religious organizations are given a broad exemption from this proposal. [Catch the significance: Dobson's organization is permitted by

this law to discriminate against homosexuals, practicing or celibate, and yet he opposed gays having protection against discrimination in other American companies.] Moreover, no business would be required to provide benefits to an employee's same-sex partner.

The employee manual for my office has for some time included a specific provision prohibiting discrimination based on sexual orientation. A majority of the "Fortune 500" companies have reached this same conclusion. It is time for this body to do the same. It is time for our laws to reflect a point of fundamental fairness: an employee should be free from discrimination at work because of personal characteristics unrelated to the successful performance of his or her job.[2]

It goes without saying that Dobson's fist-clenching, preservationist, conservative approach to public policy is a mirror image of his fist-clenching, preservationist, conservative approach to theology. He was first a man of religious thoughts and then later of political thoughts. But both are formed with exactly the same style of thought, instinct, and wording.

A bridge to the past. Obstinate resistance to change. The view that truth and stability lie behind us and our highest goal as a society is to reach back and rediscover what made us strong back in history, and then go and do that all over again. These are the ways of James Dobson. In fact, you will often hear him say that he has no greater ambition than to reconnect his society with the timeless truths of the past, those traditions that made this a strong nation of strong families. We don't need new ideas, he says repeatedly. What we need is the truth passed down to us in the wisdom of the Scriptures.

As Dobson writes his next book connecting readers to the past and as Gary Bauer lights tonight's fire in his hearth, I'm trying to discover a more balanced way to do politics. I'm trying to be a conservative liberal.

NOTES

1. Gary L. Bauer, *Our Hopes Our Dreams* (Focus on the Family, 1996), p. 4.
2. Mark O. Hatfield, *Congressional Record,* September 10, 1996.

21 ❦ A Good Republican

A question reporters frequently ask me about Jim is whether I think he will ever run for high office.

In a 1995 ABC "Day One" profile of Dobson, in which anchor Forrest Sawyer dialogued with reporter John Hockenberry, the speculation sounded like this:

Sawyer to Hockenberry: John, since he has so much influence, do you know if Dr. Dobson has any political ambitions of his own?

Hockenberry: Well, he's been asked this earlier this year and late last year, in fact. It was suggested he run on a third party sort of pro-family ticket. And it scared the republican party. But he claims he doesn't want to be a candidate. He prefers behind the scenes.

Sawyer: Do you believe it?

Hockenberry: He's an amazing figure. He has a lot of power. It's possible that his power will push him over the threshold. But at this point I do believe it. I think it would be tough for him as a candidate.[1]

In the past, Jim's answer to this question has been that he's not qualified, that he has insufficient experience for high office. True enough. But that can't be a candid response because it's never slowed him down before. Jim has no theological training and yet every day he offers himself to his constituents as a religious and moral leader. Dobson has no training in political science; in fact, many professionals have told him that he is guilty of ignorant bumbling in his political activism; that his efforts on Capitol

Hill are amateurish, disruptive, and counterproductive. Yet we don't see Jim backing off from political activism. Dobson has very little experience as a counselor or therapist. His degree is in educational psychology. And yet he offers his services regularly as an expert on counseling issues. So the reason for Jim's reluctance thus far to run for office is not that he respects the individual skill sets required of particular disciplines.

In my view, one reason he has never run for office in the past is that he enjoys so many of the features of his current status that he has been reluctant to exchange them for elected office. I've indicated previously that Jim has the amazing luxury of being accountable to almost no one for his actions and attitudes. Included in the long list of people Jim does not need to give an answer to is the national media whom he routinely stonewalls. Clearly that arrogant independence would have to change if he were to become a public servant. And surprising new information surfaced after the November 1996 elections that suggests Dobson is considering just such a change, including the possible formation of his own political party and a run for the White House.

WHAT IS ON THE AGENDA?

If James Dobson's political clout continues to grow, if he should run for office, what could we expect in the way of public policy positions? What will he campaign for? What is the America that James Dobson will strive to create?

The first answer to that question has nothing to do with Dobson's religious and moral convictions and the high-profile issues that he tackles such as abortion or prayer in school or homosexual rights. It is that James Dobson was born and raised a southern conservative and therefore he identifies economically and socially with the Republican party. James Dobson wants what any mainline conservative Republican wants. Dobson's chief political lieutenant, Gary Bauer, was candid enough to say of himself in his book *Our Hopes Our Dreams*, "What am I, without the spin? A conservative in political outlook, a Christian by faith." The same is true of Jim.

Obviously, Jim takes a slightly different approach to his politics than the straight party line. For example, he wraps his basic conservative agenda in the vestments of organized religion. Jim connects almost all social issues to religious beliefs, thereby, in his own thinking, adding somehow to the power of his arguments. In Jim's basic conservative view, we need a strong national defense. But when that belief comes out of his mouth it sounds almost like this: "It's God's will that we spend more on B2 bombers because without them the divorce rate will rise." I know that religious activists seldom use language as ridiculous as that. But I'm sincere in stating that if you study their reasoning, as I've done for many years, that is exactly where their "logic" leads them.

Dobson has spoken out vigorously against the Department of Education and the National Endowment for the Arts; he supports smaller government and lower taxes. On some of these issues a plausible bridge can be built between the particular social issue and the original agenda of Focus on the Family—strengthening the family unit within our society. It's much more difficult to build a bridge between tax policies and the Christian faith, as Jim often tries to. In listening to his broadcasts and reading his literature, you will see work in progress at all times: digging, sawing, and hammering away to build the shaky bridge between conservative politics, God's will, and the best interests of American families.

The conservative fiscal and social policy is one in which government is not a helper in society but rather stays "out of our pocketbooks and our bedrooms." Generally speaking, government should not, in Jim's view, take responsibility for caring for people or meeting their needs; government should stick to the basics of providing a strong national defense, keeping the peace, establishing the order of law, and then allowing the great engine of free enterprise to generate wealth for all (all who are smart enough, and lucky enough to master the system, like Dobson).

Dobson's agenda is so thoroughly Republican and so thoroughly antithetical to the perspectives of the Democratic party that his frequent attempts to suggest that he is somehow a political eunuch are transparently thin and often humorous.

I recall that during one of the presidential campaigns Jim offered his views on the hot issues of the day to both the Republican and the Democratic candidates by means of a lengthy letter. The Republican gave Dobson every impression his views were desired and respected. But his opponent wouldn't give Jim the time of day. He and his staff acted as if James Dobson were nobody from nowhere. It was interesting to observe how irritated that made Jim. Most of his comments about that experience and about Washington in general were heavily weighted in the direction of Republican policy, so his surprise was clearly naive.

One of the problems here is separating theological from political conservatism. The religious right does not do this very well. It tends to make the enormous mistake of wrapping itself and its large family Bible in an oversized American flag and calling the package Republican and, by the way, right. This mindless linkage between conservative faith and conservative government often leads to embarrassing contradictions and inconsistencies, breakdowns of logic toward which Dobson seems oblivious during. For example, Jesus' overriding focus of attention, as described in the Gospels, was on those in need and he had little or nothing to say about economic systems of his day. That would align him far more with the typical Democratic agenda than that of the Republicans. Jesus' famed Sermon on the Mount and the specifics of how he recruited his disciples reads like borderline socialism—leave everything, share equally, provide for the poor and the widow. It would be hard to make the case that Jesus taught free enterprise and capitalism, although those of religious right persuasion swear that the Democratic philosophy of government, tax and help, is unspeakably evil.

THE DETAILS

Perhaps it will augment your understanding of Dobson's objectives if I move beyond general political philosophies and list for you very specific political positions Jim has taken on his broadcasts, in his political magazine *Citizen* and in his other communications with his constituency.

By the way, many of the examples that follow will remind you of one of the great contradictions within the religious right political movement—when it suits them, their war cry is "Get the government off our backs!" and yet at other times their cry turns to, "Get the government into our private lifestyles."

And now, seventy-five specifics about the America James Dobson is working hard to create.

Dobson supports	Dobson opposes
Health and medicine	
• A constitutional amendment establishing the right to life of the unborn and outlawing all abortions—whether in the case of rape, incest or danger to the health of the mother • The abortion industry being blocked from all taxpayer funds • The required licensing of abortion counselors • Required parental or spousal consent prior to receiving an abortion • Fetal tissue research being severely restricted	• The inclusion in the Republican party platform of any language acknowledging that there can be an honest difference of opinion within the party on the abortion issue • Doctor-assisted suicide • School based health clinics
Government	
• Term limits • Openly using Judeo-Christian religious teachings to the exclusion of other religious teachings as the basis for public policy	• Redrawing congressional districts to change their political makeup.
Civil rights	
• Political power being exercised largely as it has been in the past • Corporate rights over individual rights • The right of religious organizations such as his to overlook the basic American civil rights of its employees, including privacy, fair labor practices, and due process, claiming a religious exception from enforcing these rights • A constitutional amendment outlawing flag burning	• Virtually all civil rights initiatives, including antidiscrimination legislation and the famed Equal Rights Amendment • Homosexual rights, women's rights, and minority rights laws
Defense and security	
• Higher levels of security clearance • A larger military • Greater protection of national sovereignty, a tougher stance against illegal immigrants	• Women serving in the military • Gays serving in the military
The judiciary	
• Strict constructionism being the prescribed judicial approach • The impeachment of judges who employ approaches other than strict constructionism	

Dobson supports	Dobson opposes
Social services	
• Welfare being reduced and restricted • Poverty being made the business of private charities, not of the government	• Social services being available to illegal immigrants or their dependents • Tax-funded day care, tax credits for not having children
Education	
• School vouchers redeemable in public or private schools • Schools that teach the mastery of English, the Declaration of Independence, the nation's history and its heroes, and the essential goodness of America • Increased curricular attention being given to how well humans have managed the earth's resources • The teaching of sexual abstinence, creationism, and the real meaning of Halloween • Bible clubs using school facilities • Schools beginning each day with the pledge, the anthem, and with prayer. "Religious values being returned to the classroom."	• The continued existence of the Department of Education • The policies of the National Education Association • The distribution of safe sex information, information about homosexuality, or condoms in schools • The distribution of information that calls into question the patriarchal approach to family leadership
The environment	
• Most environment initiatives being rejected in favor of property owners, vehicle users, and business interests	
The economy and taxation	
• Unrestrained capitalism, greater economic growth • A balanced budget • Lower taxes • Massive tax relief for couples raising children • A tax-free status for businesses like Focus on the Family, regardless of their consumption of government services or their similarity to for-profit businesses • A smaller national government	• Restricting the lobbying efforts of religious organizations

Dobson supports	Dobson opposes
Law and order	
• "A society where families no longer have to hide behind barred windows, where criminals do 'real time,' and a society where criminals aren't released on a 'whim or a technicality'"	• Any accountability to the state by religious organizations, any increased scrutiny of organizations like his
• "Drive-by shootings and 1.5 million aborted babies both being viewed as a disaster"	
• "Children playing in public parks without fear and adults walking in those parks at night"	
• A crackdown on frivolous lawsuits	
• Three-strikes laws in every state, elimination of parole and bail for violent offenders, youths suspected of adult crimes being tried as adults	
• The death penalty being used more often, exclusionary rules of evidence being reduced, more people in prison, more police on the streets	
• Drug abuse attacked more vigorously	
• Citizens being encouraged to defend themselves, gun ownership unrestricted	
• Prisons being changed from "entertainment centers" to places of punishment	
• Tougher laws to force men to pay child support	
• "A society where our daughters can go on a date without worrying about date rape"	
General morality and lifestyle	
• Divorce decrees being more difficult to obtain	• Production of crass and exploitative entertainment
• "A society where when a boy pledges to love and honor my daughter the rest of his life, the chances are he will—where children come first—where the TV is turned off in favor of family talks"	• Political correctness
	• The sale of pornographic materials in bookstores or convenience stores and the display of pornographic materials in local theaters
• Sexual themes, pornography, and violence on television or the Internet being banned and adult cable channels severely restricted, citizens being given legal standing to sue pornographers	• Government support for the arts
	• Granting benefits to same-sex partners or legalizing same-sex marriage
• Boycotting advertisers whose commercials appear on programs containing sexual or violent content	• Handouts for the poor

Dobson supports

- "A society where women who would rather be home with their children are no longer subjected to the disdain of the common culture"
- Outlawing dial-a-porn
- "Love of country becoming a virtue again"
- "Responsibilities being viewed as equal in importance to rights, contracts being sealed with a handshake"
- "The nation returning to God, whom we have forgotten"
- "Patriotism and loyalty to America"
- Vigorous restrictions on gambling

As a final observation about Jim's tendency to mix political ideology with religious dogma to create his brand of conservative Republican Christian politics: I've noticed a growing movement among American Christians distancing themselves from this God-and-country approach to politics. Leaders of a diverse and large cross section of Christendom endorsed a "Call to Renewal" position paper during 1996 on this very subject, including such highly regarded names in American religious leadership as John Hurst Adams, Louise Akers, Myron Augsburger, David and Karen Mains, Nathan Baxter, the Very Rev. Gerald Brown, the Right Rev. Edmond L. Browning, Joan Brown Campbell, Marian Wright Edelman, the Rev. Dr. Milton Efthimiou, James Wallis, and eighty others. It read, in part:

> Our times cry out for renewed political vision. And vision depends upon spiritual values. We believe that the language of morality and faith can make a critical contribution to political discourse. We believe further that the old political language and solutions of Right and Left, liberal and conservative, are almost completely dysfunctional now and helpless to lead us into a different future. But if politics will be renewed more by moral values than by partisan warfare, the religious community must play a more positive role.
>
> Christian faith must not become another casualty of the culture wars. Indeed, religious communities should be the ones calling for a cease-fire. The ideological polarization of the churches will not contribute to the spiritual discernment of politics the country most needs. Inflamed rhetoric and name calling is no substitute for real and prayerful dialogue between different constituencies with legitimate concerns and a gospel of love which can bring people together.
>
> We are Evangelical voices who seek a biblical approach to politics, not an ideological agenda. We are Catholic voices who assert our own

church's social teachings as a vital alternative to both the Left and the Right. We are Orthodox voices who have long stressed the role of spirituality in nurturing culture. We are African American, Latino, white, Asian, and Native American church voices whose commitment to personal faith and social justice leads us to visions of transformation beyond both political parties. We are voices from all the Protestant churches who feel represented neither by old religious liberalism nor new right fundamentalism.[2]

My point is not to find fault with Dobson for advocating the Republican political viewpoint. He can advance any viewpoint he chooses. But there are two areas of concern generated by his agenda: First, he spends so much time and energy denying that his is a basic right-wing conservative game plan for America. The problem here is one of credibility. And, second, he states so frequently that he speaks for God in taking his particular political positions, as if conservative Republicanism were divinely inspired.

Far better for Jim if he would do as Ralph Reed does—go ahead and attend the Republican Convention and make it clear that he is simply trying to win one more for the Gipper.

NOTES

1. "Day One," ABC Television News, October 18, 1995.
2. *Sojourners Online* 25, no. 5 (September–October 1996).

22 ❧ Abortion and Extremism

It's not widely known that Dobson's position on abortion has changed in a very significant way over the years. If you bring that to his attention, expect to prick the nerve that activates his temper.

Jim has something of a fetish about being accused of changing positions. It's part of the essential conservative temperament I described in previous chapters to be seen not as open minded, flexible, fluid, or experimental but rather as staid, steady, rock solid, unshakable. A religious youth organization I once worked for had as its motto "Geared to the times, anchored to the rock," by which they meant that some things about them changed to match the changes in youth culture but other things about them, most noticeably their religious dogma, did not. That notion of being anchored is very important to Jim. He portrays himself as understanding and communicating immutable, unchangeable truths rather than faddish social experiments. To suggest that he once took one particular immutable position only to change to a different immutable position is just a little embarrassing. This is yet another aspect of the man where he would better serve himself and us if he lightened up a little. None of us grasps perfectly the great cosmic picture of life, physical or metaphysical. All of us are, to some extent, seekers after more light. In that capacity we have two great choices: to admit that we do not have all the answers and thereby be consistent with our own inner reality, or, second, to pretend that we do while fooling no one. Jim is, I'm afraid, something of a pretender here. He would have you believe that what he knows now he's known since the beginning of his work and nothing will change that knowledge in the future because it is "anchored to the rock." One of the things he currently says he knows to be true is that abortion for any reason is wrong. What about in the case of rape? It's wrong. What about in the case of incest? It's wrong. What about when the health of the mother is threatened? It's wrong.

These common exclusions are where Jim's change has taken place. When I began working with him in the seventies his position was the standard conservative one—abortion is morally wrong and should be illegal except in those three cases. I remember clearly the point at which he moved from mainline conservative to extremist on this issue. I don't recall the year, but I can still picture the moment in the Focus on the Family radio studio when he first expressed his new, tougher position. I reacted, understandably, by stating that he had changed and, in my finest co-host announcer tones, asked him to explain his new thinking. Jim shot one of those patented looks across the studio at me as if I had just suggested that as a college student he had inhaled. He went on to try to make the case that he hadn't really changed at all, that he had always believed that exceptions to his no-abortion rule were problematic. Now, he tried to get me to believe, he was merely explaining his position more clearly. Actually, it was much simpler than all that. He had changed his mind.

ABSOLUTELY NO EXCEPTIONS

This "no exceptions" nature of Jim's position was demonstrated powerfully during 1996 when the Clinton administration had to deal with a measure that passed Congress and reached the president's desk that would have, for the first time since *Roe* v. *Wade,* outlawed partial birth abortions. It is informative as to James Dobson's character and temperament to review that specific battle within his larger war against abortion.

Several legislators proposed that America needed a law banning partial-birth abortions. They used language in their bill that did not allow the standard exception for situations where a woman's health was at risk. They openly stated that the exception was not being included because it was, in their opinion, abused. In other words, women and their doctors could not be trusted by Congress to determine when a real threat existed so Congress in its wisdom would make that decision—never. Simplistic and disrespectful arguments were made in favor of the new law, including the argument that this particular type of abortion is done for the pure convenience of a mother who has decided at the eleventh hour that she doesn't want her child.

When the legislation reached the president's desk, Clinton wisely invited several women who had actually had this medical procedure to stand with him on the lawn of the White House as he vetoed the measure, stating that women and their doctors, not government, had to make this call.

The outcry that followed from people like Dobson was deafening. They castigated Clinton's actions as irresponsible. I listened as Dobson analyzed Clinton's veto on his talk show. It lacked detail, it lacked respect for the medical and emotional complexity of the issue, and it was overly simplistic and inflammatory.

In the days that followed, I had the opportunity, as perhaps you did, to hear talk-show interviews given by some of the women who traveled to Washington to stand with the president. One of the central figures at the Clinton signing was a woman who told of being as committed to the sanctity of human life as James Dobson has ever been, and yet she determined that, in her specific situation, the partial birth abortion was the right decision. Another pro-lifer who underwent this procedure spoke with heartrending agony about the progressive insight she and her doctor were gaining during her pregnancy regarding the medical disaster that was taking place in her womb. Frankly, her description of the progressive deformity of the fetus made me sick to my stomach. Perhaps most important in the medical analysis of her situation was the determination that this child could not survive birth and separation from the womb.

With dignity as great as her emotion, with heartbreak and with intelligence, she explained her conclusion that this was not a human being inside her. Furthermore, she said, there was a medical determination made that of her two options, giving birth with the child dying immediately thereafter or using the abortion process prior to the birth, the latter procedure was safer for the mother. Therefore, she, her husband, their two children, and their doctor made the painful and very personal decision that, given the options, they would abort.

I ask you, what was irresponsible or unreasonable about her decision? What about that mother's hard choice is unacceptable or degrading to us as a society? What is un-American in terms of protecting the life of all? And what is un-Christian or (fill in the name of your own religious affiliation)? Yet this was a medical procedure that in James Dobson's America would be illegal without exception.

It seemed to me, regardless of our respective stands for or against abortion, that a bill containing language that permits zero exceptions, which was Clinton's rationale for vetoing it, is an extreme legislative idea. Senator Barbara Boxer (D-Calif.) said as much during the floor debate:

I offered an amendment to add a true life and health exception. My amendment would allow doctors, using their best medical judgment, to perform this medical procedure in cases where it would be necessary to preserve the life of the woman or avert serious adverse health consequences to the woman. This amendment narrowly failed by a vote of 47 to 51. [Therefore] I will continue my fight against this legislation.[1]

Dobson answered that very criticism of the bill on his daily radio broadcast just prior to the final vote. He said that abortion bills that included exceptions for the life or health of the woman were shams because that loophole was abused by deceptive women and dishonest doctors who constantly invent health dangers where they didn't exist. It would appear that our society, according to Dobson, is one in which doctors and women cannot be trusted, where only people like James Dobson can make the right decision.

PLAYING GOD

One of Jim's arguments against partial birth abortions is that in making such a decision a woman is "playing God." Jim would argue that the decision about who lives and who dies cannot, by definition, be a human decision. He would say that any decision about life must, in every circumstance and extremity, be a decision made on the basis that nature be allowed to take its course.

Fundamentalist Christians like Dobson have a very strange mixture of beliefs about which human endeavors are joint ventures with God and which are not. Their theology in this regard is both convoluted and irrational. In one instance they might say, "It is our human responsibility to proselytize every man, woman, boy, and girl in the world, bringing them the message of Jesus Christ and urging them to become a follower of Christ. That is our responsibility carried out in partnership with God's spirit." Fair enough. Evangelism is a joint venture between God and humans. One cannot do it without the other.

But you could question that conclusion within the realms of logic. If God is all powerful and desires that everyone be a follower of Jesus Christ, and if God's spirit is alive and well and active on planet Earth, then surely God alone could take care of that most critical issue, namely, bringing men and women into the Kingdom of Christ. Jim's response would be, of course God could, but in His wisdom he has ordained that evangelism be a joint venture between Himself and us.

However, in the very next breath people like Dobson will argue that medical concerns related to life and death cannot be a joint venture, they must be left entirely to God. Why, you might rebut, would the God of creation take great pleasure in joint venturing his most important enterprise, redemption, but not medical decisions? If you were to press this inconsistency you would discover once again the fact that for Jim Dobson the defining issue is not logic, but his personal interpretation of the Bible. Since we're all creatures of our heritage to some extent, the question is: How did Jim's Nazarene father interpret the Bible? That is the defining measurement of this issue for Jim.

Actually, Jim's newer stance on abortion is much more consistent with the way his mind works than his earlier one, which allowed for exceptions. Jim thinks in black and white; for him there are few shades of gray with respect to his political stands. To Dobson it is not for us to question but to obey. To others the central birthright we carry around with us as God's creation is to pick and probe, to pursue life's great mysteries and its never-ending grays. For us, one of the great parts of the human experience is discovering what we do not yet know. For Jim, knowing is the starting point and the journey is about persuading others. Life inside Jim's head, at least with reference to issues like abortion, homosexuality, and pornography, is a black-and-white picture on its way to becoming a black-and-white picture.

THE POWER OF AN OPEN MIND

In making that observation, I'm reminded of four adults who have helped me maintain a healthy respect for life's grays. They are stunning in their capacity to live with uncertainty and change without allowing themselves to feel as if that were a disservice to the God in whom they placed their faith. My maternal grandfather, Wilbur Powell, is said to have concluded near the end of his life that perhaps he had been wrong to view Roman Catholics as being extremely deviant in their beliefs. "I've been thinking," he told my mother, "that perhaps we are closer to each other than I've generally thought." Similarly, my father-in-law, Merton Alexander, found common ground between his Protestant heritage and Catholic brothers and sisters toward the end of his life. And my mother-in-law, Arlene Alexander, has made the journey from being a Free Methodist missionary to an active member in an Episcopal church. If you're unfamiliar with such labels all I need say is that such a journey encompasses about four trillion light years of religious relocation. It takes a lot of gray thinking to pack one's mental bags and travel that far. My mother, Dorothy Powell Moegerle, must have received a similar genetic dose of such fluid mental capacities from my grandfather. For example, after believing for nearly seventy years that divorce was always wrong and those divorced should not exercise spiritual leadership in the church, Mother changed. She did so when I divorced. Mother looked straight into the eyes of that reality, asked herself if she could apply her church's belief about divorce to her son, and was able to move the issues of divorce and remarriage into the gray area of life rather than yield to black-and-white dogma.

My point is that some live their lives applauding and probing the great mysteries of life and faith. The grays are no threat to their faith; for them God inhabits the gray as surely as the blacks and whites. But for Dobson, there is nothing quite so satisfying as a good solid black and a sure white. This is the stuff of which extremists are made.

Dennis Prager, one of my favorite thinkers and radio talk-show hosts here in Los Angeles, lists eight characteristics of extremism in his book, *Think a Second Time.* I'd like to repeat them here because every one of the characteristics he lists describes James Dobson perfectly.

"Extremists usually believe in a good value."[2]

Prager explains that one of the reasons black-and-white extremists are very effective and somewhat difficult to oppose is that the root concept within their extremism is a very good value. What is their failing, then? Not holding to that value, Prager contends, with humility and moderation. You have the Dobson position on abortion: no exceptions. Let's send people to jail. That is espousing the sanctity of human life, a good value, without humility or moderation. In contrast, walk with me into the rector's office at All Saints Episcopal Church in Pasadena and notice the small motto resting on the edge of George Reagas's desk, "Prayerfully pro-choice." Does not the message communicate a wonderfully humble and searching, "I'm really not sure when life begins, I certainly revere the gift of life as sacred, but more than anything I need to be in prayer about this and other imponderables and allow others to make the choice they feel led to make"? Moderation.

*"Extremists think you can never have too much
of a good value."*

If you're Dobson it is impossible to stop at the simple affirmation that life is sacred. You must work to make your affirmation the law of the land. Along the way you must demonize all who speak to the issue differently than you do. Why? Because *life* is a very, very good value. And fanaticism in defense of a good is not fanaticism to an extremist.

"Extremists do not acknowledge competing good values."

Prager observes with great insight that a particular value becomes so good to the extremist that it ranks higher than other goods. Instead, life must be lived on the basis of balancing goods, he urges. We must be able to say to ourselves that a very good value can, for a time, be suspended for the sake of another without being accused of abandoning that good. Otherwise we are extremists. Our nation must go to war without being accused within the community of nations of abandoning its belief in peace. We must allow ourselves that piece of pie with ice cream to festively celebrate a momentary event without browbeating ourselves that we are undisciplined when it comes to food. Our mates must give us permission to work late in special circumstances without accusing us of abandoning our commitment to marriage and family. Work is good and family is good. Neither is an exclusive good.

This characteristic of extremism reminds me of the difference between Ralph Reed's and James Dobson's approaches to the 1996 election. Reed seemed able to deal with two goods at one time—the good, from his perspective, of banning abortion and the good of winning the election. And so he embraced inclusive tolerance language in the Republican platform. Dobson held so tightly to his extremist stance that he didn't care whether a man he considers to be one of the most immoral presidents in our history would be reelected. Abortion forces on us two competing goods. One is life. The other is the essential, undeniable good of permitting individuals to determine for themselves what they believe about life's beginning and when it is right or wrong to abort. It is a good thing not to dictate such demanding and complex issues to our fellow citizens. This is precisely why two entirely different polling results can be obtained on the question of whether Americans favor abortion. If the question is "Do you personally favor abortion?" the majority of us answer no. However, if you ask "Do you favor the government controlling this issue?" the majority of us again answer no. America is either pro-choice or pro-life depending on how you ask the question. That is very good. It means, at least for now, that the majority of us are moderate. We can think about and appreciate two good things at one time, keeping them in balance.

"Extremists ignore consequences."

As I just indicated, Jim would gladly forfeit a presidential election to an undesirable candidate so long as he was true to his beliefs. As Prager points out, extremism drives people to ignore consequences in their blind focus on their pet value.

"Extremists cannot compromise."

You'll recall the story told earlier of the compromise Barry Lynn proposed to Dobson regarding children having access to dial-a-porn—that adults could still use the services, which Dobson opposed, but children would be blocked by means of the issuing of PIN numbers available only to adults. It is better in the minds of extremists that they win nothing while standing for a good than that they accept "half a loaf" and appear to compromise their good. And so they often forfeit available gains.

"Extremists think they have the advantage of 'purity.' "

Prager suggests that you can spot extremists by their criticism of those who hold the exact same view but without their intensity. Extremists will question the commitment and the purity of conviction of allies if such allies are not consumed with campaigning for that good. Listen to the words of James Dobson to his constituents immediately following the August 1996 political conventions: "Moral relativism was certainly evident last month in the way political leaders conducted their conventions and how they positioned their candidates. None of the leading parties dealt with the great moral issues facing our nation. Instead, the parties bragged about their newfound 'tolerance' and 'inclusiveness' and congratulated each other on the 'big tents' they had erected."

I seem to recall that the religious right got its way on virtually all of its issues within the Republican platform. And the platform was approved by the convention. I guess that's not pure enough. Dole proclaimed himself pro-life, but I guess he didn't do so loudly enough or long enough for Dobson. Perhaps it was the Republicans' horrendous crime of permitting Colin Powell to thank the party for including a pro-choice person like himself that caused the extremist James Dobson to complain that Dole wasn't pure enough.

"Extremism is often a response to extremism."

Prager points out that we must all guard against allowing extremists to make extremists of us. I see evidence of this in Jim's work. It could easily be argued that it has been extremism on the left that has enticed Dobson to extremism on the right. And once drawn into conflict, he has lost sight of the beauty of moderation and reason and of the central tenet of his own faith: "They shall know we are Christians by our love (not by our contention for the good)." The answer to extremism is not extremism.

"Extremism is more comfortable than moderation."

Jim goes ballistic when people accuse him of using political activism to enhance his fund raising. But the point here is that you do not raise donations for charities on the basis of ambiguities and uncertainties. Black-and-white positions raise money. They motivate a large portion of our fellow citizens. Prager is right: many of us march more readily to the simple staccato beat of the extremist drummer who says, "This way, I know this is the way," than to the moderate who says, "I'm not completely sure. Let's go explore the gray together."

The August 19, 1996, issue of *Newsweek* spoke eloquently to Prager's point. It said of the struggle by Republican moderates like California governor Pete Wilson to keep the party centrist during its 1996 convention: "Part of the moderates' problem lies in the very nature of moderation. The banner of 'tolerance' all but precludes banners; to march and shout for moderation is almost a contradiction in terms. Even when he was threatening a convention-floor debate over abortion, Bill Weld [delegate to the convention]) kept referring to it as a 'floor discussion' as if fighting over tolerance would undermine it."[3]

🌿 🌿 🌿

The danger we all face is that one day an extremist like Dobson may become powerful enough to throw a monkey wrench of intolerance into the machinery of consensus building and threaten the entire system by which we confront issues like abortion and move forward as a society.

NOTES

1. Barbara Boxer, *Congressional Record*, September 26, 1996.
2. Dennis Prager, *Think a Second Time* (New York: HarperCollins, 1995).
3. "The Passion Gap," *Newsweek*, August 19, 1996, p. 68.

23 ✤ Church and State

When I spoke in the fall of 1996 with Barry Lynn, the man Dobson loves most to hate, I asked him about a constitutional issue that is at the heart of any discussion of the religious right, the separation of church and state. It seemed to me that any book attempting to analyze Dobson's political activism should address the question: Does Jim cross the constitutional line separating the church and the government?

Gil: Obviously at some point in your career, you decided to devote yourself to this issue of the separation of church and state. Can you give me a little background on what would so concern you that you would lead Americans United for the Separation of Church and State, an organization devoted to just that issue?

Barry: There's one incident that I recall from my days in college which I've often described as the first time I thought seriously about what would happen if a religious group with an essentially religious viewpoint were to completely control moral decision making.

It had to do with a friend and the friend's need to have a woman friend of his obtain an abortion. At the time I would have characterized myself as a pro-life person. So although I didn't approve of what was going on, I realized the difficulty of actually having to go out of the United States at that time—this would have been in 1969 before *Roe* v. *Wade*—to go to another country to see a doctor you had never heard of before to obtain what in this person's mind was simply a medical procedure that she was entitled to have. And although I didn't agree with her decision, I thought that it was essentially her moral decision.

When you have a government taking these decisions away from you and your spiritual advisors and dictating your decision, you eliminate real morality because you eliminate the possibility of making moral choices and living with the consequences of those choices. I think that incident long ago led me to see that danger in a way that I had never seen it before, of government making what are essentially moral choices and then simply telling you that if you have a difference of moral opinion you can't exercise it.

Later, when I went to seminary at Boston University, I began to look at the intersection between government and the Church. Both during and after seminary I worked for the United Church of Christ's lobbying office on Capitol Hill and I began to see a conflict between government and the Church when the two became too closely aligned. It was one thing to take a moral message to government—I want churches to do that—but this idea that the Church should expect anything in return, that the church should become a partner with government, creates serious problems for the integrity of the ministry of the Church. I found it to be an uneasy relationship, whether it was conservative churches or liberal churches that became heavily involved in public policy. I found myself concerned by what you seem to lose as the Church when your mission became so focused on political victories.

Just as Lynn recalls his first thoughts about this issue, so do I. I remember vividly the feelings of fear I experienced in my adolescent years as the conservative Protestant Christians around me discussed what would happen if the Roman Catholic John Kennedy were elected president. Alarmist rumors ran rampant that a Catholic president would be bound by some mysterious obligation to Rome to do whatever the pope wanted him to do. I recall images going through my mind of phone calls coming from some hushed, incense-filled corner of Saint Peter's Basilica to the White House with instructions that Kennedy must raise taxes or include Catholic dogma in public schools. And in my imagination there was no way that Kennedy could say no because no Catholic said no to the pope. In that vulnerable way that children soak up the emotions of adults closest to them, I became afraid because those around me were afraid.

Clearly, our anxiety was based on ignorance. Kennedy was elected and, in hindsight, it's humorous to imagine that there was some danger in electing him to high office. To some extent we owe a debt of gratitude to Kennedy for modeling for our culture the true meaning of the separation of church and state. I have in my files one of his statements on this subject, from a source unknown to me, that makes it clear that he sensed its importance. He said, "I believe in an America where the separation of church and state is absolute—where no Catholic prelate would tell the president, should he be a Catholic, how to act, and no Protestant minister would tell his parishioners for whom to vote."

A similar type of fear exists today among those who are not ultra-orthodox, right-wing Protestants regarding the power surge of the religious right. The circumstances are very similar and the anxiety is quite understandable—a concern that someone of a different faith will gain a degree of power that touches our individual lives and then that their religion will, in some way, be imposed on us against our will. It's one thing for a politician to mess with our taxes, forcing us to part with more of our hard-earned income. But when we begin to perceive that a political movement such as the religious right is trying to direct our lives based on some alien religious dogma, we feel much more than anger, we feel genuine fear.

How should we view our fear? Were we wrong to fear Kennedy but correct to fear the religious right? Did Kennedy do the church-state thing right but are Robertson and Dobson doing it wrong? If they are wrong, how exactly? They're Americans like you and me. They have as much right as we to speak out on the issues of the day, to organize and mobilize for their causes. There can be no wrong in stating that one opposes a certain measure or favors another. There can be no right in stating that people of strong religious conviction should not speak in the public square. Power brokering is neither unconstitutional nor a sin. Leveraging one's own position on the issues of the day into a greater force than one vote is, in some ways, the very definition of politics.

In short, what do we mean as Americans when we say there is an important line drawn in the sand of our democracy that states: Congress shall make no law that abridges or restricts freedom of religion and Congress shall make no law regarding the establishment of religion? And how do we evaluate the actions of people like Dobson with respect to that line?

If you think about it for a moment, the issue of how cultures balance the authority and influence of the church with the authority and influence of the state is one of the more potent international political issues of our time. The central question is whether nations will take a "separated" path, the church focusing on spiritual matters and the state on secular matters and each respecting the other's realm of influence, or a "combined" path, the church serving as the state, as is the case, for example, in Iran. I suggest to you for starters that we cannot talk about these two fundamental alternatives on the basis of determining which is right or wrong, but rather on the basis of which we prefer as a society and whether the American way of "separation" warrants changing.

It is my view that James Dobson prefers the "combined" approach to government, with the Protestant Christian church, as represented by him, dictating public policy based on sectarian religious positions. Furthermore, I believe he crosses the line within our current "separation" system and violates the First Amendment.

To illustrate, I return to my 1996 conversation with Barry Lynn.

Gil: It seems to me that we're dealing here, on the subject of church and state, with a line drawn in the sand that becomes fuzzy at times and hard to understand.

There is a sense in which James Dobson has as much right as any citizen of this country to be active politically. But then there's the sense you get that he's doing some things that violate our system of government. Help me understand that line.

Barry: It's obviously a very important issue. Let me talk about it first without reference to Dobson. You may know that Americans United recently started something called Project Fair Play, which was intended to ask our members and indeed any Americans who see an individual church in their community crossing the line between simply speaking about moral issues into direct advocacy of the election or the defeat of a candidate, to report those activities to us and we would help them in appropriate cases to complain; to file a formal complaint with the Internal Revenue Service. To me that's the clearest way of describing the line.

Endorsement of candidates is something that nonprofit organizations, including 501(c)3 organizations, which include every church, is absolutely barred from doing. Our churches cannot work to elect or defeat candidates. That is a breach of the separation of church and state. So when someone from the pulpit says, Vote for my friend Bill Jones, that's wrong under the tax laws of the United States. When people violate those laws and are not willing to play by the same rules as other groups, then I think that violation of our system is worthy of being reported to the proper authorities.

Similarly, when a church distributes information so biased as to lead to a conclusion that candidate A is clearly the person to vote for and candidate B is the person to oppose, the distribution of that kind of material also crosses the line between speaking a moral message and telling people whom they should vote for in a particular election for public office.

My problem with Dobson is not that he does that. He does not do that, at least as far as I know. For example, he does not do what the Christian Coalition has done with regard to distributing voter guides which are now under attack and properly so by the Federal Election Commission and the Internal Revenue Service. [The Christian Coalition has allegedly distributed voter guides so clearly biased in favor of Republican candidates that their 501(c) tax-exempt status is being questioned.]

My problem with the way Dobson functions is that he has what is essentially a radio ministry, and in the best sense. I know a lot of people who, before they learned of Dobson's political leanings, turned to his radio program and to his books for advice about how to raise their children. It becomes a kind of long distance pastoral relationship supplemented by what you learn from the telephone counselors when you call.

Then these individuals find themselves getting material that's not about how to raise their children, it's now about political issues. I don't believe that it violates his tax exemption to talk about political issues, or breaches the separation of church and state. I just think it is terribly inappropriate to take a pastoral relationship and turn it into a political relationship by beginning to send literature that increasingly tells you what you should tell your Congress people to do on abolishing the Department of Education or defunding Planned Parenthood or removing books from a library. And the fact that Dr. Dobson is not ordained makes no difference. His is very much a religious Christian message and then, all of a sudden, this Christian pastoral message becomes one of Christian politics.

That's offensive even if it's not illegal. And just because something is legal does not mean that it is right. I think Mr. Dobson has crossed *that* line, the line between right and wrong.

Does the "separate" approach mean, by definition, that one sphere of influence cannot communicate with or influence the other in any way? Obviously not. The state has messages for the church which need to be heard. They include, for example, how the standards of society are applied inside the four walls of the religious institution. Is tort law also the "law of the land" in the church building? Yes, it is, with some exceptions. Likewise, the church has many messages for the state, including its important call to employ a high moral standard when making the laws of the land.

Does this separate approach mean, by definition, that no religious people are allowed across the line into the area of the state to work there? Clearly not. Dobson has a right to go to Washington and twist as many arms as he can grab. And the president has a right to call religious leaders into his office and make the case for new legislation he advocates and for which he needs their support. The wall of separation here is clearly not a communications barrier. That was part of Lynn's point.

Then where is the danger? Why should anyone be concerned about the political activism of Robertson or Dobson or, before them, Falwell?

THE DANGER ZONE

First, there is the danger Lynn pointed out, that people like Reed and Dobson will, in their zeal, cross the line into endorsing candidates and supporting campaigns.

Second, there is the more subtle danger in any democracy that a trend will begin, fueled by people who don't know their history, to undermine our fragile experiment to deliver maximum personal freedom to the individual while maintaining a controlled society through nonreligious law. Dobson's particular faith, the Church of the Nazarene, has historically taken a strong stand relative to "keeping the Lord's Day holy," which has at various times in history included not shopping on Sunday, not going to sporting events, not watching TV, and even not engaging in certain private family activities. We have no guarantee, other than our vigilance, that a Nazarene zealot like Dobson will never build a political coalition strong enough to reenact the old blue laws of New England that were designed to enforce certain moral and religious standards prohibiting specified forms of entertainment on Sunday. I believe it is precisely the same thinking—public policy driven by sectarian belief—that is behind his positions on abortion, pornography, and homosexuality.

The larger problem Jim represents is that, in his heart, he intends for his America to be a Christian nation. Will we be a nation whose public-policy consensus is strongly influenced by Christian values? Always. But a Christian nation? Never, in my view, unless Jim should prevail. Jim is angry about the degree to which his particular religion is not openly revered as the fountainhead of public policy. He is upset with those who, in his opinion, are causing the country to be something other than distinctly Christian. Rather than being content to be a Christian American and valuing the contributions that Christians like him are making to American society; rather than wanting simply to be a person who contributes to the presence of Christian faith and perspective in society, seasoning the stew of a diverse democracy, Jim's passions run in the direction of controlling society in such a manner that we have a Christian government. That is his most dangerous mistake.

During his November 25, 1996, radio broadcast, Dobson dissected the results of the recent general election with the help of Gary Bauer. Listening to the precise words they used to characterize what they believed to be the good and bad news from that election, I was struck once again by the awareness that Jim is encouraging the creation of a distinctly Christian rather than a nonsectarian government. For example, he said, with Bauer's enthusiastic support, "Some of those new guys [speaking of successful candidates for the Senate and the House] are really going to be outstanding. John Thume is a new Republican, pro-life, pro-family, *a strong Christian.* Jim Ryan, a Republican from Kansas, has been on this radio program. He's a wonderful *Christian man*; great family values. There's one [new Congressman] right after another *like that.*"

That crosses the line. It sounds suspiciously like a man whose political goals include creating a Christian government rather than supporting America's traditional view that we are best served, to borrow once more from Dennis Prager, by "a government that is completely secular and permits complete religious freedom for the individual."

I mentioned in the last chapter Prager's checklist to help us identify extremism. Dennis applied his test to this very issue. He reminds us that belief in the separation of church and state is itself a good that is subject to the abuses of extremism.

Prager suggests, in *Think a Second Time,*[1] that there are two mistakes to be avoided here—religious and secular extremism. The former believes that the wall of separation is good because religion cannot possibly be too strong in a society. The latter believes that the wall is good because secularism cannot possibly be too strong in a society. Prager suggests that examples of such extremes would be secularists attempting to get the oath to God removed from the Boy Scout pledge and religionists trying to block gays from having protection from basic discrimination.

The answer to extremism is moderation and balance. The answer to church and state is a reasonable wall. And the answer to Jim and his type is no.

NOTE

1. Dennis Prager, *Think a Second Time* (New York: Regan Books, 1995), pp. 159–65.

24 ❧ Case in Chief

It is important to ask if we want James Dobson's private attitudes and conduct, as well as his powerful dispositions, to shape our public policy. If Dobson is prepared, for example, to invade Joyce Landorf's privacy and to strong-arm her publisher into ending its business dealings with her, or to muzzle Gary Warner, what might he do with increased power within the Washington, D.C., beltway? What further abuses of power might he entertain? I've already stated, but it bears repeating, that I see a great difference between the work of James Dobson the marriage and child-raising guru to millions and James Dobson the national morality spokesman and political power broker. My intention in this book has been to support Jim's work as an advisor to families and to call into question his work as an advisor to governments. I believe that Jim is without credibility in the public policy arena, but that he has a great contribution to make in the family life arena. My motive has been to applaud him on one front and question him on the other. My challenge to his political endeavors arises from four basic concerns: First, Dobson seems not to understand or be able to function within the essential framework of public policy formation—that of building consensus solutions in a pluralistic society based on compromise. Second, he demonstrates significant blind spots on essential, fundamental social needs relative to civil rights. Third, while coveting enormous political power, he refuses customary accountability to the public by way of the media. Fourth, he brings to the political process a heavy religious message, advocating an agenda that would, in effect, turn the country into a singularly Christian nation, violating the all-important separation of church and state outlined in our Constitution.

229

My Case in Chief

In the following chapters I want to illustrate further, in a very personal way, the second of those four concerns. This is a man who does not respect individual rights and existing civil law.

For some time I have believed that I witnessed uncivil conduct inside Focus on the Family that warranted the public's attention and consideration, especially as Dobson becomes more and more powerful. I have wanted to write this book for years. But until now, publishers have advised me that my motives would be viewed as too suspect for a book like this to be credible. However, each of the publishers who offered that view functions inside the niche-market religious-commercial world that Jim dominates, the "Christian Booksellers Association" and the "National Religious Broadcasters" marketplace. So I've often asked myself whether their motives were all that pure. Why don't they want a book published that calls into question some of the attitudes and behaviors of the top-selling author and most listened-to broadcaster in their marketplace? How many of their tables does Dobson put food on—religious publishing staffs, religious bookstore staffs, religious radio station staffs—so that no one wants to deal with the shadow side of this golden goose?

But in 1996 Prometheus Books, a secularist publisher outside Dobson's marketplace, asked for this account of James Dobson. They did so because of their interest in how religion and politics coexist within our society and where and when one gets a little too close to the other for our common good. In addition, they observed that James Dobson was rising in political influence. And yet few outside Dobson's religious community knew much about him.

As I've recounted, Focus on the Family began while I was living in Chicago and Jim in Los Angeles. I was vice president of the Domain Advertising Agency, headed by Doug and Faith Mains, two of the distinguished pioneers of religious radio in this country. If every industry has its good and bad guys, and American religious broadcasting surely does, then Doug and Faith and their son, broadcaster David Mains, represent the finest in that field.

All the services needed to broadcast the Focus on the Family radio program, publish its magazine, conduct its fund raising, manage its mailing list, and support its related activities were being created each day by the Domain staff. The excitement generated by the account was contagious; it electrified the agency office. We knew from day one that Dobson had tremendous potential as a communicator and that there was significant public interest in what he offered. One of the most enjoyable images I carry around in my memory is that of the affable, highly respected president of the agency, Doug Mains, standing by a desk talking to a station manager in some faraway city, pitching the new Dobson broadcast to someone who, in those days, knew nothing of James Dobson, but who respected Doug's judgment in programming and booked the broadcast on that basis. We watched with excitement as the young Dobson radio network began to grow from ten stations to twenty-five to fifty.

There is one other book that describes these beginning days of Focus on the Family. It is written by Dobson and his vice president of publishing, Rolf Zettersten. To Jim's great shame, he never once mentions Doug and Faith or Domain in his history of the organization, but pays tribute instead to his later agent in southern California. That is a snapshot of the shadow side of Jim Dobson: his tendency to write off people who cross him. In this case Doug and Faith have been written out of the official Focus story, given my former role at Domain, because of the volcanic falling out between Jim and me.

Because Dobson was in L.A. and Domain in Chicago, the most common scenario for meetings between Jim and me in those early days was that I would fly to the coast once a month to discuss business and to record new radio programs. Occasionally Jim would fly east. It was on one such trip by Jim to Chicago that the following scene occurred.

HIS TRUE COLORS

An organization had given Focus on the Family a sizable grant to produce a series of thirteen half-hour television programs similar in content to our new radio program. Of all the exciting bits and pieces of the Dobson enterprise in those days, none was more exciting to me than to be handed that grant and told by Doug, Faith, and Jim to go make some great TV. I set about contracting the people at the historic WGN television facility in downtown Chicago to arrange for studios, crews, and studio audiences. We were offered the Phil Donahue studios, since our production work would take place in the evenings while his was done during the day. We arranged the taping schedule so that Jim would come to town for two or three days at a time. Each evening we would bring an audience into the Donahue studio and tape three half hours that combined questions and answers between Dobson and me with interaction between Dobson and the audience.

One night after a taping session, as I was accompanying Jim and his wife back to their hotel, we found ourselves at the top of the lobby esca-lator, where I would typically say goodnight and return to my car for the trip home. This time Jim asked if we could speak about an important per-sonal matter. Shirley said good night and went on to their room. Then Jim revealed to me for the first time what I consider to be one of the worst sides to his personality—a compulsion to encourage people to share with him private and even intimate information and then to impart that infor-mation to others or take action based on it in a manner that is extremely inappropriate.

On this occasion Jim stated that my wife had asked for a private meeting with him and had told him that we were experiencing marital problems; that her marriage to me was an unhappy one for her. You could have knocked me over with the proverbial feather. I was stunned that my wife would seek out my client and use him as the recipient of her marital frustrations. It felt to me like an incredible display of disloyalty and dis-respect. I was equally shocked that Jim would permit her to do so. I had known for some time that my wife was unhappy in the marriage and I'd been trying to discover the root cause of the frustration and to help resolve it. I knew I was a garden-variety husband and father, neither per-fect nor irresponsible, but the cause of her discontent had thus far eluded me. I would have never guessed that this confusing and difficult situation would be discussed by and with a business client.

The most dangerous signal Dobson communicated that night, one which I completely missed until much later in our relationship, was that he perceived nothing amiss in that meeting with my wife.

Jim plunged ahead, suggesting that my wife and I get counseling. Specifically he referred me to a good friend of his, Paul Roberts, at Asso-ciated Psychological Services in Pasadena, California. Did Jim recom-mend that clinic so that he could keep tabs on my private life just as he had done on Joyce Landorf's? I will never know for sure. My wife and I did indeed begin therapy with Roberts, scheduling intensive, multiple sessions on my trips to California. And shortly afterward, Dobson had Paul Roberts as a guest on the broadcast, creating once again the strange mingling of relationships between Dobson, Associated Psychological Services, and patient referrals.

When it became unmanageable to try to do therapy with a counselor so far from home, my wife and I switched to a therapist in Chicago. And with that, I wish I could tell you that my experience with Jim crossing the line into my private life ended. In fact, I had no idea what lay ahead in terms of Jim's disrespect for that line.

25 🌾 Invasion of Privacy

In 1980 I resigned from the agency to accept the position of Focus on the Family vice president. My wife and I packed up our home and moved to Los Angeles so that I could lead an in-house creative services staff that replaced most of the professional services Focus had been purchasing from Domain.

Three years had gone by since that night in the hotel at the top of the escalator without further incident. Despite therapy and our best efforts, my wife and I were moving closer to the dreaded precipice of separation and divorce. But we were both still searching for a magic formula to fix the relationship. When we moved to California, we looked for another marriage counselor and Jim referred us to his good friend Neil Warren of, you guessed it, Associated Psychological Services in Pasadena. Soon thereafter the nightmare of Dobson's disrespect for this employee's privacy resurfaced.

One afternoon Jim asked me to stop by his office. As I seated myself in one of the two soft, low-backed guest chairs that sat opposite his grand mahogany desk, surrounded by custom-made rich wood bookcases, pictures, and plaques heralding the accomplishments of this man of rising stature, Jim said, "Gil, I've had a talk with your wife." My mind began to race as the ghost of that first conversation in Chicago floated before my eyes. Here was not my client, but my boss, my employer, wanting to discuss my private life. "I asked her for examples of what seems to be the problem with your marriage. And one impression that I got was that she has difficulty getting your cooperation regarding matters such as routine legal documents the two of you need to transact as a married couple. Why are you so difficult to deal with? You know you're much more verbal than your wife. Why do you make it so difficult for her? She tells me she has made a reasonable and simple request that you sign the California Homestead Act?* But she says you refuse to sign it. What's going on here?"

Dobson paused and looked at me, waiting for an answer. I was so taken off guard, I responded by defending what was a strictly private decision. I told him I didn't sign legal documents without first gaining the advice of an attorney, but that I had intended to seek the advice of the corporate attorney the next time I saw him. Dobson waved a hand, "You don't need to do that, Gil," he said. "Shirley and I have signed one and trust me, it's fine." Then he reached into the middle of a stack of papers and pulled something out. "In fact, I asked your wife to leave the legal form with me and I told her I'd take care of it for her. Here, I'd like you to sign it now." He then slid the document across the desk with a pen. I refused to sign, but was so stunned I felt I was moving in slow motion as I picked up the unsigned document and stood to go, mumbling something about seeing the attorney as soon as possible.

THE LADIES ARE GOING TO TALK

Several weeks later, the executive staff and their wives were scheduled to go on retreat to Mammoth Lakes where Jim and Shirley owned a resort condominium. The afternoon before we left town, Jim told me in the hallway that he wanted me to find a ride with one of the other executives because my wife was going to be making the six-hour drive to and from Mammoth with Shirley so that the women could "talk." I was obviously concerned about what Jim had arranged but, again, I did not protest, for reasons I will explain momentarily.

On yet another afternoon, as I was finishing up at my desk, Jim suddenly walked in. I assumed I knew why. As I've described, Jim's favorite time of the day was the bewitching hour of 6:00 or 6:30 P.M., when either he strolled from office to office looking for evidence that we had experienced another record-shattering day or we walked into his office for our executive ritual of mutual back patting. Very quickly he announced his purpose. "Gil, I've been talking to your wife." Those dreaded words. I braced myself. "Tell me something," he continued, "could it be true that

---

*A law preventing creditors from seizing a person's house in the case of a bankruptcy.

you are tight-fisted with your family finances, so much so that your wife has no idea where the family stands in terms of income and debts?" "No, that's not true," I replied.

Jim was not satisfied. He followed up. "Do you, by chance, keep your family financial records here at the office instead of keeping them at home where your wife can review them at will?" I responded, "Yes, I do." I went on to explain that I had just purchased one of the very first personal computers and I was so excited about using it that I kept it at my desk so I could write business memos and do spreadsheets on it. I indicated that I also kept the family budget on it so my records were, at least for the moment, at work. Jim was still not satisfied. He asked me to open my desk and show my personal records to him. I dutifully slid open the drawer and did so. Jim proceeded to lecture me about how disregarded a woman feels when her husband is not forthcoming and communicative, and with that he left my office.

WHERE IS THE LINE?

Jim was completely oblivious to the incredible degree of invasiveness that these and other confrontations indicated and the unbearable stress it placed on me to have my employer attempt to hold me accountable for my private life. He seemed to have crossed the privacy line with no warning signals going off in his head. I knew I couldn't afford to lose my job, so I was unsure how hard to resist Dobson's decision to make my business his business. My family was in terrible pain, my children were crying themselves to sleep at night, fearful of what it meant that Mom and Dad did not get along, and my own heart was breaking. I didn't have the emotional resources to search for a new career, nor could the family absorb a financial disruption. I was afraid that if I drew a hard line in the sand, Dobson would overreact and terminate the working relationship. I felt a responsibility to myself and my family not to add unemployment to what was an already overwhelming stress load. So I decided on a two-pronged approach. I would give Jim enough information to back him off and, at the same time, try to stem the tide of his offensive invasive onslaught by an occasional mild protest. I remember on many occasions, when I'd express disapproval of him talking behind my back to my wife, he'd respond, "So what have you got to hide, Gil?" For this man, the only reason an employee would not want his boss talking to his wife about his private life was that he had something to hide.

Things grew worse. One day, Jim passed me in the hall and stopped to say, "Gil, Neil tells me you're not cooperating with therapy. Stop by my office when you get a moment. I'd like to chat."

Now my therapist? I had never signed a Release of Confidentiality form authorizing Neil to talk to Dobson. But when I later met Jim for that conversation, it was clear he and my counselor were talking.

In the summer of 1985, when Jim's pattern of probing my marriage was in high gear, I wrote him the following: "I simply do not have the emotional stamina to dispute with you the details of my handling of my family after having wrestled over the same details with both my wife and my counselor. I can't do it." Dobson never gave the slightest indication he respected those words.

I can hear you saying that such a protest should never have been necessary in the first place. Indeed it should not have, given the fact that the boss in question was a licensed psychologist schooled in the issue of confidentiality, trained to understand the extraordinary emotional and psychological pressure it would place on an employee to have to deal with a deteriorating marriage and family at home and then be forced to explain all that as a part of his job. If any CEO on the planet should have known not to probe into an employee's private life, James Dobson should have understood the issue of "emotional stamina" I placed before his eyes in my memo. But he didn't. He kept advancing. From my checkbook to my bedroom and everything in between: it was all fair game for Dobson.

Later, his response to my concerns about this period in our relationship was that I had invited him into the private areas of my life, as if, to a trained psychologist, that is a reasonable excuse. Does Jim support psychologists using the defense, when charged with having sex with their patients, "Gosh, she invited me to"? I asked him that question once and got no response.

Into this fray Dobson introduced yet another element as his invasion continued. Jim and Shirley invited my wife and me to dinner. I accepted on the condition that they not attempt to discuss our marriage in a public restaurant. Jim agreed. However, when the main course was served, both he and Shirley began soliciting from my wife her various complaints about the problems in our marriage. Shocked and betrayed, I bowed out of the conversation altogether and remained silent. Later Jim wrote me in a memo that my silence at dinner was proof to him that I knew I was guilty of all the things my wife had accused me of. He told me that it was clear to him that I had realized this under the weight of her accusations.

But of all my experiences with Jim's invasiveness, perhaps the high water mark of his excesses took place when my marriage reached its distressing end and the legal process of separation commenced.

To the Courthouse

During the summer of 1985 my wife formally announced in a statement Neil Warren helped her draft that she had concluded the marriage was over and she wanted a divorce. That fall she told the children and me on several occasions that she intended to leave California and return to her home state, and that she wanted to take our young son with her, assuming the girls would want to live with me. This speech routinely reduced our daughters to tears at the thought of being separated from their mother as well as their brother. In November of that year, in another of her secret meetings with Dobson, she repeated her intention to divorce me and leave the state. That was the exact day it was announced that my services would no longer be needed in the radio studio as co-host. Yet I had not actually been served with legal papers by my wife.

I believed my wife when she announced her decision to divorce me. But part of growing up in my conservative religious community included a distrust of attorneys just as my dad distrusted doctors and therapists. I suspect that was why I procrastinated in seeking legal advice about what to expect when my marriage ended. One day, I accidentally saw a receipt lying on a shelf in my home showing fees paid by my wife to a law firm for "divorce consultations." It scared me. I remember feeling an enormous sense of dread. Any irrational fantasy I harbored, namely, that the lack of a filing of papers might mean hope for reconciliation, ended abruptly.

I telephoned an attorney Dobson and I had interviewed on our talk show and made an appointment for my first consultation. It was horribly distressing. Why does the heart keep hoping and wishing and refusing to let go long after it knows the object of its attachment is dead and buried? I was never nervous walking into our radio studio and addressing an audience estimated in the millions. But I was filled with anxiety walking into the attorney's office, as if I were about to be sentenced to jail for some horrendous deed. And the words Greg said to me that day did nothing to relieve my anxiety. I had intended only to open an account with him so that, when I was served with papers, I would know exactly what to do next.

A TIME TO ACT

Instead, after I brought him up to speed on the events of the previous six months, Greg told me that the advice my wife was undoubtedly receiving from her attorney was to get on a plane, with my son, leave the state for her new home, and then file the divorce action there. He indicated that no court in that state would order her back to California and that she would receive custody of the child who was with her.

The thought of losing contact with my little boy almost killed me. When I asked Greg what legal options I had, he indicated that his professional advice was that I file a restraining order to keep all our children in California until a judge could assign custody. He told me, however, that a restraining order of this kind could not stand alone, it had to be attached to a motion either for separation or for divorce. He indicated that there was no guarantee that I would be granted custody of my son, but this process was my only shot at it. I could not file fast enough. But even then I could not set aside my religious conviction not to divorce. So I authorized a filing requesting a legal separation. It was a routine filing, composed of the customary legal stuff, including the restraining order regarding the children. Jim's relationship with my wife had become so unmanageable that I also included an order restraining her from speaking to Dobson. The filing took place in February 1986.

Without my knowledge, Jim obtained a copy of that court document the very day it was filed. The next morning, sitting on my desk, was the following Dobson memo. I'll explain its background as we go, so you can follow its ghastly content.

> Gilbert,
>
> You and I have been friends and brothers for nine years and it really hurts me to write the note that follows.
>
> Nevertheless, I have a profound sense of justice and I've never been able to remain silent when a weaker or disadvantaged individual was being wounded or devastated.
>
> If I understand correctly your present circumstances at home, you have just dealt a *crushing* [emphasis Jim's, as all italics will be] blow to [your wife]. I received a call from one of her friends last night who told me about the papers you served on [her] yesterday. I couldn't believe what I heard. Here are the provisions you apparently worked out with your lawyer:

Before we go further, to grasp the folly of Jim's memo the first time through you need to know that he was reacting to the standard language and set of requests that are contained in any petition to the court for a separation or a divorce. Legally, there would follow my wife's petition containing her version of how various issues should be resolved, such as the custody of the children and the division of property. Finally, there would be a hearing in which the judge would take testimony and then make the court's ruling on these issues. All we have on the table at this moment is my petition indicating to the court what I thought would be best for myself, my wife, and my children.

(1) You are attempting to take all three children away from [your wife]. You, the consummate workaholic, are hoping to gain custody of an ambitious toddler to be raised in a child care center or who knows where for ten hours a day instead of being with his mother. I can't believe it.

(2) You obtained testimonials from your girls against their mother. . . . What an incredibly vicious thing to do. [Your wife] has said all along that your permissiveness and overindulgence with [your daughters] was designed to turn them against her—presenting yourself as the "good guy" and her as the devil. Now it looks like there was yet another motive—to use them in the battle for [your son].

Given the natural competitiveness and antagonism between adolescent girls and their mothers, it would not be difficult to turn that friction into hatred. I could *easily* have done that to Shirley if I'd wanted to get custody of [our daughter] and her brother. I pray that I'm wrong in assessing your motives at this point but it sure looks nasty.

(3) [Your wife] is to be out of her home by February 28! Come on, Gil. What kind of a man would throw his wife—a lifetime homemaker with minimal employment skills—out of her house in one month? Again, the word "vicious" is the only one that comes to mind.

(4) The individual who shared all this information with me was a little uncertain as to the support you were proposing that [your wife] get. He thought it was $200 per month. God help us!

You make $60,000 per year and you're going to give $2,400 to [your wife]? Say it isn't so, Gil. *Please* tell me I'm wrong. [Your wife] couldn't find a chicken coop for $200 per month. Who will feed her? Who will pay her medical bills? Who will put gas in her car? How could you do this?

To help you understand the bizarre nature of all this: The actual proposal was that while my wife remained in our home I would provide her with $200 per month in cash, on top of paying all her bills and then, when we separated I offered to pay whatever the court deemed appropriate. And I proposed to the court that I would like the three children to be able to remain together in their home, to minimize the trauma. Therefore, I proposed that my wife find an apartment.

> (5) Perhaps *most* important, you got the judge to issue a restraining order saying she couldn't talk to me. You, Gilbert, who have always had an open book with me—allowing me to talk to [your wife], Neil Warren or anyone I wished, have now gagged [your wife] by legal decree. Given the circumstances, I don't blame you! I have never seen a man stick it to his wife more than you have in this instance.
>
> Relevant to item 5, it is interesting that you said nothing to Paul [Focus executive vice president] or me about these plans. I saw you at chapel yesterday and you talked to Miriam [Paul's secretary] at 4:00 P.M. You must have known for a week or more that you had mailed a package of dynamite to [your wife]. The sound of silence is deafening! You flew home with Peb [Focus vice president] last week and said nothing!!

These words by Jim provide you with a key insight into this period. You can see for yourself the kind of response Jim gave to my protests regarding his invasive ways. I call to your attention the fact that he labeled it the single most important part of his memo that he was outraged that I had cut off his access to my wife and that I had neglected to "tell all" about the court filing to him, to Paul Nelson, to Peb Jackson, and even to a Focus secretary. This was a man who demanded information. This was a man with no respect for the line between the public and the private lives of those who worked for him or, for that matter, of people like Joyce Landorf and Stan Mooneyham, who did not.

> Gilbert, I am so disappointed in you. [Your wife] has said for years that you were mean at home—a ruthless infighter. I've refused to believe it. For six years I supported you blindly. Even after [your wife] was here and the story she told looked so incriminating, I said, there *must* be two sides to that conflict. I looked hard for your point of view.
>
> It looks like you're going for the jugular. [Your wife] is defenseless. She's lost her home, three children, income, self-respect—and even the right to plead her case! You've destroyed her, Gil!

One of the remarkable characteristics of James Dobson's thinking you have just witnessed is Jim's strange, compulsive need to be a savior to women. Notice how many times he leaps to the sexist assumption that women, by definition, must be the victims in any difficult situation. That's because Jim views women as essentially weak, defenseless, and needy. Men, by definition, are the strong ones, the providers, who are charged with making things right. If men do the right thing in their marriages, then their marriages will work out because women always follow along when the man does it right. Examples of this viewpoint abound in this memo:

- If a man takes legal action against a woman it is victimizing her. But Jim had known for six months that my wife was planning legal action against me, and yet does not characterize those intentions as victimizing me.
- It was inappropriate, in Jim's view, for me to use day care, but it was all right for my wife.
- Men should feed the women who leave them, pay their medical bills, put gas in their cars. They couldn't possibly do that on their own.
- I was destroying my wife by filing for a legal separation, but she was not destroying me by planning a divorce.

Notice also Jim's naïveté about family law court procedures. Is this the man who consults with Congress and presidents about how to improve the laws of the land? He writes as if the simple act of filing my petition meant that everything I asked for would be granted by the court. No need to wait on the court's ruling. It was over simply because I had filed.

I would argue that you have before you exhibit A regarding Jim's overly controlling temperament. Here you see him telling an employee exactly what he can and cannot do in his private life. Can there be any question that the issues discussed in this memo are strictly between my wife and myself? But Jim was not done. Not by a long shot.

26 ✤ Breach of Confidentiality

I reacted to Dobson's memo in the way I had become accustomed to dealing with his other intrusions. I wrote him a note indicating that I was available to answer the questions he had raised in it. I know. That cooperative style of response makes no sense in hindsight; that is, until you factor in the emotional disorientation of losing one's first marriage and, perhaps, one's children.

When the appointed day and time came for the followup meeting, at approximately two o'clock in the afternoon of February 14, 1986, I walked into the office of the CEO of Focus on the Family to be greeted by Jim, Paul Nelson, and, if you can believe it, my therapist. Jim had called Neil Warren and invited him to participate in this confrontation over my filing for legal separation and Neil had accepted. What followed was the spectacle of my boss and my therapist making demands about the language in my separation filing with a fellow vice president looking on.

As the conversation began, Jim and my therapist did the talking. I took notes and, for some reason, saved them. They read as follows:

> Neil stated that the end of my marriage was a tragedy for all concerned; that, in this time of tragedy, he wanted me to take his advice about how to handle the legal aspects of the end of the marriage.
>
> He said (in front of my employer and another executive) that my contribution to the end of the marriage had been as large as my wife's.
>
> Neil stated that he wanted me to propose to my wife that I would accept custody of the girls and give her custody of our son. Next, he indicated that I should support my wife's desire to move back to her home state and to take our son with her.

243

I recall Jim offering statements in support of each of these points by Neil.

Neil asked me to rise above the law in terms of how the marriage ended; to have what he called a "Christian divorce," which, he said, meant treating everyone with dignity and resolving things without a court hearing.

He said he and Jim were concerned about a bitter fight taking place in court that would wreck my wife's chances of restoring her relationship with our daughters.

My notes indicate that Jim then spoke not only in support of Neil, but offered several new thoughts of his own:

Jim would tolerate a divorce between me and my wife, but he would do so only if it was carried out with what he called "civility." He indicated that my filing violated this value and my initial court positions would not be tolerated.

And then Neil spoke again.

He asked me to preserve all that I could of my wife's dignity and her relationships with the three children. He concluded by calling on me to circumvent all the "legal junk" that could be bypassed.

Years later, these comments by two trained and licensed psychologists seem grotesque. But, at that moment, I recall not being able to articulate my feelings, although I indicated that I would give their statements my thought. As quickly as I could, I asked to be excused. As I stumbled from the office, I noticed Paul Nelson ahead of me in the hallway, heading for his office. I followed him inside and closed the door, slumping into one of his guest chairs. "Paul," I said, "Could you verify for me that Jim just threatened to terminate my employment at Focus on the Family unless I give up custody of my son? Is my job on the line here?" Paul, whose duties included responsibility for all employment issues at Focus, answered, "Yes."

Paul has since gone on to the position of president of the Evangelical Council on Financial Accountability, the private agency that assures to the donating public and, in a manner of speaking, to our government, that nonprofit organizations like Dobson's raise and spend money by the highest of ethical standards. He's an ethics czar, in order words. Yet there was apparently nothing unethical about that meeting, from his perspective, nor about Dobson's threat to terminate an employee for seeking custody of his young son. My filing remained as written and, for reasons Jim never explained, I was not terminated—for the moment.

PANIC

Let's take a moment before we go further to speculate about why Jim was invading my private life in such an out-of-control and unprofessional manner. My best guess is that Dobson panicked for personal reasons. I believe Jim perceived some irrational threat to his own personal image and that of his company if the public who donated to him and bought his products drew the conclusion that Dobson's principles of marriage didn't work because his closest associate got divorced. I suspect that he worried that donors might lose faith in him, concluding that Dobson and his associates don't really believe what they preach. When you analyze it, this panic is an expression of disrespect for his constituency, assuming as it does that they are incapable of understanding that it takes two people to hold together a marriage; that marriages cannot be maintained on the basis of one spouse's beliefs or conduct alone; and that divorced staff members can be viewed as believing in lifelong marriage, just as single and nondivorced employees can be. Because of his lack of self-discipline regarding the line between people's private and public lives, Dobson leapt across it, grasping for some way to force my wife and me to appease his panic.

In that regard, one of the most astonishing moments that I experienced with Jim during these months came during a week when the Focus board of directors was in town. I was told that Jim would be informing the board at this meeting that I was experiencing marital difficulties. Dobson called me into his office one evening at the end of a day of board sessions. To my surprise, he informed me that after he had discussed my marital difficulties with the board, one of its members asked if the problems my wife and I were experiencing were related to financial pressures. Jim answered by saying that all marital problems are related in one way or another to finances, but that he was not aware of any specific financial component to our problems other than the routine financial pressures of a family of five living in southern California on a single income. At that point one of the members of the board stated that he thought the board should do something financially for me to help save my marriage. After some discussion, it was determined that rather than the board authorizing the corporation to make a financial gesture toward me, individual members would help.

As Jim and I stood in the middle of his office, he reached into his pocket and pulled out four personal checks that four board members had written to me on their personal accounts. Each was for twenty-five thousand dollars. Jim was holding in his hand a gift of one hundred thousand dollars.

Since nothing like that had ever happened to me, I had no point of reference from which to instantly evaluate the emotions of the moment. I did not come from a wealthy family. The thought that my mother and father had struggled for thirty years to meet their obligations, including their house payment, prior to reaching the point where their home was paid off, but that I was being handed four twenty-five-thousand-dollar checks that could pay off my mortgage that afternoon, was more than I could contemplate or analyze. I knew instinctively that it was going to be impossible to evaluate whether to take the money or not without allowing some time to pass.

When I regained by composure, I told Jim that I had to think about the board's offer for a day or so; the four unbelievably generous checks were causing me strangely mixed feelings that I could not instantly assess. I remember the stunned look on Jim's face that I was not simply pocketing the offer. I recall that he then linked the gift to God's will, stating that he wanted me to see this gesture as God telling me to pay off the mortgage on my home and thus reduce the pressures on my marriage.

THROW A LITTLE MONEY AT IT

Jim believed in solving problems with money. He stated that belief to me very pointedly on numerous occasions. I recall, for example, that during the first year that my family and I lived in southern California my family experienced very strong feelings of culture shock and homesickness. To move from Chicago to Los Angeles is not unlike moving from Chicago to Saudi Arabia, so great is the difference in culture. Having grown up in Pennsylvania and having never been further west than Denver I spent twelve months fighting the emotional equivalent of a body rejecting a tissue transplant. I would put my children to bed at night amid tears over how much they disliked California and missed their Illinois friends. From time to time, I would tell Jim of this difficulty. On one occasion I stated to him that I wasn't sure my family was going to succeed in making the adjustment to California living, that I might be forced to resign, pack up, and return my family to Illinois. Jim stated that it was his practice, when faced with family problems, to see if throwing money at them might solve things. So he encouraged me to think about whether there was something that money could buy that would help my family make the adjustment. He offered me a personal loan to make possible such a purchase. Because of such exchanges, it was abundantly clear to me that he viewed my marital problems as something money might help fix. One of my reservations was that I knew that wasn't true of these particular problems.

I remember the drive home that evening and sitting alone in the dark in our family room pondering all that money. The realization that slowly came into focus was that one of the reasons I had been uncomfortable accepting those four checks was that I had already been experiencing James Dobson, the control junkie, without $100,000 of financial indebtedness. How much worse might it get if he was able to say in response to a situation where he wanted his way in my private life, "But, Gil, what about the hundred thousand we gave you?"

I wrote Jim and the board a memo several days later turning down their gift. I said, among other things: "I've wrestled intensely with whether to accept the offer. There are several reasons I cannot. First I'm concerned about interpersonal jealousies with my peers, even though we have the finest of working relationships at this time." (I had been asking myself how I would feel if I learned the board had given another vice president a hundred thousand dollars but not me.) "Second, I was raised to be self-sufficient in family financial matters and I feel responsible to solve my own problems rather than accept assistance from others. Third, I have been reviewing over and over again the nature of my family's problems and whether such assistance would really accomplish the purpose for which it is given. I don't believe it will."

I didn't realize it at the time, but the pronouns in my memo were all singular. In other words, I stated that "I" could not accept the gift because "I" was uncomfortable doing so, but "I" was grateful for the gesture. Jim noticed. He wrote back a fiery note indicating that those singular pronouns were clear evidence to him of the truth of the concerns expressed to him by my wife, that I cut her out of all family financial matters. He said, "Did [your wife] play any part in this decision? You know, Gil, I believe she didn't. Without beating you over the head with yet another disturbing note I see in this response a further example of the point I've tried to make. [Your wife] seems not to be a co-equal with you." Once again, my private life was not to Jim's liking.

The truth was that my wife and I did discuss the gift. She thought we should accept it immediately and I thought we should not. After giving consideration to her views, I chose to make this particular decision based on my perspective. I did so believing that we were not dealing with a random gift to the two of us but, rather, one emanating from my boss and my board of directors and directly related to my job. Allow me to be even more blunt. I thought the gift represented a serious case of poor judgment by the board. Jim did not notice any of its unnatural, unwise, entangling factors, only that a fix had been put on the table and I had stubbornly refused to accept it.

A SINGLE FATHER

Somehow Jim and I survived the spring of the fiery memos, the confrontation with him and my therapist, and the four checks. My wife and I separated in early summer. Her legal response to the petition that had so angered Jim reached me: In it she told the court she did not agree to my request for a legal separation, that she wanted a divorce instead.

That summer I experienced the strange happiness that can sometimes come to those broken by divorce. My wife and I had struggled for so long; the air of tension and discomfort in our home had been so thick that getting on with life brought a strange relief. I was a grateful single father with custody of two and one-half children and I had survived. And then it happened. That fall, as I was developing a new film and video department for Focus, a woman by the name of Carolyn Alexander applied for the position of production assistant. I didn't know it the day she walked through my office door for her interview, but we were to fall in love and marry nine months later. Conservative Christians sometimes use a strange sounding phrase from the Old Testament about "God restoring the years that the locust ate." By that we mean that God has a gracious way not of saving us from trials and tribulations, but of helping us through them and then, afterward, of dropping in our laps special pleasures, bonus blessings, as if God were leaning over the banister of heaven and saying, "I know it's been tough for a while. Now it's party time." Meeting Carolyn began party time in those places of this man's heart where only love, respect, and the intimacy of female companionship can restore the years the locusts had eaten. Carolyn did just that.

But the locusts were not done eating.

27 ✤ Wrongful Termination

There are all shades and varieties of marital situations represented on the staff and board of directors of Focus on the Family, including those who are single; those who are married for the first, second or third time; those who are in transition into or out of marriages; and even those who get pregnant out of wedlock. In other words, the staff was like any grouping of Americans. There is no policy at Focus on the Family that precludes from employment certain general categories of married or unmarried people. There were board members, as well as vice presidents and others throughout the organization, who had divorced and remarried. The exact circumstances of these divorces and remarriages were seldom, if ever, a topic of discussion let alone investigation. We took people at their word that they were working with us because they believed in lifelong marriage regardless of how their individual marriages had turned out—for better or for worse.

The key consideration here was the word "belief." We believed in and were committed to preserving marriages, starting with our own. The only two people who would not have fit in at Focus on the Family would have been the person who was flip and careless about whether or not their marriage stood the test of time and the person who believed in same-sex marriage.

An example of exactly how wide an assortment of marital conditions we housed would be found in the story of an applicant for employment I will call Bill Smith to respect his privacy. We hired Bill knowing he was divorced and put him to work in our computer department. To the great excitement of the entire staff, Bill fell in love with a Focus on the Family secretary and married her, to the applause of everyone from Dobson on down. Single, married, separated, divorced, remarried: we employed them all.

But Bill's story definitely had a few more twists and turns than the usual. It was Jim who personally proposed to the cabinet that we hire Bill. Even though specific candidates for jobs were rarely reviewed at the cabinet level of the company, it was natural that Jim put this one on our agenda that day because Bill was Dobson's longtime friend. Smith, as Jim told us at that cabinet meeting, had just gone through a painful divorce. The cause of the divorce, Jim continued, included the unfortunate fact that Bill had had an affair with a live-in maid. Bill repented, Jim assured us, and Dobson personally vouched for Bill's compatibility with our belief in lifelong marriage, our policies and procedures, and our values. I recall every single member of the cabinet supporting Jim's perspective regarding Bill.

FALLING IN LOVE

Because of this Focus marital smorgasbord it came as a jolting surprise to me when my own marital situation changed and Jim decided to deal differently with me than our employment policies and procedures dictated; in other words, to discriminate against me.

I was aware of the general policy used by most companies that individuals who were romantically involved could not work together in the same department or certainly not in a supervisor-subordinate relationship. So, as I discovered myself falling in love with a staff member, I called Jim's home one evening during the Christmas season of 1986 and asked if I could drive over for a short talk. He was available. Jim's home had a small office just off the front door, and when I arrived he ushered me in and closed the door. I felt both nervous and exhilarated. Is there a finer feeling on the face of the earth than new love? I began my story, explaining that I wanted him to know that I had begun to have feelings for Carolyn and that I knew I would want to date her eventually. I asked how he wanted us to handle that situation in terms of departmental assignments. Carolyn is a writer of children's books, I reminded him, and Focus on the Family had a publishing division that was beginning to investigate that market. It seemed logical to me that we would transfer Carolyn to that area of the company in advance of any dating relationship. I should add that the divorce decree had been delayed from September to January due to legal technicalities. Dobson and I were both aware that night that I was just days away from legally being a single man.

Jim began by indicating that he was not surprised in the least; that he saw Carolyn as a beautiful, bright woman and he could understand fully how I would find her attractive. He suggested no assignment changes of any type, asking only that we keep our dating relationship discreet. I recall his words, "Just don't be seen flaunting your newfound bachelorhood by showing up at some party with Carolyn on your arm." My response was, "I'm a little brighter than that."

The divorce decree was issued, and Carolyn and I began to date but without anyone other than our immediate families knowing.

By Easter, Carolyn and I knew this was true love. On Easter Eve I knelt at the couch in my bachelor condo, my girls and son fast asleep on the second floor, and asked Carolyn to marry me, offering to add the great "Alexander" name to mine if she would add mine to hers.

THE RUDE AWAKENING

We arranged a dinner with Jim and Shirley to share the good news of our engagement and to decide how to handle the staffing assignment issues it would surely raise. I had no reason to expect anything but congratulations. It had been four months since my meeting with Jim in his home office. During that period he had not asked a single followup question about our relationship. I assumed one reason was because Carolyn and I had fulfilled his only request—we had been very discreet. When we announced our engagement to colleagues with whom we had worked side by side every day during our courtship, not one of them had guessed what was happening.

I can still picture the look on Dobson's face when I said the words, "We plan to marry." Shock. Bewilderment. Concern. The words that came out of his mouth sounded as if he had been struck with an anxiety attack. Instead of toasts of best wishes all around, I was greeted with a somber warning that a cabinet meeting would have to be convened the next day to assess the situation. What situation? I was to learn the troubling answer almost immediately.

It is important to take note here of a national news event that was unfolding on the very day Carolyn and I were having dinner with Jim and Shirley. The media were breaking the story of the indictment of Jim Bakker for fraud. The full magnitude of the misconduct represented by

Jim and Tammy Faye Bakker's leadership of the PTL organization was just surfacing. Allegations of the misuse of donor funds were lead stories across the country. And there were the stories about air-conditioned dog houses and lavish personal expenditures which appeared to represent a complete insensitivity by the Bakkers to their contributors. And then, of course, there were the allegations of sexual misconduct. It was at this exact point in 1987 that Carolyn and I announced our plans to marry. The following day I watched Jim fixate on the PTL debacle, as though it represented an immediate danger to him. I saw a paranoid fear develop that the evil liberal press were probably boarding the first plane out of South Carolina for Louisiana, where they would burn at the stake Jimmy Swaggart, and then it was on to Arcadia for the next course in their "feeding frenzy." That spring's three-course media meal was going to be Jimmy Bakker, Jimmy Swaggart, and Jimmy Dobson. It was completely irrational.

Jim called an emerging meeting of the cabinet, but barred me from attending for reasons that were never explained. I was told that the group considered several options in response to my engagement, several of which included terminating Carolyn's employment and mine. Next, Jim informed me that the cabinet's options were being sent to the board of directors in a letter and that they would quickly convene a telephone board meeting to decide on our fate. Jim's board letter read in part:

> Gil informed me that he plans to marry. Two overriding issues are now presented to us that require a response. The first is theological, i.e., does Gil have biblical grounds for remarriage? [Since Focus policy did not prohibit remarried individuals from working there, it is impossible to explain why Jim began his letter this way.]
>
> I'm not . . . qualified or authorized to make this determination. It is between Gil and Carolyn and the Lord. I have chosen, therefore, not to deal with the theological implications. [Remember this line because later in the book you will see Jim state the exact opposite.]
>
> There is a second issue, however, which may be entirely independent of the first. Here the question relates to the ministry of Focus on the Family and how this marriage will affect the work we have been called to do. Even if the marriage is not wrong it may be judged to be so by our constituents. And as always perception is reality for the perceiver.
>
> Other questions emerge such as how will our staff respond to this development? And how will it effect my credibility? And what is the potential for national exposure? All signs point to a danger signal for us.

What danger signal? Many times during the ten years I worked with Jim we were alerted by listeners in different parts of the country to rumors circulating that Jim was getting a divorce. We had a policy for handling such false rumors that Jim and I personally executed. Dobson would inform me at the beginning of a radio program recording session that he wanted to save five minutes at the end to respond to a false rumor. About twenty-five minutes into the taping I would say, "Well, Doctor, before we run out of time today, I know you have a special issue you want to bring up. Let's turn to that now." And Jim would respond, "Yes, Gil, we've received word that a number of churches in the Orlando area have made announcements to their congregations that Shirley and I are getting a divorce and to pray for us. I need to give those friends and others the good news that there is no truth to that rumor whatsoever. We're blessed with a wonderful relationship. I have no idea how such rumors began, but all is well at the Dobson household. Naturally, I assumed that this same rumor control procedure would have been used regarding false gossip about my own private life."

FEAR OF THE UNKNOWN

Jim continued in his letter to the board:

> Several circumstances converge to make this situation even more explosive. The greatest concern is in the appearance of wrong doing! By Gil marrying his secretary only five months after his divorce was final one might assume that an affair had been ongoing and played a role in the marital demise.
>
> I can guarantee that did not occur, that Gil and Carolyn did not know each other until September 4. That was seven months after the legal separation. Carolyn began working for Gil on October 5. Again, there has been no hanky-panky here. The question remains, how will the marriage be seen? The concoction is right for a witch's brew.
>
> Our cabinet met this morning to discuss the options before us. There was unanimity that the reputation of Christian ministries including our own must be protected from scandal—even baseless scandal. Enough damage has been done in other ministries of late. Reluctantly, everyone agreed tentatively that Gil and Carolyn should resign quickly.
>
> Just as he did on the broadcast, Gil has done a marvelous job in the film department. I have never known a more creative man. Please make this decision a matter of fervent prayer.

Hard to comprehend, isn't it? Essentially Jim has just said that Carolyn and I had done nothing wrong, but we had to go because of his fear of personal and corporate damage from possible false rumors. Again, the reason I include this story is to ask you this question: If Dobson handles the civil rights of employees in this fashion, if the basic right to privacy and to be treated consistent with company employment policies can so easily be abridged, should such a CEO be encouraged to enter the larger arena of public policy to help the nation fashion the policies by which we all live and work together?

THE VOTE

Within twenty-four hours Jim had set up a conference call with the board and I was informed that I would be given ten minutes to address them and then asked once to leave the room—again, for reasons that were not explained. As with the cabinet meeting, Carolyn was not even invited. In fact, throughout these momentous days I had to keep reminding Jim that he was talking of terminating Carolyn but not talking to Carolyn about it.

The conference call was an eerie experience. Around the table were the cold stares of men who had for so long been my friends and colleagues, many of whom I had hired and trained. The room had been sucked empty of camaraderie. I stumbled through an explanation of what I've already described and, after only six minutes, was told to excuse myself.

I waited outside the boardroom, and Carolyn across the street in the film department, to learn of the board's vote. Some time later I was told that Jim was waiting for me in his office. He was not behind his desk, his customary station, but rather was seated in one of the two guest chairs immediately in front of it. He motioned to me to sit in the other. He had a very grave and somber look in his face as he began. "Gil," he said, "both the cabinet and the board have concluded that you and Carolyn must resign and leave the organization."

He talked once again about the dangers of false rumors, concluding with a line I'll never forget nor refrain from challenging: "Gil, the institution is more important than the individual. When forced to make the hard choice between the needs of the institution and those of the individual, the institution must come first."

I protested. I stated that the decision was incomprehensible, that he was basing this action solely on the chance that an admittedly false rumor might start at some unknown time ahead. Jim asked, "So what are you saying, Gil? That if the cabinet and board ask for your resignation you're not going to leave?" To which I responded, "Well, I suppose if you put it that way we have no choice. But it is still a mistake."

Jim had offered a slight glimmer of a compromise solution. He said that two board members had suggested that if Carolyn and I would agree to postpone our marriage one year they might view their votes differently. But Jim emphasized that these two had not specifically said such a postponement would definitely change their vote. Besides, the vote had been 7 to 0. Two votes for us would make no difference. My parting appeal for reconsideration was the fact that if the exact same circumstances were applied to Jim's employment at Focus, the company's response would be to go on the air and refute the rumor. I asked Jim why he wasn't prepared to defend Carolyn and me in the same fashion in which I supported him when rumors circulated about him. His response was simply, "We can't do that. Once it's out of the bottle you can never get it back in."

I returned to Jim's office the next day and offered the organization a compromise we hoped would save our jobs. We did not offer to wait a year to marry but rather three months. During the next forty-eight hours, Carolyn and I waited for word of a second vote taken among the board by telephone. Paul Nelson called me in the film department every time a member's vote came in. No change. Our resignations were required immediately. And that we did, quietly, having been given no choice but to clear our desks.

Several days after the cabinet and board votes, a meeting of our entire staff took place at which Jim announced our departures from the organization. He said, in part:

> This may be the most difficult moment in the ten-year history of Focus on the Family. It relates to Gil Moegerle. Going back to 1985 when Gil left the studio some of you knew that there were some family stresses; that Gil and his wife were going through a difficult time and that Gil left the studio because of the pressure of it but also because integrity has to be so important in a ministry of this nature.
>
> There were no skeletons in the closet; there was no infidelity, none of those kinds of things; they were just two people who could not make it work. I believe every effort was made to try to preserve that marriage. It continued to deteriorate and in February of last year a legal separation occurred. In January of this year the divorce was final.
>
> Three weeks ago a new development occurred and Gil and Carolyn Alexander took me and Shirley to dinner and announced their intention of being married. That presented new problems for us . . . having to do with the perception of wrongdoing. For people out there perception is reality. It doesn't matter what reality is.
>
> I can absolutely guarantee you 100 percent that Carolyn and Gil's relationship had nothing to do with the deterioration of Gil's marriage. There was no entanglement, no triangle, nothing there. And yet we do

have a situation with the Jim Bakker affair and the Oral Roberts mess [Roberts had just issued his announcement that God was going to kill him if his latest fund-raising letter didn't raise enough money] and everything else going on right now where integrity becomes paramount. The situation is built for radical misunderstanding.

Our cabinet felt Gil and Carolyn should resign. The board felt unanimously that Gil and Carolyn should resign. There seems to be no other solution.

My great concern is with the people out there disillusioned in the past few weeks in a devastating way. Some will lose their faith over it and will go to hell. That's my great concern. That some people are already thinking there are no honest ministries that live according to what they teach—there are none left. We cannot give that message to them. We have to have integrity.

By the way, this public statement also contained the same disclaimer found in the board letter—that theology was not a part of this decision.

When Jim concluded, staff members were in tears, Carolyn and I stood in a middle aisle hugging friends and crying for over an hour. Strangely, Jim did not say goodbye, nor did any other member of the senior staff who had voted for our departures.

WEDDING BELLS

Several weeks later, in a beautiful back yard in Sierra Madre, California, belonging to some wonderful friends, Carolyn and I stood before an Episcopal priest to join our lives. With close friends and family seated on white wooden chairs around a small pool topped by floating flower arrangements, as a harpist played, we began our marriage, filled with bliss and oblivious to the drama that lay ahead. I shall always treasure one moment at the end of the wedding ceremony when the Rev. Bob Schaper wrapped our joined hands in his beautiful white and gold stole as a symbol of God wrapping our marriage in his loving arms. I knew as I stood there, as every divorced person knows, that there were no powers in heaven or on earth that could absolutely bind two people together forever, that lifelong marriage flows out of more than a belief; it flows out of individual decisions made by each partner day after day, for a lifetime.

Carolyn and I left Focus on the Family quietly and peacefully. I emphasize that fact because you're about to learn that a full-blown war broke out between Jim and me less than a year later, one that was to end with Jim standing trial on charges of invasion of privacy, wrongful termination, and related violations of civil law. But on that June day in 1987, as Carolyn and I left southern California for our honeymoon in a rustic cabin on Anvil Island off Vancouver, we said goodbye to James Dobson without the slightest thought of attorneys or due process.

28 🌿 Unrelenting Encroachment

In December 1987, eight months after our departures and six months after our wedding, the phone rang in Jim's office. On the other end of the line was Neil Warren. He was calling to report to Dobson that he had heard, incorrectly, that I was abusing my former wife, harassing her legally, and reneging on child-support payments. It was to be a conversation that would change forever my relationship with James Dobson.

Prior to that call, any conduct by Jim that I thought to be inappropriate I confronted privately or absorbed. We conservative Christians do a lot of absorbing. It's a virtue to us. And so we often pay a very heavy price for the passivity of our relationships.

In fact, I will offer you at this point one of the central reasons Carolyn and I decided that the time had come to write this book. As we've struggled to find a pathway between godly friends who advised us that a book like this would be viewed as nothing more than an act of revenge and those who said "go for it" but had little understanding of the price you can pay for confronting a very powerful person, I heard myself say to Carolyn one day, "Our refusal to confront Dobson is our gift of pain to his next victim." Prior to December 1987, we had done very little confronting and a great deal of absorbing. But all that changed when Neil called Jim and, one more time, Jim came dashing across the line into my private life.

Jim went ballistic. He swung the mighty arm of Focus on the Family into swift action to defend my supposedly abused first wife. The next word Carolyn and I received was that my former wife had been hired by Dobson and was working in the same department where Carolyn had once worked, among Carolyn's very closest friends. The sense of insult, for me and for Carolyn, was overwhelming.

MAKING IT UP AS WE GO

I couldn't work at Focus, an organization I helped to start, because someone might start a damaging rumor that I didn't believe in lifelong marriage. Carolyn couldn't work at Focus because people might falsely conclude that she, too, didn't believe in lifelong marriage even though her marriage to me was her first. But my first wife, who had personally informed Jim that she was ending her lifelong marriage, could work at Focus on the Family.

My initial sense of outrage was nothing compared to the level of affront and fury Dobson generated just twenty-four hours later. According to a phone call I received from Focus radio co-host Mike Trout, when Jim and my former colleagues on the cabinet learned of my angry reaction, Jim defended his hiring decision by repeating in an official Focus staff meeting everything that Neil had told him. None of these accusations was true and none had been checked with me by Jim before his speech to the cabinet.

The realization that Jim was once again up to his old tricks, gathering information about my private life behind my back, even though I was no longer on his staff, talking about my private life inaccurately and in a defamatory fashion in an official Focus meeting, and hiring my former wife after terminating Carolyn and me, made me a believer forever in constructive confrontation. A principle that a theologian friend named Larry Richards offered me from the Old Testament has been my cry ever since: "Never ignore wrong." In the days that followed, I wrote his board of directors telling the entire story of Jim's invasive conduct over the preceding years: the conversation in Chicago, the demands that I sign the Homestead Act papers, the requirement that I show him my family financial files, the conversations with my therapist, the criticism that I wasn't responding to therapy the way he wanted me to, the requirement that I abandon custody of my son, and now his latest venture into my private life. I demanded that the board investigate Dobson's misconduct and inform me of the steps they were taking to ensure that my privacy would henceforth be respected and that all employees would be protected from any future recurrence of the search-and-seizure method of managing to which I had been subjected.

The board's response was inept and irresponsible. Sidestepping altogether our central complaint that Dobson had invaded our privacy, they spoke only to two issues in a return letter, a document so confused that it was impossible at first to fully decipher. It read:

> First, is the matter of [your wife's] short employment at Focus on the Family. This has been settled by [her] leaving. . . . [Focus found another job for her at a similar organization several miles away.]
>
> Second, there is your question of the possibility that you might be associated in some capacity by Focus on the Family in the future. [The demand for your resignations] has been reaffirmed unanimously as of this date and we want you to understand that we are firm in this decision.

This second comment was the confusing part of the letter. The board addressed an issue that had not appeared in my letter, a supposed interest in returning to Focus. And the letter completely sidestepped the complaint about the invasion of my privacy.

When I telephoned and asked a board member why the letter didn't respond to my central concern, he had no response. When I demanded to know if the board planned to investigate my allegations he said that he had "no response beyond the board letter" and that "there had been no in-depth discussion of that issue," but that "the board was sure that Jim's motives had been pure."

These individual board members had been my personal friends. Many of us had worked hard to build Focus on the Family for ten years. The group included such stalwart names within conservative Protestant Christendom as Ted Engstrom. And yet when I appealed to them to investigate Dobson's invasive conduct, they walked away. To this day, board members as renowned as Adrian Rogers, Bill Hybels, and Susan Baker, wife of our former secretary of state, have not even proposed, let alone agreed to, an independent binding grievance process by which the conduct of the man whom they are charged to oversee might be scrutinized.

INTERFERENCE WITH BUSINESS

During that spring Jim's anger over my protest letter to his board expressed itself in several ways. He notified us that we were banned from coming onto Focus property. Freelance production work my former film department staff and I were planning was stopped. I was notified that I was not to use the name "James Dobson" or "Focus on the Family" in any of my personal professional literature. (Presumably, my résumé was to read: "from 1977 to 1987 I was gainfully employed, but I can't tell you where.") Communications projects I was attempting to develop with organizations closely aligned with Dobson were scuttled. My largest film project while at Focus was shown in prime-time television here in Los Angeles but with my credit as executive producer removed. I became concerned that I would soon be unable to support my family within the religious broadcasting field, so quickly were rumors spreading from Focus executives of the falling out with Dobson.

As Carolyn and I attempted to analyze our next step, one of the people we approached for advice was a well-known broadcasting friend in southern California by the name of John Stewart. He seemed like a superb candidate to advise us on our dilemma. John was an evangelical broadcaster who understood Jim's temperament and the makeup of Focus on the Family. He was a practicing attorney and law school professor. John was also an ordained minister with a very impressive body of knowledge about the Christian faith. One afternoon, we drove south on a freeway near our home to a restaurant where John was waiting to advise us. As Carolyn, John, and I sat at the table reviewing the events of recent weeks, and as I added the accounts of Jim's invasive conduct over the past several years, I pulled out a pen and yellow legal pad to capture the assessment offered. To my surprise, John's immediate response was that our story contained four or five specific areas of potential violation of civil law by Dobson.

Until that moment, we had experienced Jim's dark side as conduct that causes one frustration, anger, a feeling of being invaded and manipulated. But we were not lawyers and had no experience in matters of civil law. Therefore, we had not contemplated that the conduct might also be illegal. John very calmly, in the matter-of-fact manner common to attorneys, advised us that the remedy for Jim's misconduct toward our family might be found in court.

Allow me to offer you another brief lesson in the thinking of conservative American Christians. To that group, courts are evil. You could easily draw the conclusion as you listen to members of this religious group that there are no attorneys, judges, or court staffs who are responsible and godly. Attorneys operate an industry that is viewed much the same as gambling or night clubs. When I was growing up, no Christian I knew ever went to court for any reason. No Christian aspired to be a member of the legal profession.

But Stewart regarded it as a responsible service available within society for precisely the circumstances in which Carolyn and I found ourselves. He spoke as if litigation could be responsible behavior. Sometimes people find themselves unable to resolve serious matters directly with their adversaries, he advised, and appeal to the court to hear and judge their case. For me, it was a breathtaking experience. To hear an attorney/clergyman say that our concerns should be given a hearing in a court of law and that redress and even restitution might be available was eye-opening to say the least.

CHURCH DISCIPLINE

Carolyn and I were not quite ready to seek that remedy. Instead, we decided to try to find an organization that provided private Christian arbitration services. We selected a man by the name of Sam Ericcson, executive director of the Christian Legal Society, an association of Christians in the legal profession who assist fellow Christians with conflict resolution. To our great pleasure, Sam was available to help. After reviewing our allegations and evidence, Sam said almost exactly what John had: that it was possible that the conduct in question had violated civil law and that he would take our case in the sense of working with us to establish a private hearing at which an independent panel of Christian lawyers or judges would hear both sides and render a decision. Sam described a type of process that would last one day and be held in a meeting room in a local church. We would state our case and Jim could rebut. There would be simple rules of evidence. A decision would be reached. The plan sounded wonderful. We were available. But Jim was not.

Dobson said no. In a formal letter of rejection dated May 31, 1988, and signed by Focus's corporate attorney Stephen Reed, we were told, "After due consideration, the board and Dr. Dobson have concluded that nothing will be gained, either for you or for Focus on the Family and Dr. Dobson, by resort to arbitration or mediation. Accordingly, your previous proposals for such procedures are declined."

Ericcson was disturbed by Jim's rejection. He spoke with Dobson and wrote him, critical of his refusal to do what Sam had been invited on the Dobson radio broadcast just months before to propose to other Christian organizations: private Christian arbitration rather than expensive public litigation. In response to Sam's criticism, Jim instructed his staff to remove all Christian Legal Society literature from the Focus warehouse and discontinue distributing it or re-airing previous Ericcson interviews.

That fall, on the very day that the statute of limitations would have expired for us, Carolyn and I took the big step. We authorized attorney David Warren to file in Los Angeles Superior Court, Pomona Branch, lawsuits against James Dobson and Focus on the Family. The complaints: First, Jim and Focus had wrongfully terminated Carolyn's employment contract and mine. Second, Jim and Focus had invaded my privacy. Third, Jim and Focus had interfered with my business dealings after leaving Focus. And fourth, Jim and Focus had intentionally inflicted emotional distress by the three actions above.

The battle was joined. We had asked for our day in court.

29 ❧ Obstruction of Justice

When we filed the lawsuit, the very first thing Jim did represents one of the great ironies of this entire story. It's probably true that what he didn't do was equally telling. He did not respond like a man who values peace or understands negotiation and compromise. He made no gesture regarding wanting to reconsider Ericcson's proposal of a private arbitration process. He proposed no alternative idea for avoiding court. One could argue, based on reviewing Focus on the Family's response to the court filing, that Dobson views conflict as unavoidable, inescapable, and irresolvable apart from moving straight ahead through the long, expensive legal process. Whereas most adults and corporations knowledgeable in conflict management would set about searching for a quiet path to resolution, especially when they have learned that their adversary is serious about his complaint, Jim and the Focus board showed no signs of such a commitment to nonlegal dispute resolution.

Jim personally wrote a national press release on December 20, 1988, regarding our lawsuits. It said:

> Focus on the Family today acknowledged that two former Focus employees who had resigned in early 1987 recently filed civil suits against the Pomona-based ministry.
>
> Gilbert Alexander-Moegerle and his wife Carolyn had been employed at Focus on the Family. They resigned shortly after Gil Moegerle's divorce and engagement to Carolyn who served as his secretary. They authored, signed and submitted a voluntary resignation letter on April 27, 1987. The suits pertain to the termination of their employment.

Focus on the Family denies any inappropriate dealings with the Alexander-Moegerles. Dr. Dobson stated, "Frankly, we are somewhat perplexed by this action. The relationship between Focus and the Alexander-Moegerles was amiable at the time of separation, with no hint of conflict for many months. Although we feel their complaint is frivolous we have attempted to resolve it by mediation through the Christian Legal Society. Having rejected that possibility, the Alexander-Moegerles have chosen to take the matter into the courts. We have little choice in this development."

I'm sure it's disheartening, if you are a devoted fan of Dobson's, to see a champion of morality play fast and loose with the truth, consciously creating impressions Jim knew to be untrue. However, here is the great irony. Do you recall that the central reason Jim gave for the decision by the cabinet and board to terminate our employment? It was the fear of an admittedly false rumor about us that would hurt his reputation and that of the company. In his press release Jim himself had started that very rumor to create the impression that we and our lawsuit were irresponsible. The rumor to which I refer is the oldest sexual slur in the books—executive falls in love with beautiful secretary, dumps wife to marry her: "They resigned shortly after Gil Moegerle's divorce and engagement to Carolyn who served as his secretary." I assure you that in the religious world of conservative Christians and in the broadcasting community serving that market, nothing could have been more deadly to my reputation than the impression Jim crafted as he wrote those sixteen words. It is one of the reasons I no longer work in that field.

PRETRIAL HEARINGS

There followed the amazing pretrial exercises as the two law firms, Rutan and Tucker of Irvine, California, representing Dobson, and Smith and Warren of Sierra Madre, California, representing Carolyn and me, exchanged demands for discovery, interrogatory questionnaires, motions and responses to motions. Depositions began, including all the drama of coming face to face with Jim, Focus executives, and board members across law office conference room tables. Early in the proceedings, Dobson appealed to the court for a gag order prohibiting me from telling you what took place in those depositions. Our twin cases are therefore sealed in boxes of files in the basement archives of the L.A. Superior Court, Pomona Branch. But public aspects of the case can still be told.

The first critical turning point came in the fall of 1990 and focused on a routine step in the legal process called "summary judgment." In layman's terms, a summary judgment is a request of the court, made by all defense attorneys, that asks the judge to prevent the plaintiff from having his day in court. We have the fundamental right as Americans to take our civil grievances before a jury of our peers and petition them for redress if we feel we've been wronged. But in order to screen out frivolous and nonsensical petitions, the law provides a preliminary step where the defense can make a reasonable argument why a particular complaint is without merit and the plaintiff must pass at least a minimal test of having a case to present. We reached that stage in September 1990.

The first argument Dobson made went like this: All complaints against him were without merit. He offered several reasons that bore the unmistakable imprint of the language of his December 1988 press release: playing fast and loose with the truth. For example, in a declaration to the court dated September 5, 1989, Jim said the following in a document that bears his personal signature and ends with those weighty words, "I declare under penalty of perjury under the laws of the State of California that the foregoing is true and correct":

- The sole purpose of Focus on the Family is to propagate the Gospel of Jesus Christ.

- In August of 1986 Gilbert filed a stipulation transforming his legal separation into a divorce proceeding.

- Plaintiff's marriage [to Carolyn] created disturbing theological and institutional problems for Focus on the Family. [Remember Jim telling his board and his staff that theology was not a part of the decision to require our resignations?] Several biblical passages, the authenticity of which Focus on the Family is founded on, decry divorce.

- It is believed generally within mainline Evangelical Christian circles that remarriage after a divorce constitutes a form of adultery in the eyes of God.

- Gilbert and Carolyn's conduct was grossly inconsistent with the value of permanent marriage as espoused by Focus on the Family. Moreover, it violated accepted norms of conduct for Focus on the Family employees.

- Plaintiffs' marriage constituted a direct repudiation of the Focus on the Family message. Therefore, plaintiffs' continued employment in the organization threatened to destroy the organization's credibility.

- Gilbert and Carolyn's conduct was in direct conflict with biblical and organizational teaching against divorce.

- A formal request for resignation [was never] made. Plaintiffs resigned voluntarily.

FIRST AMENDMENT PROTECTIONS

Jim's second summary judgment argument was that, as a religious organization, the First Amendment and its separation of church and state clause prohibited the court from hearing our complaint, since Jim had a protected right as CEO of a religious corporation to establish theological guidelines for employment that matched his faith. Specifically, he argued that he had taken the two steps in our complaint, terminating us and crossing the line into our private lives, for religious reasons and therefore the court couldn't hear our case.

You could not have convinced me by any argument that Jim's position would have prevailed with a fair-minded judge. But on September 10, 1990, Judge Theodore Piatt issued the following ruling on summary judgment. The court found that Focus on the Family was a "religious organization" entitled to First Amendment protection from prosecution on certain charges in a civil court:

> The services of our courts may not be invoked to resolve clearly ecclesiastical differences or conformity to standards of morality.

The court found that our complaint of wrongful termination was such an "ecclesiastical" matter. With those words, Carolyn's lawsuit died completely, since it revolved around her termination, and the termination portion of my lawsuit died as well.

There is confusion about the frequently used phrase "The charges were thrown out of court." The phrase is a deliberate attempt by defendants to make themselves look good. Instead of stating that a charge was ruled inadmissible, they imply that the charge had no merit. The court found only that "ecclesiastical" rather than civil authorities would have to judge whether Focus properly or improperly applied its religious standards when terminating our employment. Naturally that fact did not restrain Dobson from injecting a fine spin into the press release he distributed upon receiving the court's summary judgment order.